Iowa Pastel Landscapes

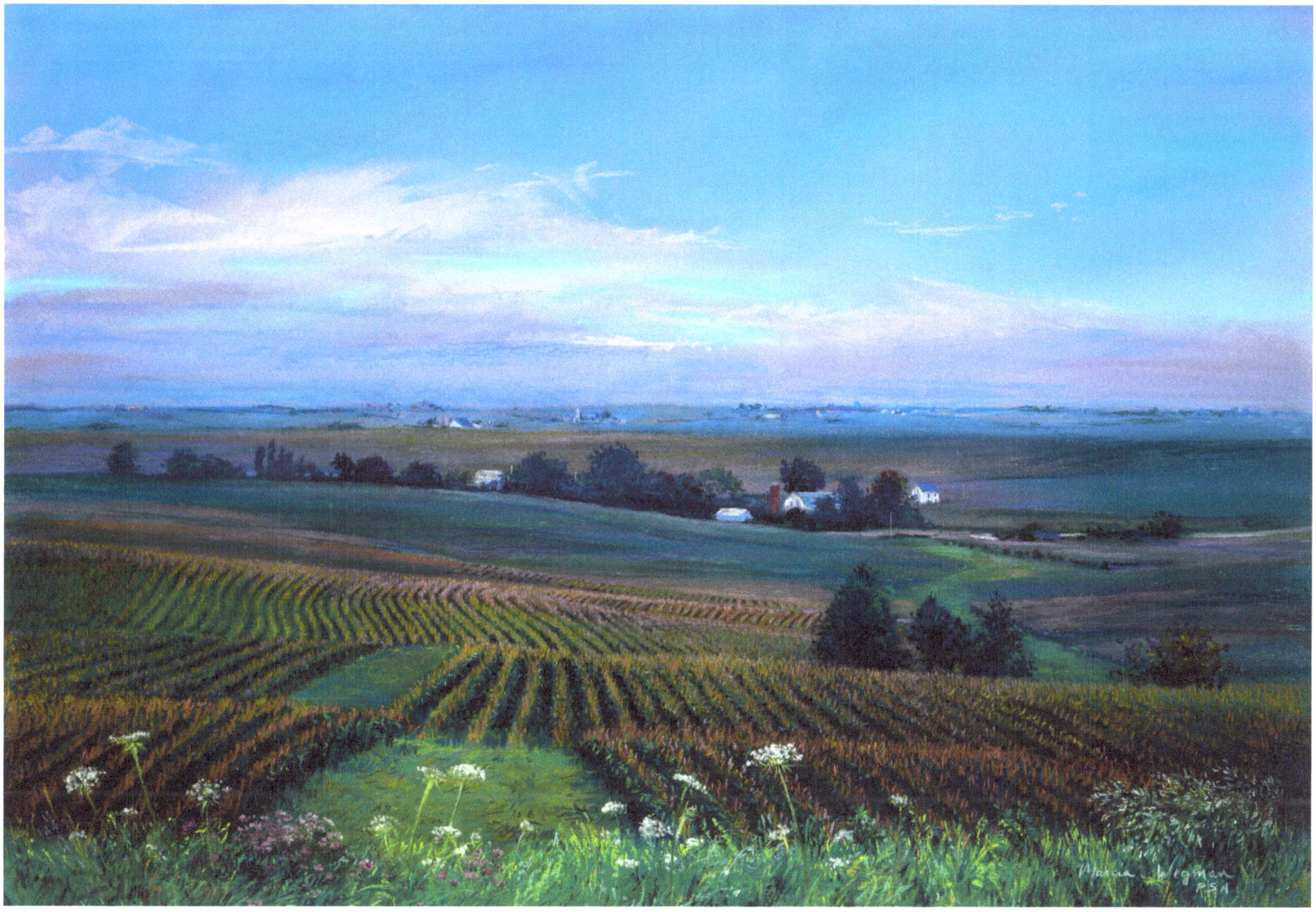

Maquoketa Cornfields 14 x 21 in.

MARCIA WEGMAN

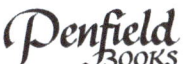

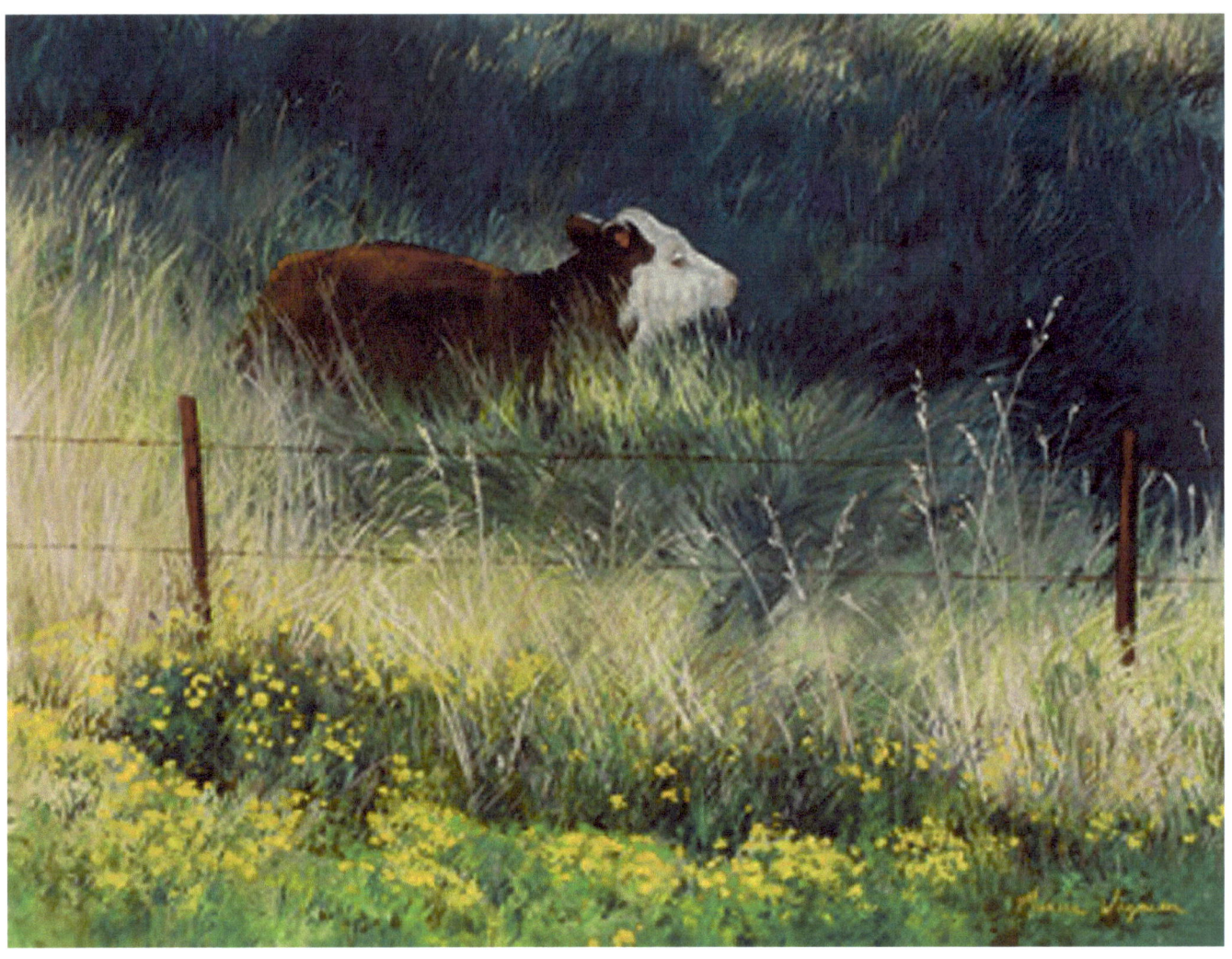

Resting Calf 18 x 24 in.

Acknowledgments

Front cover: View from the Road 27 x 21 in.

Back cover: Winter Home 12 x 18 in.

A special thank you for Charlene Trawick, photographer of all the landscape pastels in this book.

Edited by Joan Liffring-Zug Bourret, Melinda Bradnan, Miriam Canter, Deb Schense, and Mary Sharp

Graphic design by Molly Cook, MACook Design

All rights reserved by Penfield Books

© 2013 pastels by Marcia Wegman   © 2013 *The Infinite Beauty of Iowa,* David W. Wright

Penfield Books, 215 Brown Street, Iowa City, Iowa 52245

Printed in the U.S.A. by Tru Art Color Graphics, Iowa City, Iowa, with Rodger Rufer

ISBN-13: 9781932043952

Contents

Preface 2
Triptych at Kirkwood Community College 3
Creating a Life and Art in Iowa 5
The Infinite Beauty of Iowa 7
Iowa Farms 11
Cattle 25
Wild Flowers and Grass 35
Sky 43
Rivers, Lakes, and Creeks 61
Spring 67
Summer 73
Fall 89
Winter 97
Roads and Trails 107
Diptych, Triptych, and Quadriptych 116
Use of Photographs for Developing Paintings 119

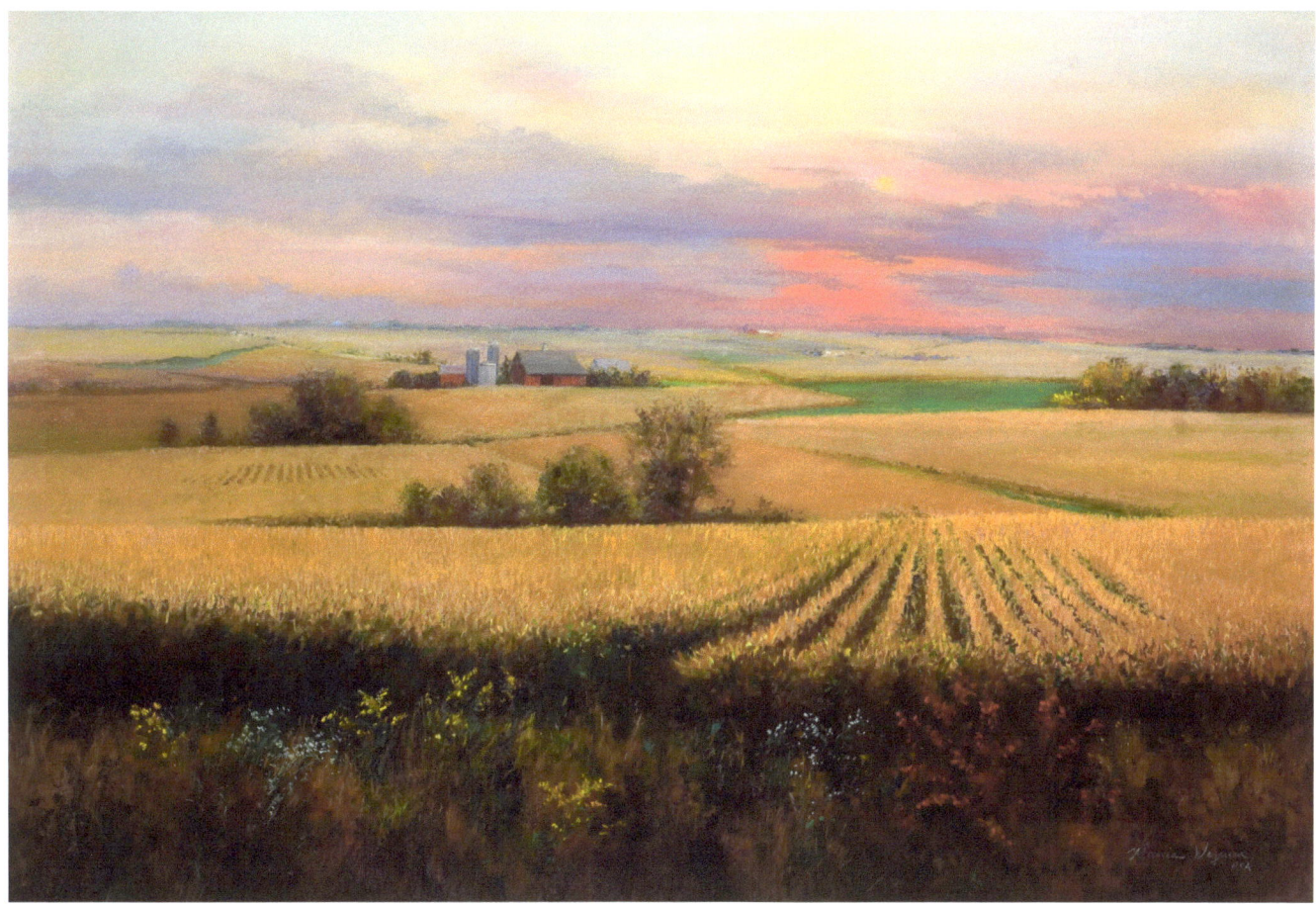

Autumn Light 24 x 36 in.

Preface

When looking at one of Marcia Wegman's works, one cannot help but be drawn in. This is true of her abstract paintings as well as her pastels of the landscape. Both invite the viewer into another world. While the abstract works draw one into a world of expansive interiority, her landscape compositions draw the viewer into a world that is seemingly familiar.

These two worlds, both similar and different, are based on the same thing—nature. Nature is the foundation of all that Wegman creates, and she even admits as much: "Nature, whether realistic or abstract, underlies everything I do." An avid traveler and hiker, Wegman seeks out opportunities to be in nature, recording them for future use. It is that constant and persistent pursuit of the underlying qualities of nature that drives her and finds its way into all of her work, whether representational or abstracted.

In speaking about how she deals with the sky in her works, Wegman says, "Although I always use a photo reference, I have much more freedom to play with shapes, colors, and patterns with the sky part of the composition."

But it is exactly these elements of shapes, colors, and patterns that Wegman finds in all of nature that inspire all her works.

One can see it in the rolling hills she depicts, or in the rows of corn, or the line of telephone poles, or in the paths that lead the viewer back into her compositions. These elements are both the basis of nature and the foundation of her works. Wegman sees and records this, adding her own interpretations and changes to the items that nature gave her in the landscape.

Wegman has no qualms in combining the sky from one day and the place with the hills from another and the road and telephone poles from a third. In this way, Wegman, like every artist, is a creator.

Marcia Wegman, like nature itself, is creating something for us to behold.

Sean M. Ulmer
Interim Executive Director
and Curator of Collections and Exhibitions
Cedar Rapids Museum of Art
Cedar Rapids, Iowa

Marcia Wegman's capacity to distill the beauty of the Iowa landscape is firmly rooted in a lifelong love for its pastoral grandeur and a passionately refined skill that captures the familiar and renders it transcendent.

Trained at the University of Iowa, Wegman has spent her career drawing and painting both the mundane and the iconic as informed by her peripatetic travels throughout the world. Now at the height of her expressive power, the artist's fluency bridges naturalism and abstraction in paintings and drawings that resonate with the vivacity of "Iowa"—translated from the language of its first inhabitants, "beautiful land."

Priscilla Steele
Artist, teacher and gallery owner
Campbell Steele Gallery
Marion, Iowa

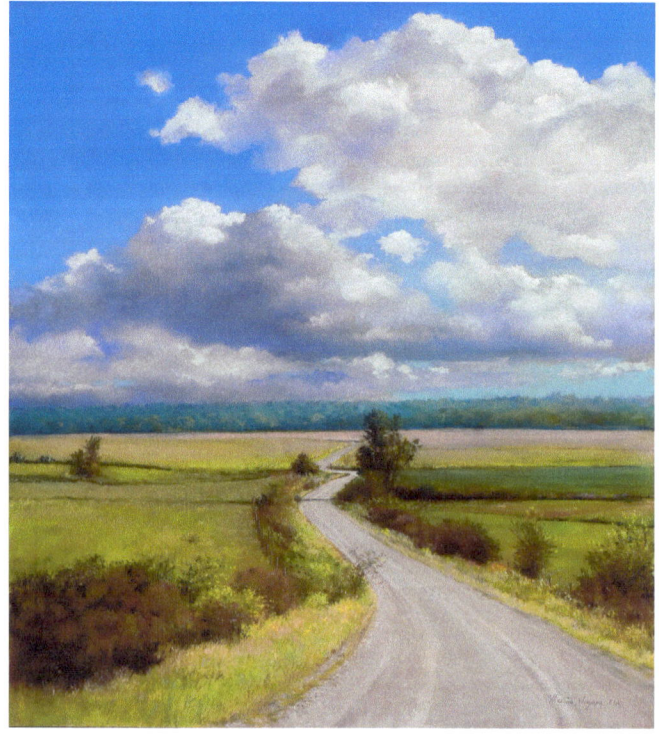

Road to River 17 x 34 in.

Triptych at Kirkwood Community College

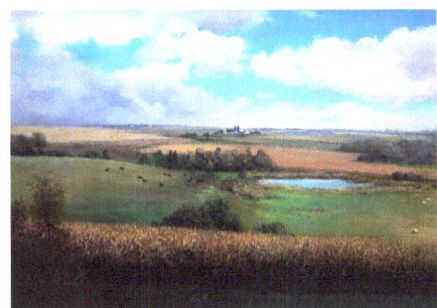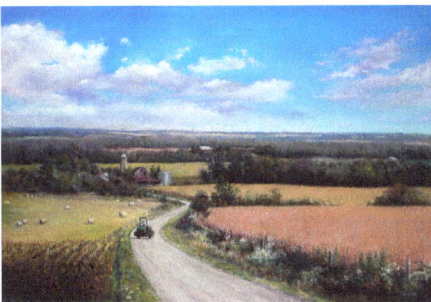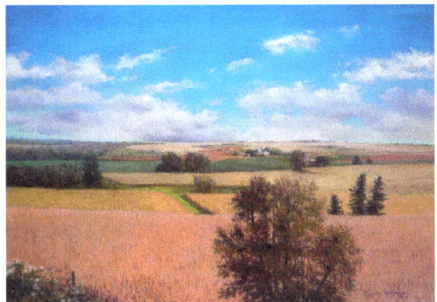

Iowa Fall Fields 24 x 36 in. Linn County Regional Center, Hiawatha, Iowa

It has been a pleasure for me to see Marcia Wegman's paintings in various galleries the past few years and to see her shifts in focus as a painter. Subtle changes in technique and mood throughout her landscape paintings and complete gear shifts in the genre of abstract painting provide much visual interest. I have purchased both types of work for new building projects at Kirkwood Community College. The wonderful relationships of time and space, color, mood, form, shape, texture, and surface are qualities that serve well this quintessential Iowa painter and all who are fortunate to enter her rich world that is so much about Iowa.

Arbe Bareis
Curator, Professor of Painting
Kirkwood Community College
Cedar Rapids, Iowa

Besides being the inspirational muse to many of our artists and owners with her store, Things Things & Things, Marcia Wegman was first known to our customers through her handmade flax paper jewelry. Incorporating crystals into the dyed, folded, locally made paper, each was unique and found a certain audience.

More than a decade ago, Marcia switched her focus to pastel landscapes of Johnson County. Suddenly, she became a gallery rock star. Customers eagerly awaited her work!

On more than one occasion, we'd hear a story about what precipitated the sale. "That was my family's barn. Yes, really." This customer had returned from her current home in China to close an estate. The farm was to be sold. She walked in the gallery and saw the image of the barn, which clearly held emotional resonance for her. There was no doubt about what to do. The piece was purchased and shipped abroad. Marcia's work has accompanied Iowa ex-pats to their homes across the world, feeding their much-loved, sometimes nostalgic, connections to their homeland.

At the gallery, we appreciate Marcia's energy, dedication, modesty, and creativity when it comes to venturing into new territory. As others have so adroitly mentioned, we have seen her master technique and subject over the years, drawing intense admiration from viewers and fellow artists. We revel in her achievements and awards in national shows, including our Art-in-Embassies program. We are honored to be able to celebrate her accomplishments with a contribution to this book.

Astrid Hilger Bennett, Co-owner
For the owners and staff of Iowa Artisans Gallery
Iowa City, Iowa

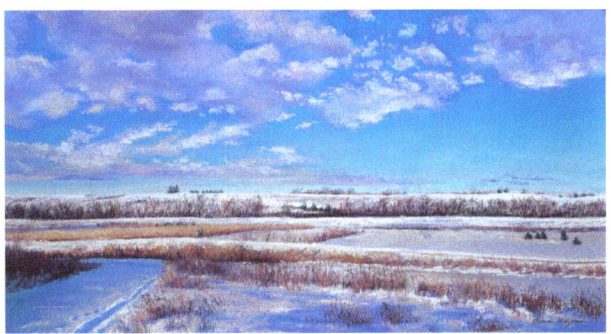

Winter at Waterworks Park 17 x 24 in.

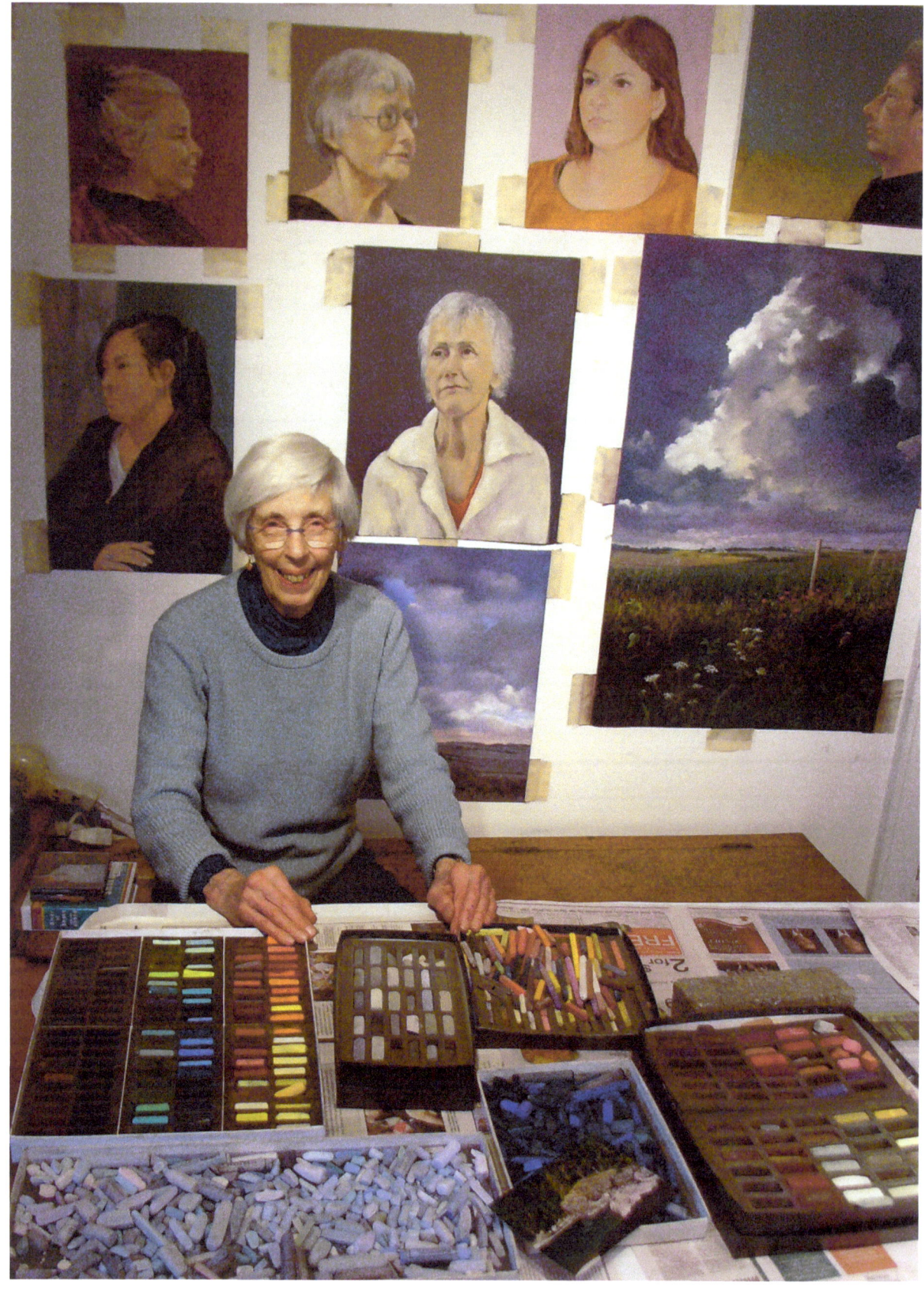

Joan Liffring-Zug Bourret photograph

Marcia Wegman is shown in her Iowa City studio with a landscape similar to the one on the front cover and also portraits she has done.

Creating a Life and Art in Iowa

As far back as I can remember, I have been drawing and painting.

Columbus, Ohio, was home. Miami University of Ohio, where I majored in graphic design, was the beginning of my art education. This gave me a good foundation with emphasis on technique and composition, all the elements of art. An excellent teacher in printmaking diverted me from thinking of fashion illustration as my future profession. And the office manager for whom I worked part-time throughout my college days, a native of Iowa City, brought my attention to the University of Iowa's highly ranked printmaking department. I owe a lot to Dorothy Pownall for my landing in Iowa City, where I have lived for fifty-five years.

I did take one year out of those wonderfully rich years to live in Chicago while my new husband, Tom Wegman, attended the Chicago Art Institute for his second year. We returned to Iowa City where Tom began work in graduate school as a painting major. I received my master's in fine arts in printmaking in 1961. I never made another print.

For a few years, I continued to paint and draw. First the birth of a son, Kyle, then the creation of our store, Things & Things & Things, in downtown Iowa City, which we ran together for thirty-four years (with the addition of Tom's sister, Doris Marchael, as our business partner), and finally the birth of our daughter, Syril, all made it very hard to find time for the artwork.

It was a difficult decision when I found it necessary for myself and my family and my business to give up my artwork. I knew it would be for a period of time before I would be able to return to it. That period of time grew to fifteen years.

What I found during that fifteen-year hiatus is that a lot was going on inside my head. I was looking at art in museums, galleries, and books, I was maturing as an individual with a more developed consciousness, and I was observing the world around me. I was deeply growing in a spiritual dimension due to the death of my twelve-year-old son in the crash of a small private plane in 1975.

All these factors meant that when I was able to return to making art, by taking a drawing, then a watercolor, class through the university, I was able to be creative at a new, higher level. It took very little time for me to regain the technical skills.

Over the years, I have worked in a variety of mediums: oil, watercolor, acrylic, mixed media collage, handmade paper art and jewelry, and finally pastel. Nature, whether realistic or abstract, underlies everything I do.

From my earliest childhood days, being out in nature while walking, hiking, camping, backpacking and gardening is what fills me up, speaks to my soul, and connects me spiritually with all that is.

But it wasn't until I began working with pastels in 1999 that I felt I had truly found my medium. What especially appealed to me about pastels was being able to use them as a combination of painting and drawing. And the Iowa landscape in all seasons was the perfect subject for this new discovery. I credit Iowa-born artist Ellen Wagoner for showing me both the possibilities of pastel and the infinite beauty of Iowa. Credit also must go to Mary Lea Kruse, an Iowa City art consultant. My first pastel landscape, not of Iowa but of the Lake District in England, was done for a client of Mary Lea's.

Any landscape artist will tell you it is all about the light and how light illuminates and colors land, plant, and architectural forms. My landscape paintings begin with a foray out into the country, primarily in Johnson County, but also in other parts of Iowa. The early morning or evening, when the light creates the opportunity for more colorful and dynamic compositions, is my favorite time to travel down the small gravel roads looking for interesting views to photograph.

Back in my studio, the photos are stored in my computer. Later, when ready to begin a new painting, I print out the selected photo or photos, given that I often use two or three different views or a different sky for one painting. I have learned to keep a little digital camera in my car to be ready to snap a picture if an interesting cloud formation appears. I have taken sky pictures through the windshield of my car while at a stoplight, which I later turned into significant parts of some paintings.

My working method is to paint quickly and directly, with no preliminary planning and drawing, as I prefer working out the compositional problems on the paper. Weekly sessions with both figure and portrait drawing, and painting with live models, have helped me develop my ability to see and the hand/eye coordination to record with expressiveness.

The support for my pastel paintings is heavy archival sanded paper made expressly for pastel artists. It holds many layers of pastel and is easy to wipe out and change, one of the great advantages of the pastel medium. The biggest disadvantage in painting with pastels is not being able to mix the precise color and hue on a palette, as can be done with oil, acrylic, and watercolor. This results in a huge quantity of pastel sticks from a number of different manufacturers, in differing degrees of softness. Knowing which one to use for a desired effect comes with practice.

People looking at my paintings often comment that they look like photographs. I then ask them to look very closely in order to see how quickly and gesturally they are done. I like to think this approach adds a certain energy to the painting as a whole. I rarely spend more than five days of about three hours each on a painting, regardless of size.

Nothing brings me more pleasure than being in my small, bright studio, surrounded with drawings taped up all around the space, a couple of newly finished paintings taped to one wall, my two black cats snuggled side by side in two baskets holding reference material, and a recorded book playing. It is here that I daily carry out an expression of my passion for the beauty of the land called Iowa.

—Marcia Wegman, Iowa City, 2013

Marcia Wegman paintings are in many private and public collections. They include:
University of Iowa Hospitals and Clinics, Iowa City
University of Iowa College of Dentistry, Iowa City
University of Iowa College of Medicine, Iowa City
Fred Riddle, D.D.S., Iowa City
Mercy Hospital, Iowa City
Mount Mercy College, Cedar Rapids
MidWest*One* Bank, Iowa City
Pediatric Associates, Iowa City
Kirkwood Community College, Agriculture Sciences, Cedar Rapids
City Workplace Uniforms & Mats, Cedar Rapids
Benchmark, Inc., Cedar Rapids
Cedar Rapids Museum of Art

Honored Pastels

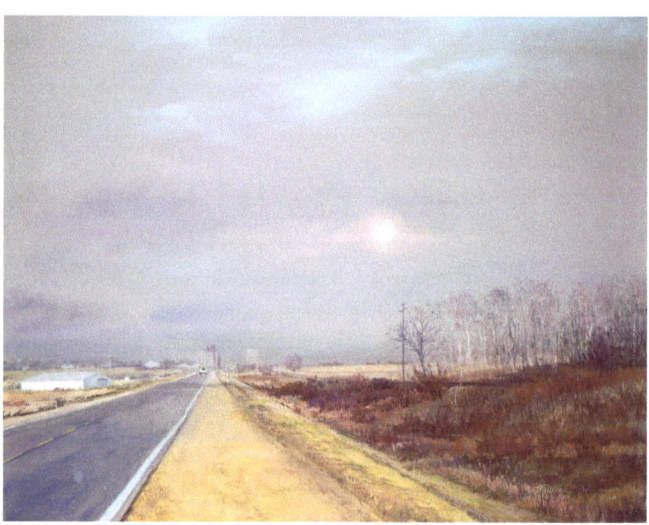

Morning Fog Along Route 30 III 21 x 27 in.
Dubuque Museum of Art Biennial Juried Show, 2013

Summer Wildflowers and Corn (Summer) Dubuque Museum of Art Biennial Juried Show, 2011

Maquoketa Cornfields (Summer) Demonstration painting for feature article in *Pastel Journal,* December 2013

White Farm (Farm) Finalist *International Artist Magazine,* December/January 2013

July Weather (Summer) Finalist *International Artist Magazine,* August/September 2010

Summer Wildflowers and Corn (Summer), *The Artist's Magazine,* winner in the "Over 60" competition

Herd (Cattle) Pastel Society of America, 2010 Annual Members' Juried Exhibition

November Farm (Farm) Pastel Society of America, 2011 Annual Members' Juried Exhibition

Books by Marcia Wegman:
Lula Belle
Latvia and Lithuania
Iowa Pastel Landscapes
Available from Penfield Books, Amazon, and Prairie Lights

The Infinite Beauty of Iowa

By David W. Wright

"I delight in showing with my paintings that Iowa is anything but boring…"
—Marcia Wegman

In the eyes of the world, the landscape of Iowa is forever captured in Grant Wood's sensuous images of fertile fields and undulating hills. Wood's depictions stand in a long line of memorable images of Iowa, stretching back to the first half of the nineteenth century when artists John Caspar Wild and George Catlin responded to the beauty of this land between the rivers.

Marcia Wegman builds upon this artistic legacy, now employing the challenging medium of pastel to explore the magical effects of sky, earth, and light of this place called Iowa.

Before Europeans discovered it, this land was fully occupied by native hunters and gatherers, people who first inhabited this region nearly thirteen thousand years ago. Science tells us that Iowa soil has been used for the cultivation of domesticated plants for nearly three thousand years. Our valleys and hills echo with the venerable history of agricultural endeavor. Our most recent history includes Iowa's leading role in feeding the world. The clouds and sky over Iowa, memorably shown in Wegman's images, look down upon a landscape shaped by ice, wind, and rivers. The timeless flow of waters—springs, creeks, streams, and majestic rivers—carve out the prairies, hills, and valleys that she

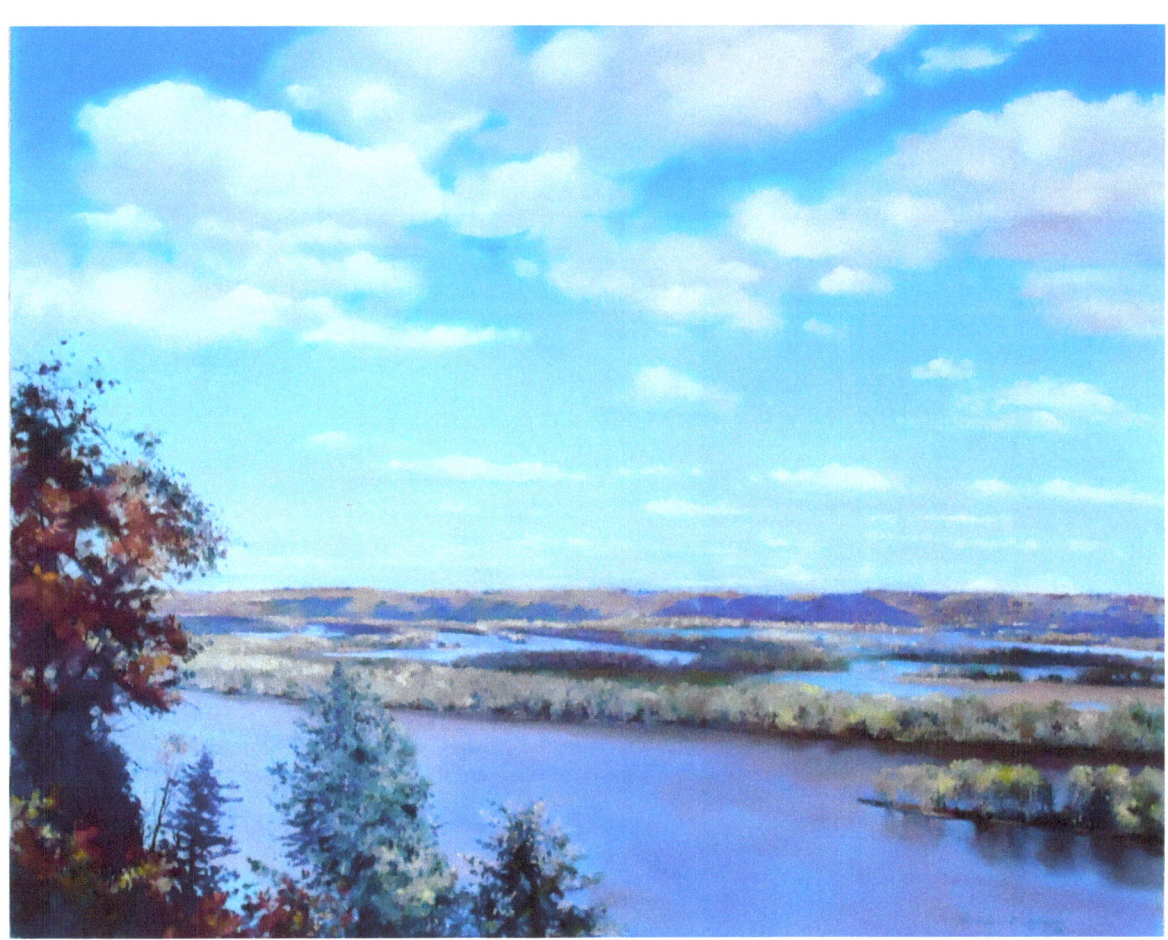

Mississippi Overlook 21 x 27 in.
View from Pike's Peak State Park north of the Wisconsin River

captures in pastels.

Marcia Wegman's pastel portraits of Iowa demonstrate the picturesque diversity of Iowa's landscapes. How many of us know that this land is generally not flat? Its varied topography ranges from the Loess Hills in the west to the Driftless zone of steep hills and valleys in the east, from prairie to forest, and from plateau to cold-water cave. Some visible Iowa bedrock formations are 1.6 billion years old—the familiar limestone that we all know dates to a paltry five hundred million years of age. Glacial advances and retreats formed our land; airborne silt and resulting prairies produced some of the richest soil on earth here.

This Iowa, a terrain of fertile ground, gently rolling hills, and ample precipitation, is the only state bordered by rivers—two great rivers, the Missouri and the Mississippi, forming its west and east boundaries. While the flow of rivers is one of Iowa's primarily geologic features, the state also proudly stands at the bridge between the forests of the eastern states and the grasslands to the west.

Iowa's landscape today, with its domesticated aspect of farms and roads, bears little resemblance to its ancient appearance. Less than one percent of its native grasslands remain. Yet some regions retain the wilderness that was known to those inhabitants of centuries ago. In the eastern part of the state, which often inspires Wegman's pastels, the palisades along wild rivers were formed more than four hundred fifty million years ago. Wild landscapes include the scenic valleys that tumble down to the Mississippi.

The dramatic beauty of eastern Iowa is captured in Wegman's work. She knows well the Karst topography and its springs, caves, and underground streams. She has studied the Mississippi landscape as did Mark Twain and Zebulon Pike. She well knows the spot of the confluence of the Wisconsin River with the Mississippi, and the view from Iowa's Pike's Peak, one of the most impressive prospects in North America.

That beautiful prospect marks the location of a great historic moment, the first sight by Europeans of what would become known as Iowa. In 1673, nearly three hundred and fifty years ago, a mere blink of an eye in geologic terms, Jacques Marquette and Louis Jolliet floated down the Wisconsin River, the first Europeans to see the Upper Mississippi and the land across it to the west. The European discovery of Iowa is but a moment in time; we who now live in Iowa would do well to remember that this region was the home of ancient inhabitants for thousands of years before us.

The timeless beauty of Iowa's earth and sky, with fog, sunlight, and shadow, is well captured in the medium of pastel and its pure, powdered pigment. Marcia Wegman discovered this for herself: "Pastels lend themselves to developing the ephemeral aspects of light and color in the landscape."

Wegman is at work with the ancient artistic medium used to great effect by her predecessor, Mary Cassatt, whose memorable pastel images of a century ago still inspire. Yet works in pastel are notoriously difficult to execute, demanding an unusual dexterity, color sense, and artistic insight. Wegman has developed her special affinity that links this demanding and dynamic artistic medium with her subject matter.

In her work, Wegman has captured, as she puts it, the "infinite beauty of Iowa" in every season and aspect. Her special affinity for drawing clouds and sky is a modern marvel. Exploring fields, farms, and forests, she sees and records with a clarity and skill that reflect all the enduring qualities of Iowa's immortal landscape.

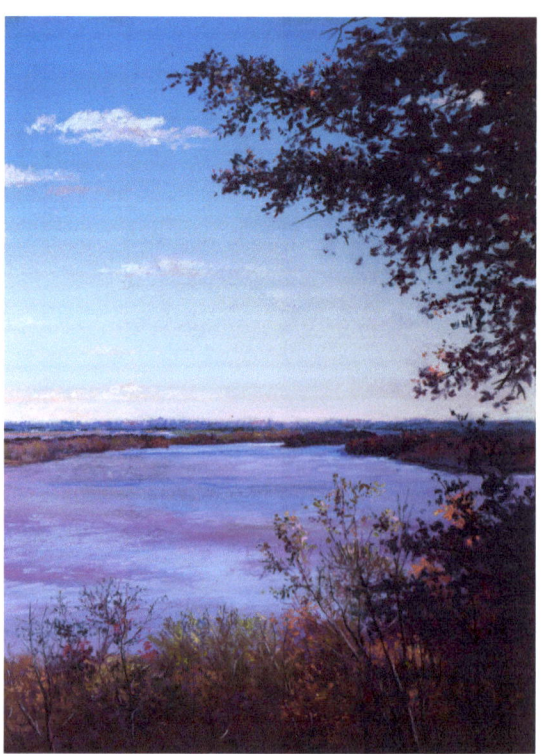

The Mississippi at Burlington 17 x 12 in.

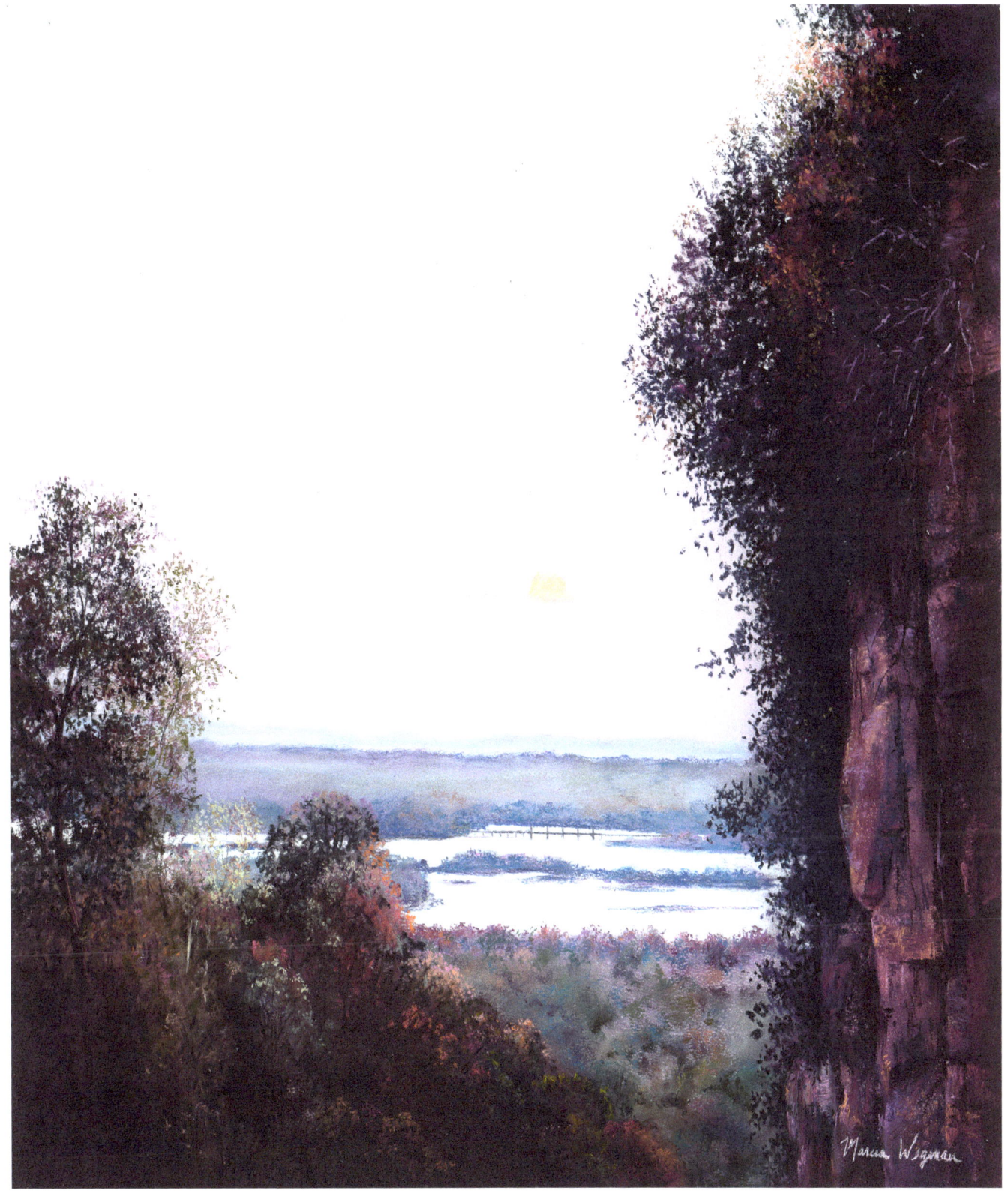

Looking Back at Guttenberg 24 x 28 in. A view of the Mississippi River from Iowa with Wisconsin in the background

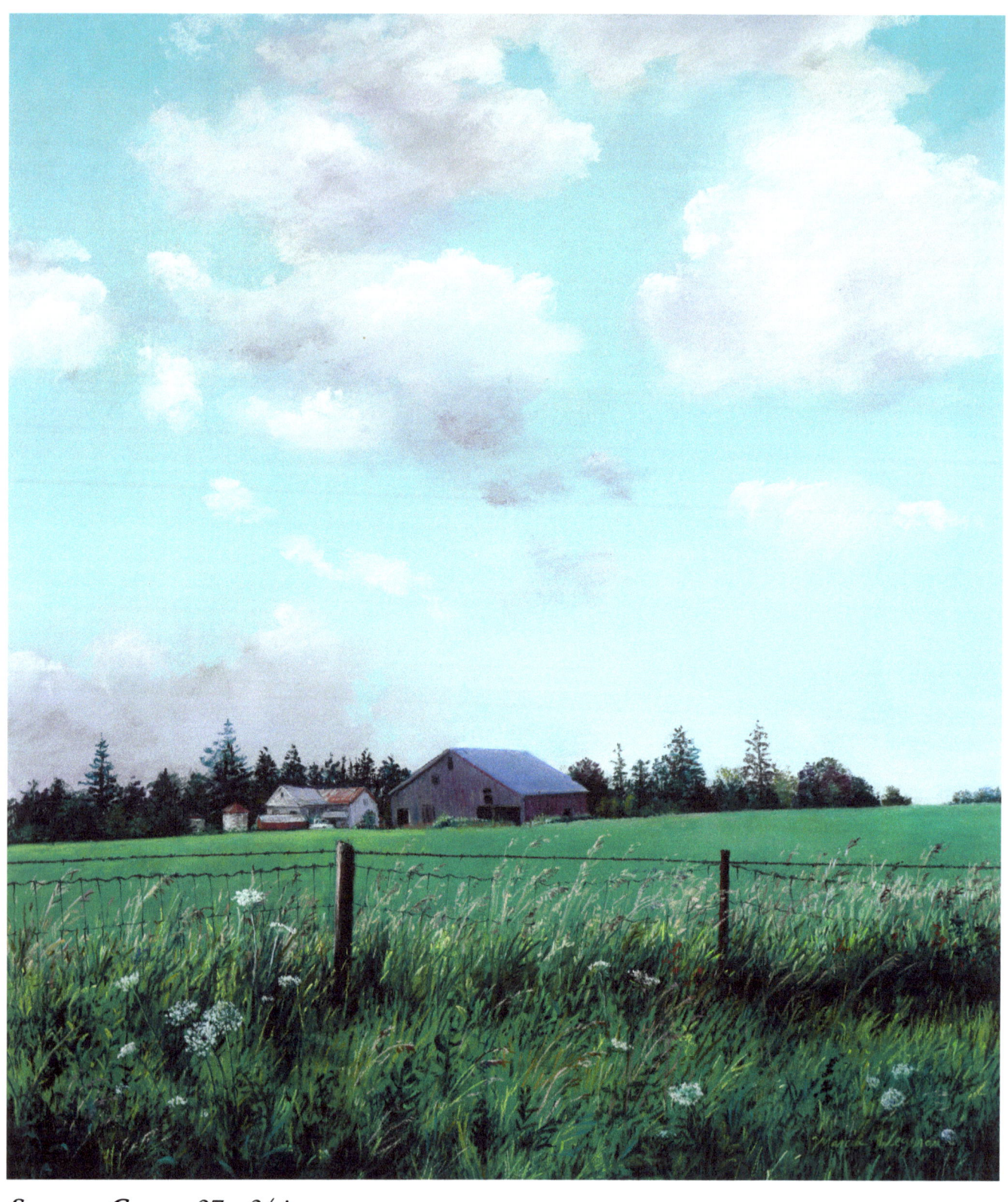

Summer Greens 27 x 24 in.

Iowa Farms

A favorite scene to paint is a long horizontal band of land silhouetted against the sky with periodic accents of farms nestled among tall trees. I love this aspect of the Iowa country. The close-up view of farms I find equally intriguing, as no two farms are laid out alike.

The relationship of shapes and colors is what makes for a good painting with a combination of squares, rectangles, triangles, and cylinders in either muted or bright colors. The accent of straight light and telephone poles is also a nice design element.

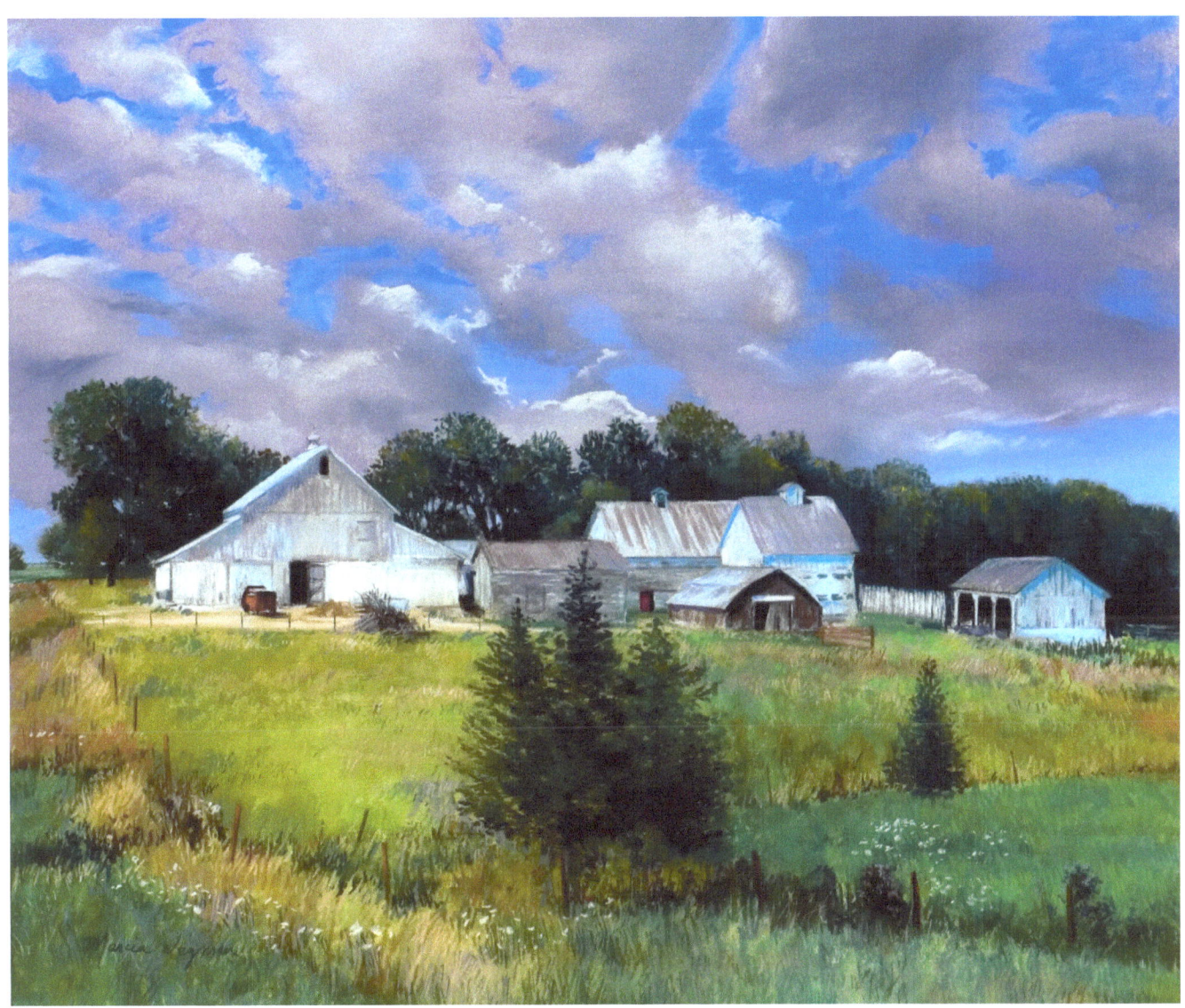

Blue Farm 20 x 24 in.

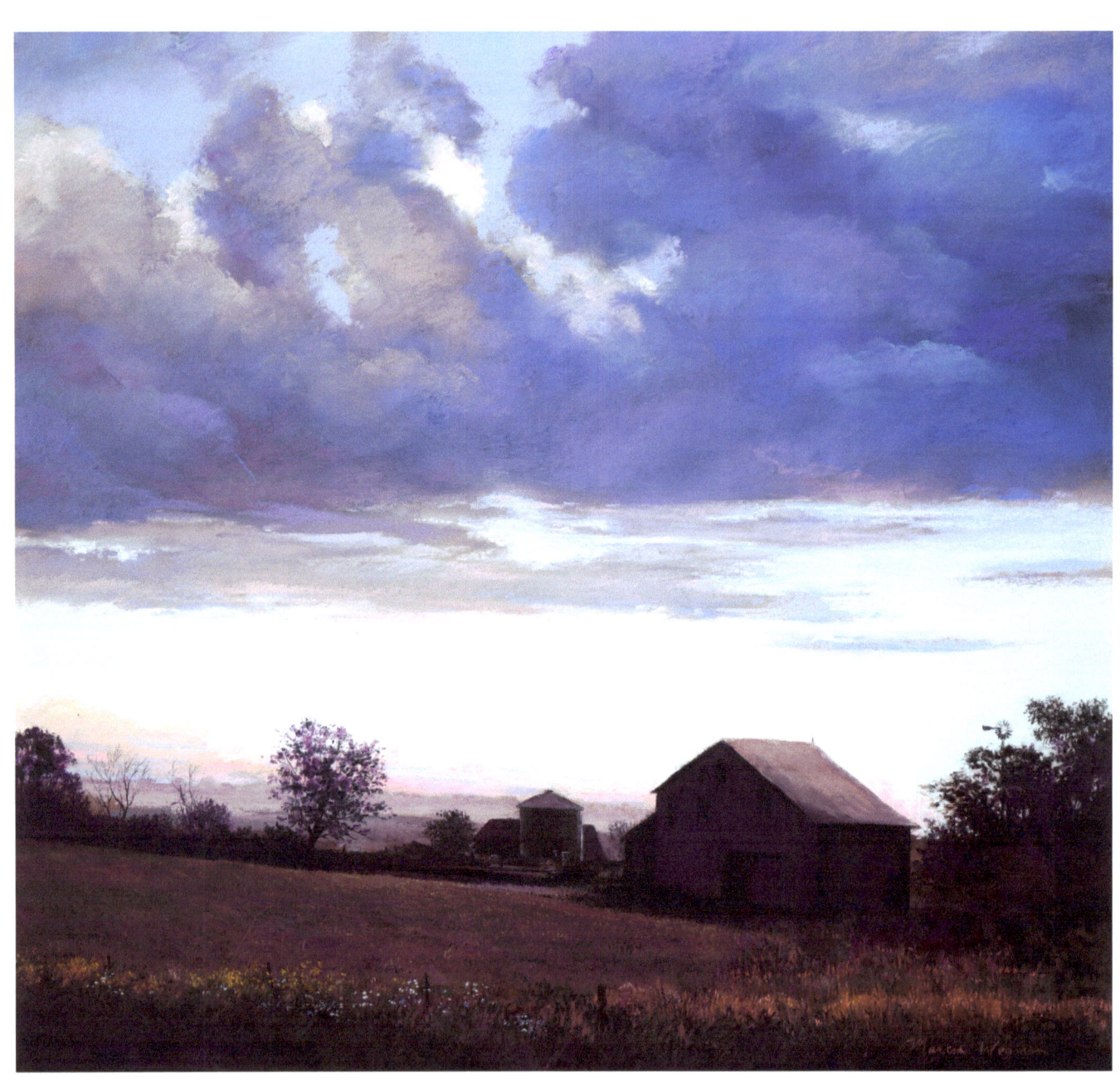

Evening Grays 24 x 24 in.

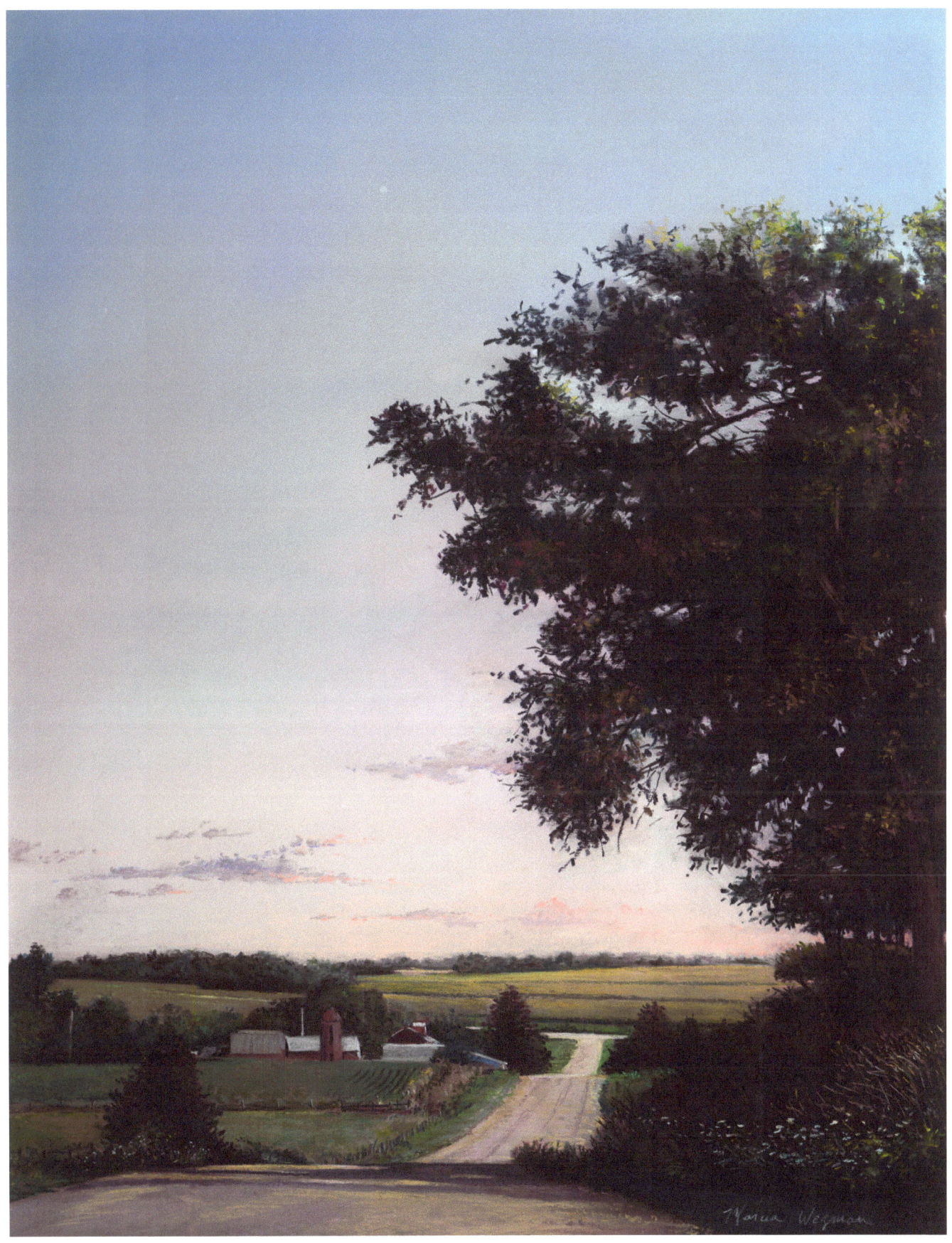

Dawn 27 x 21 in.

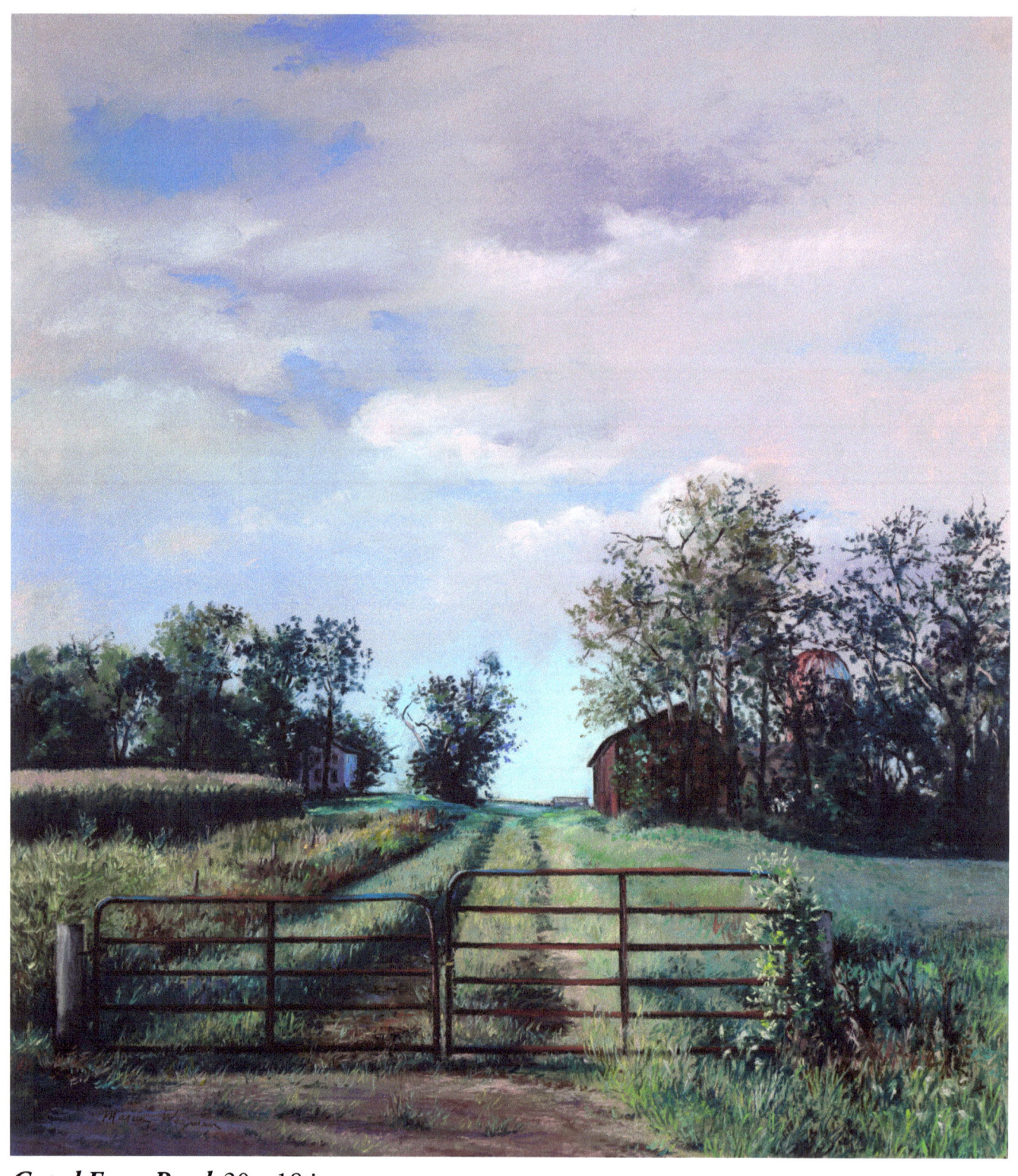

Gated Farm Road 20 x 18 in.

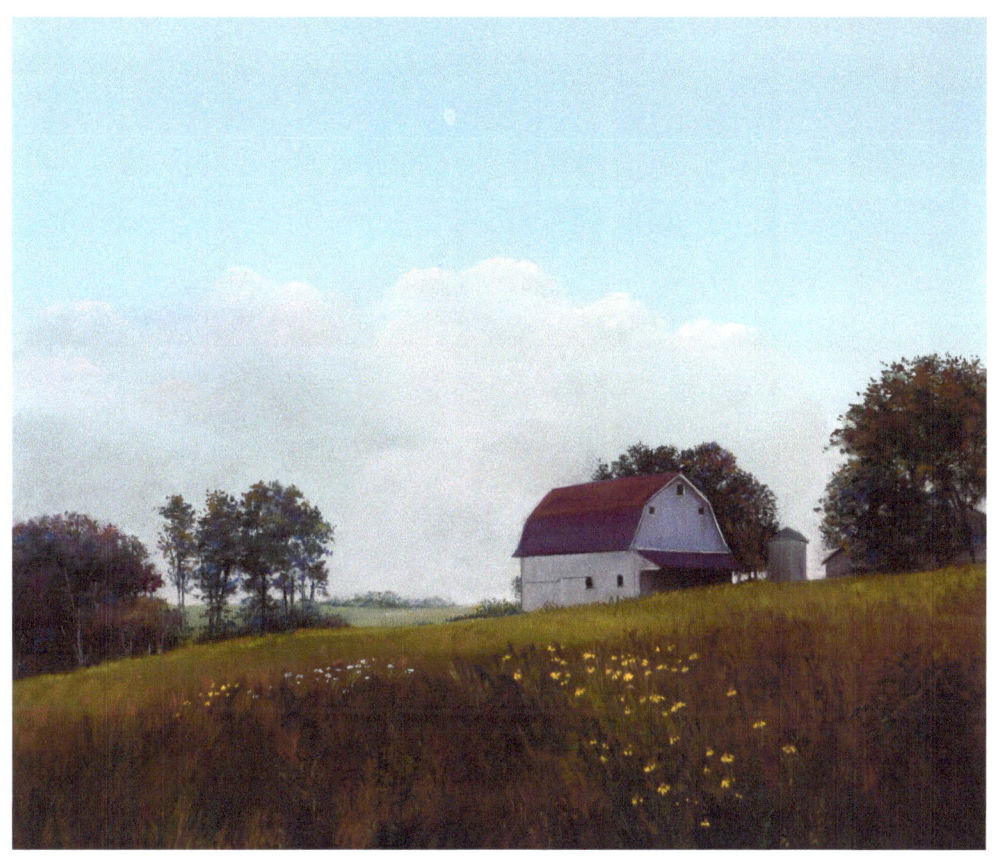

Farm and Flowers 24 x 36 in.

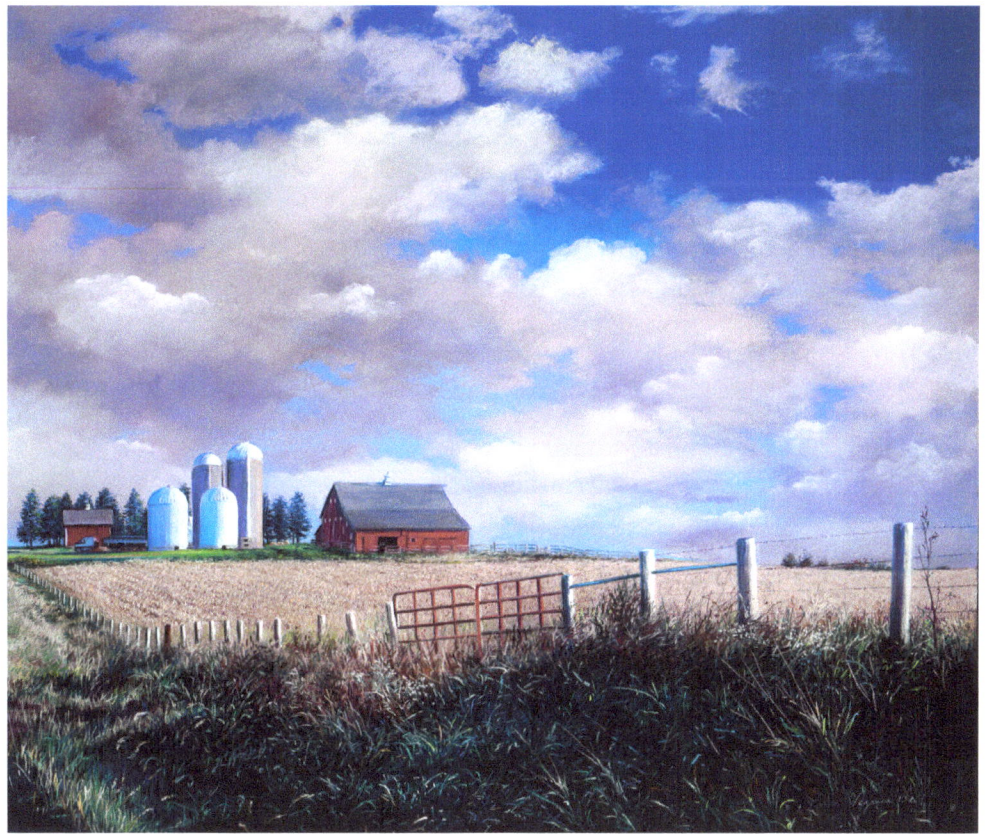

Farm and Field 28 x 34 in.

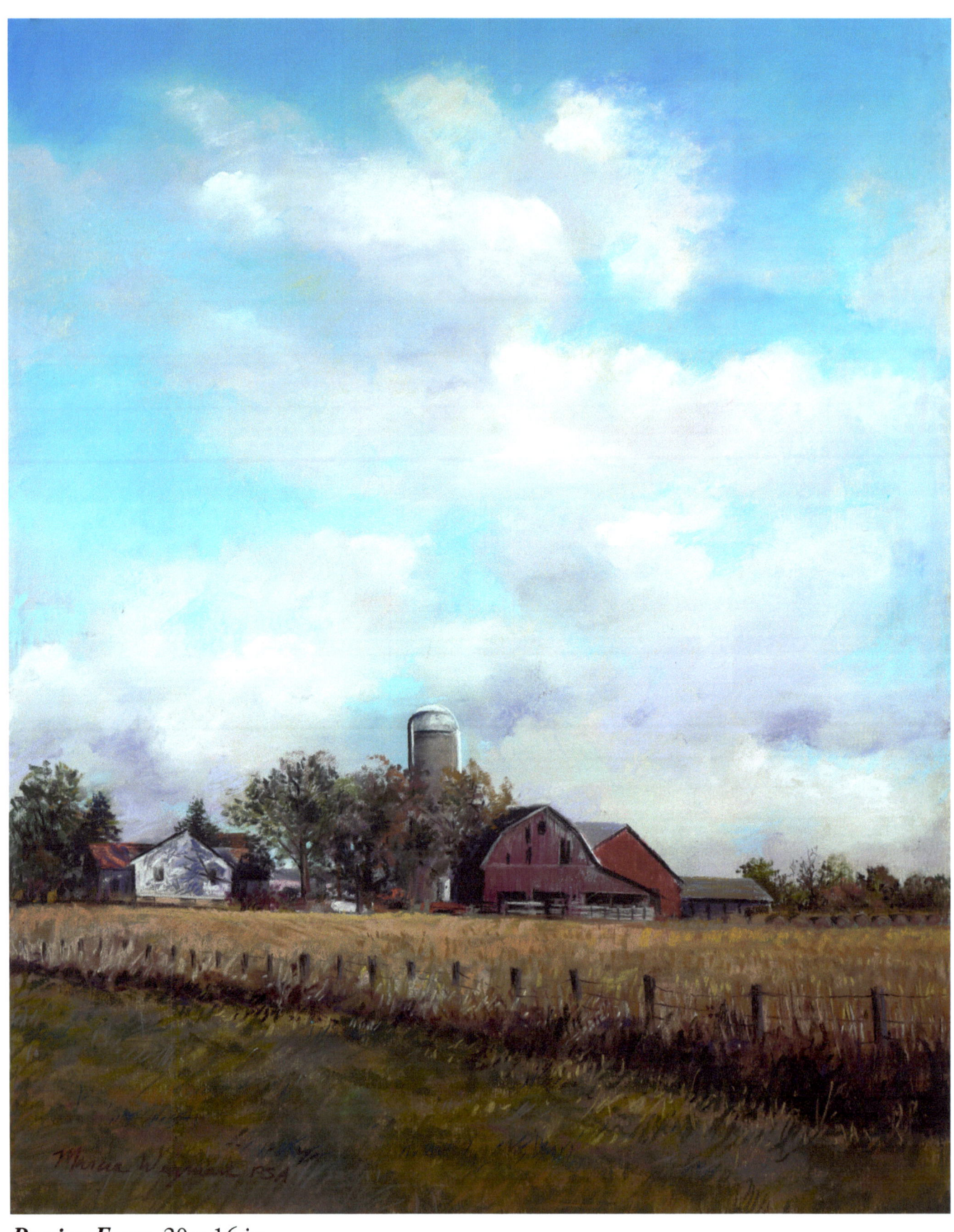

Passing Farm 20 x 16 in.

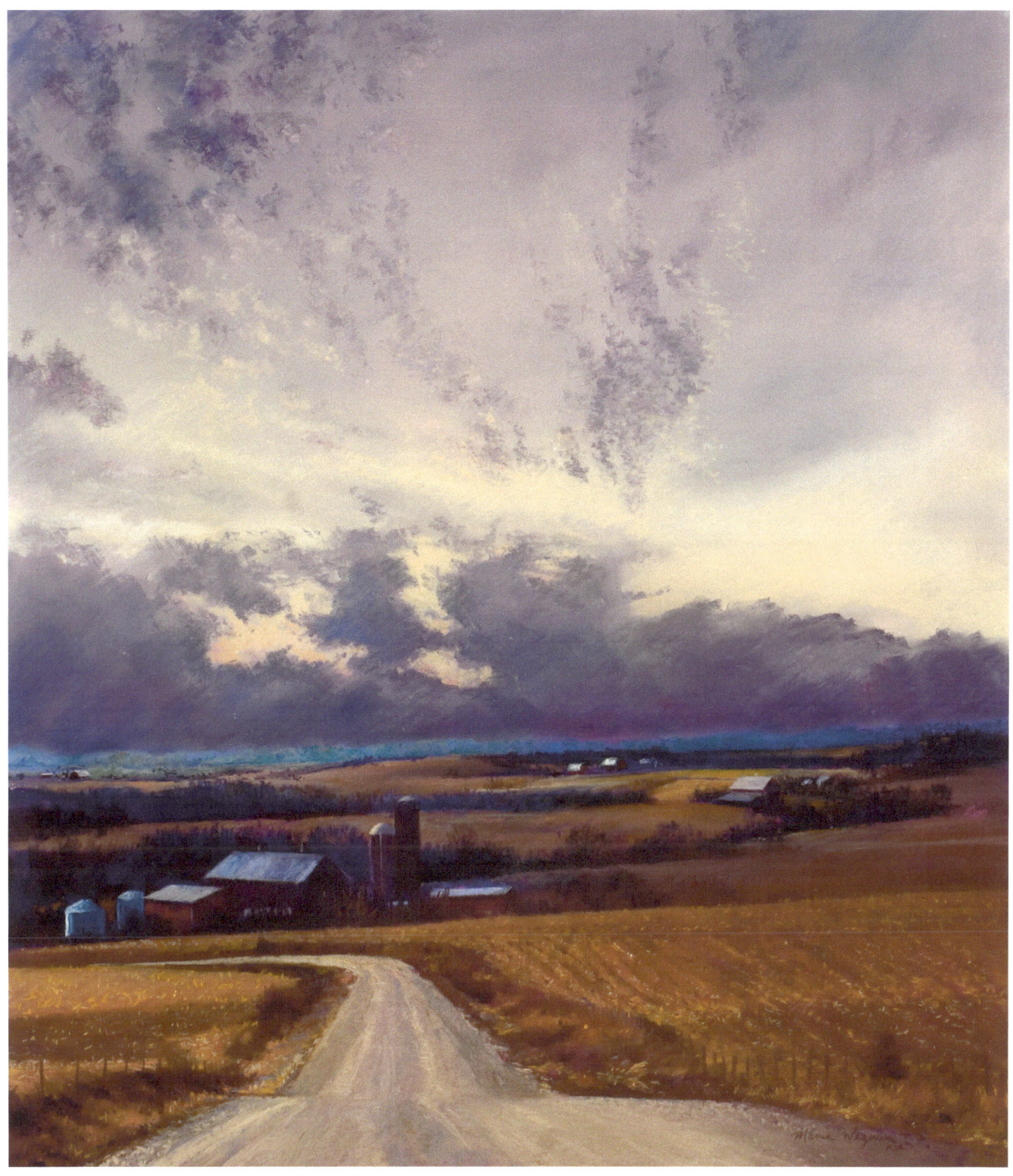

November Country 27 x 24 in.

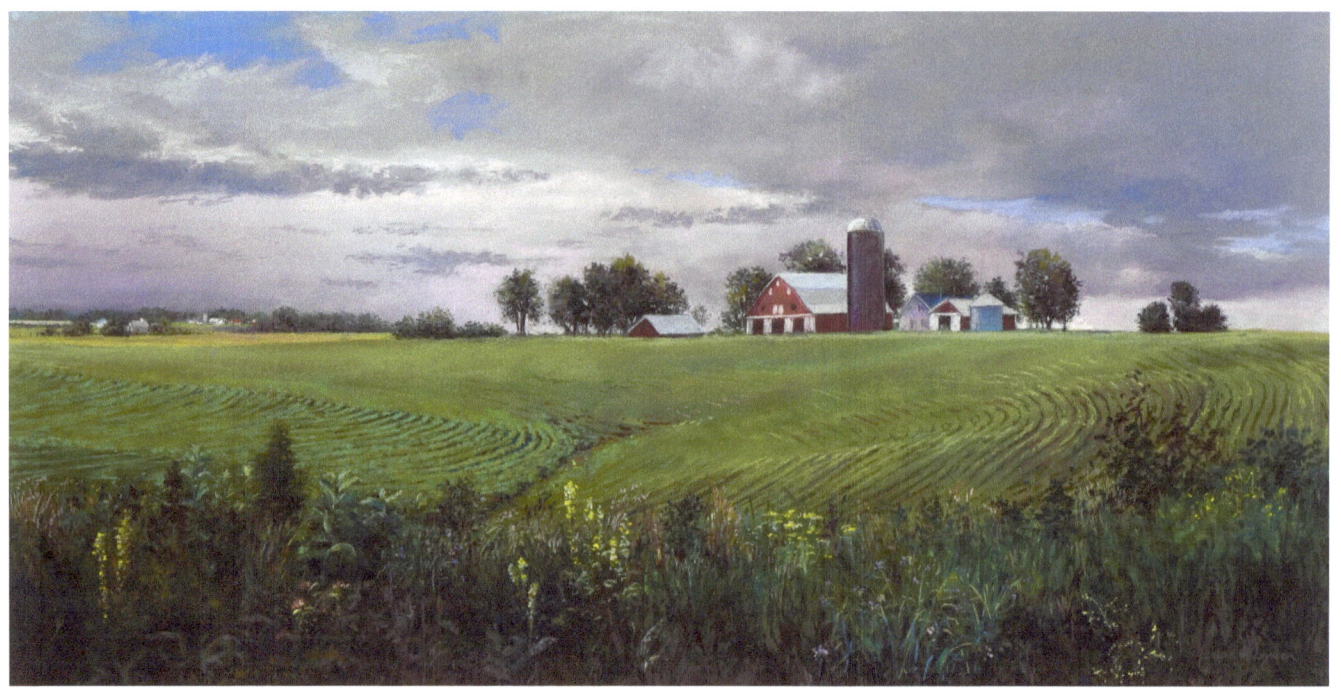

Beginning of Summer in Iowa 17 x 36 in.

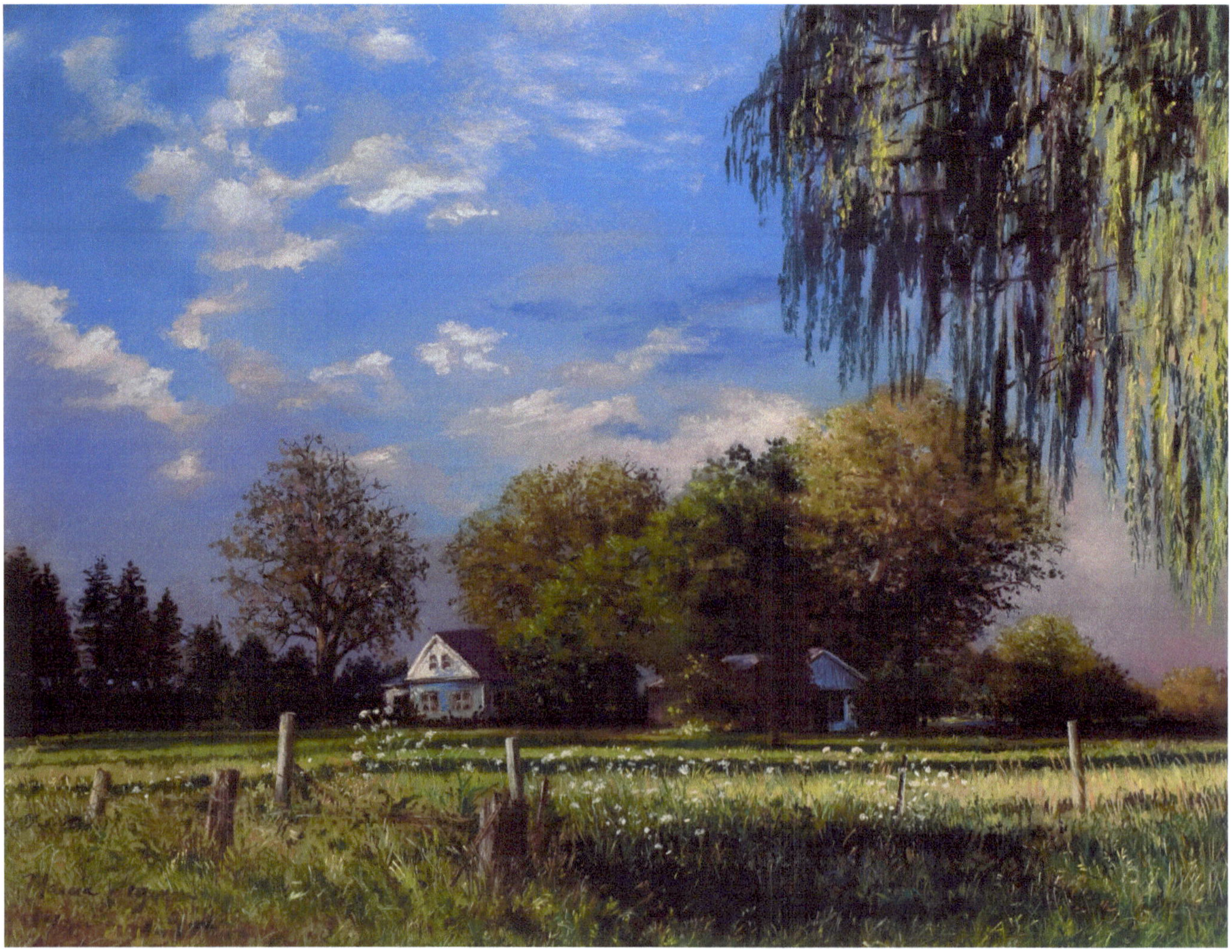

Farm Home from the Road 18 x 24 in.

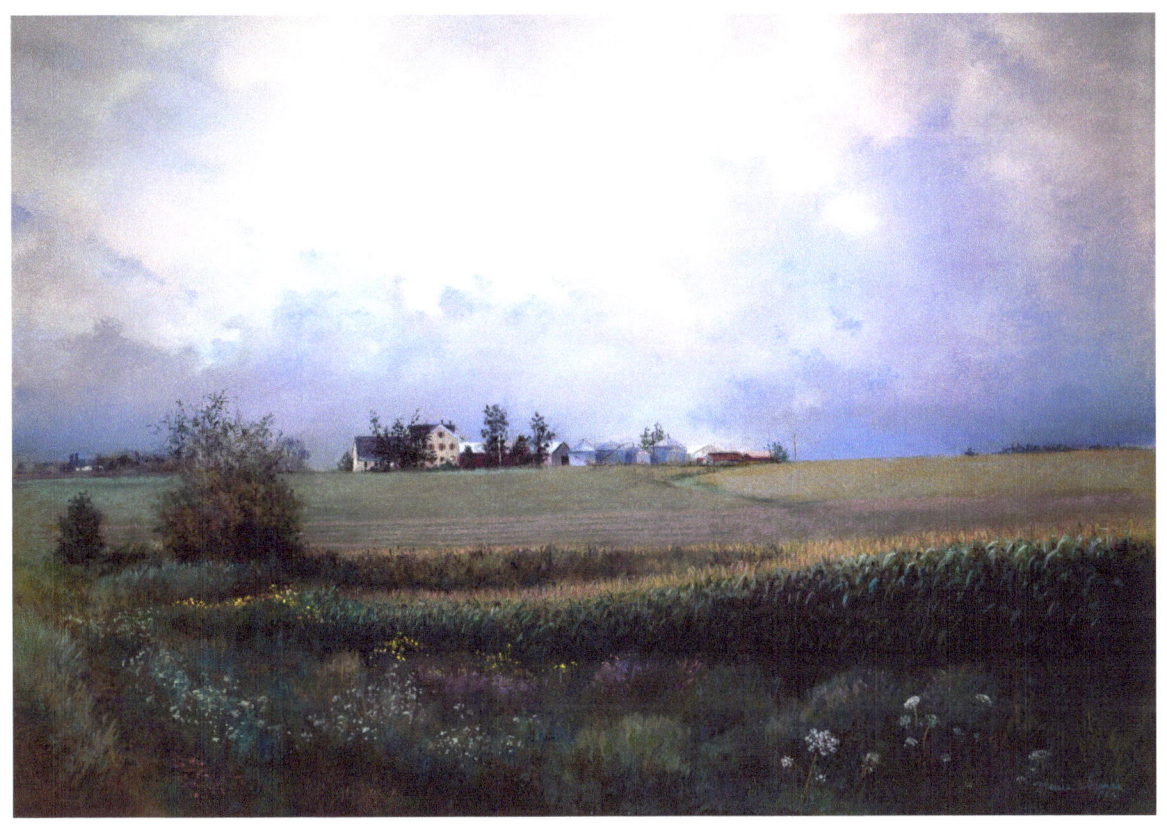

Iowa Farm and Field 27 x 40 in.

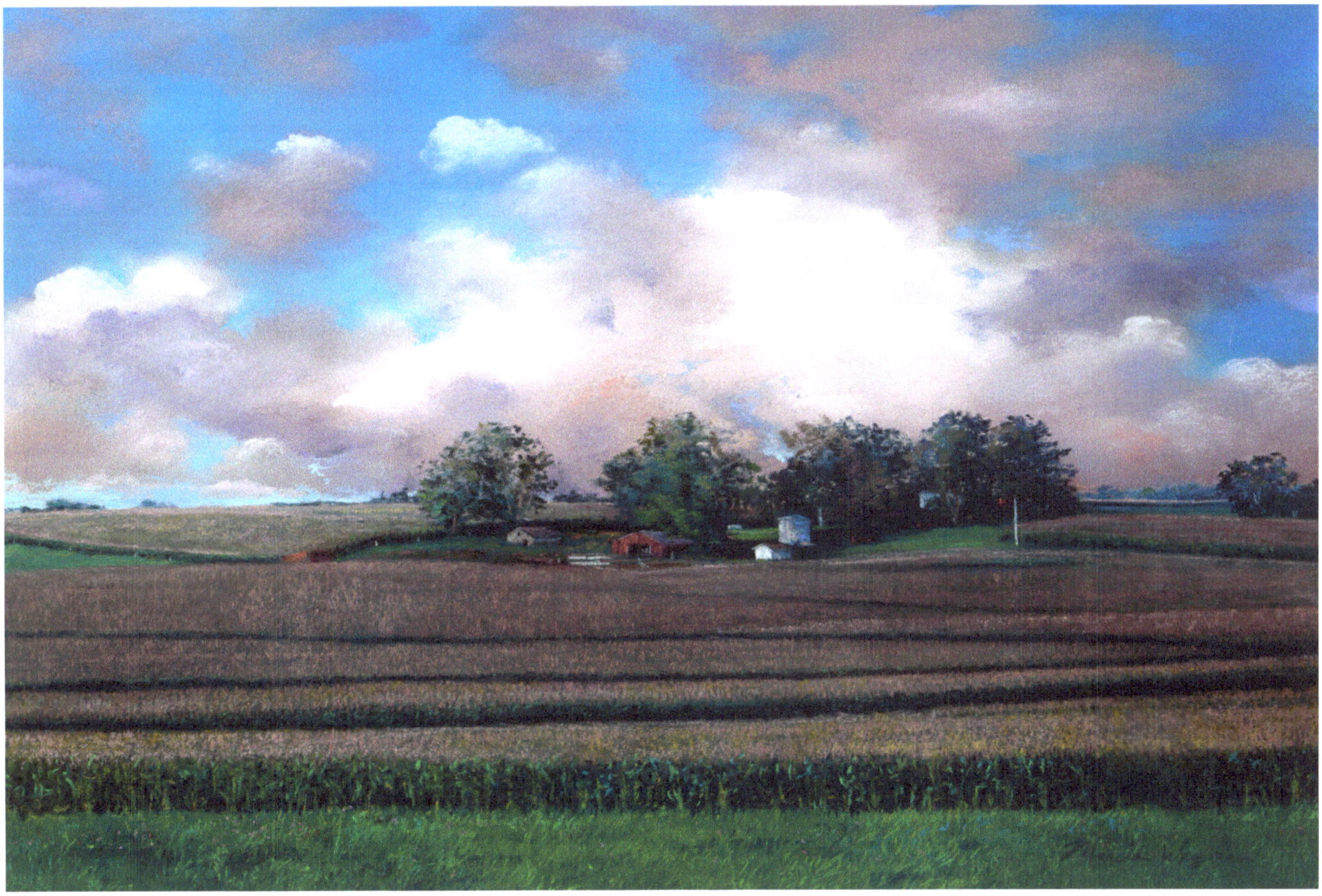

Iowa Farm 21 x 18 in.

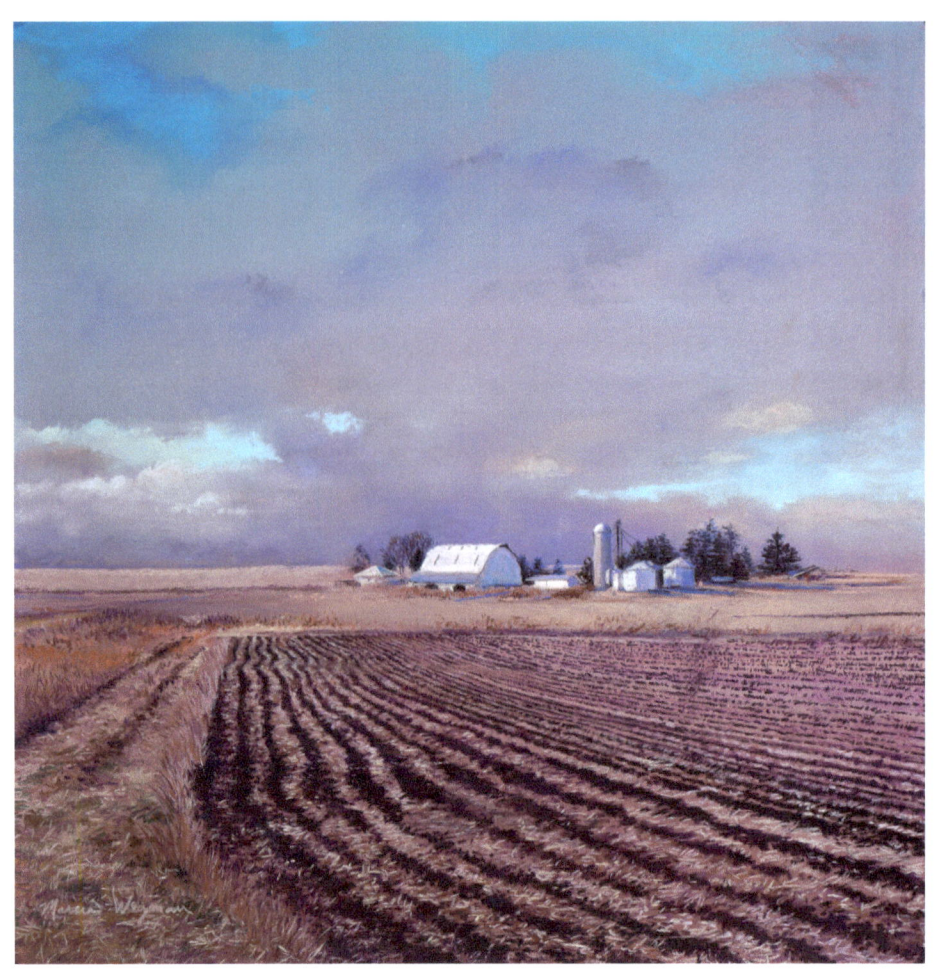

November Farm 18 x 18 in.

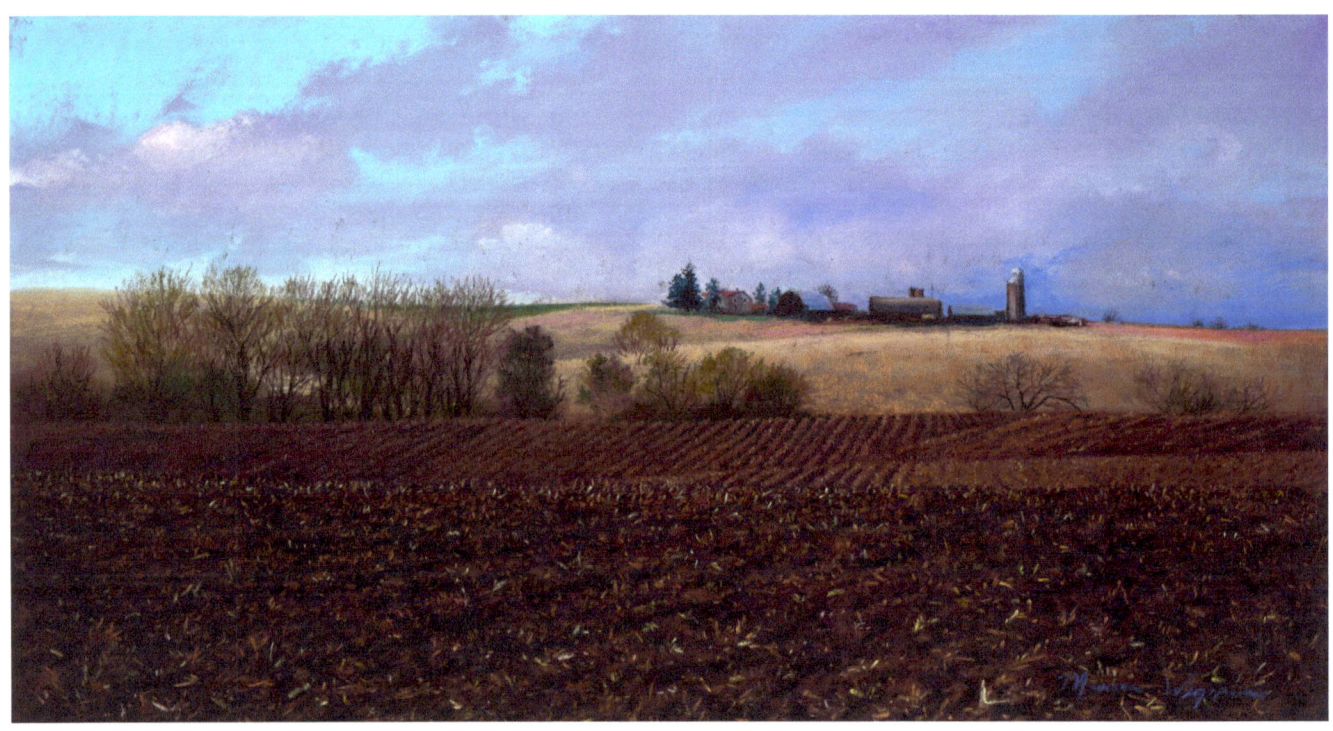

Plowed Fields 12 x 22 in.

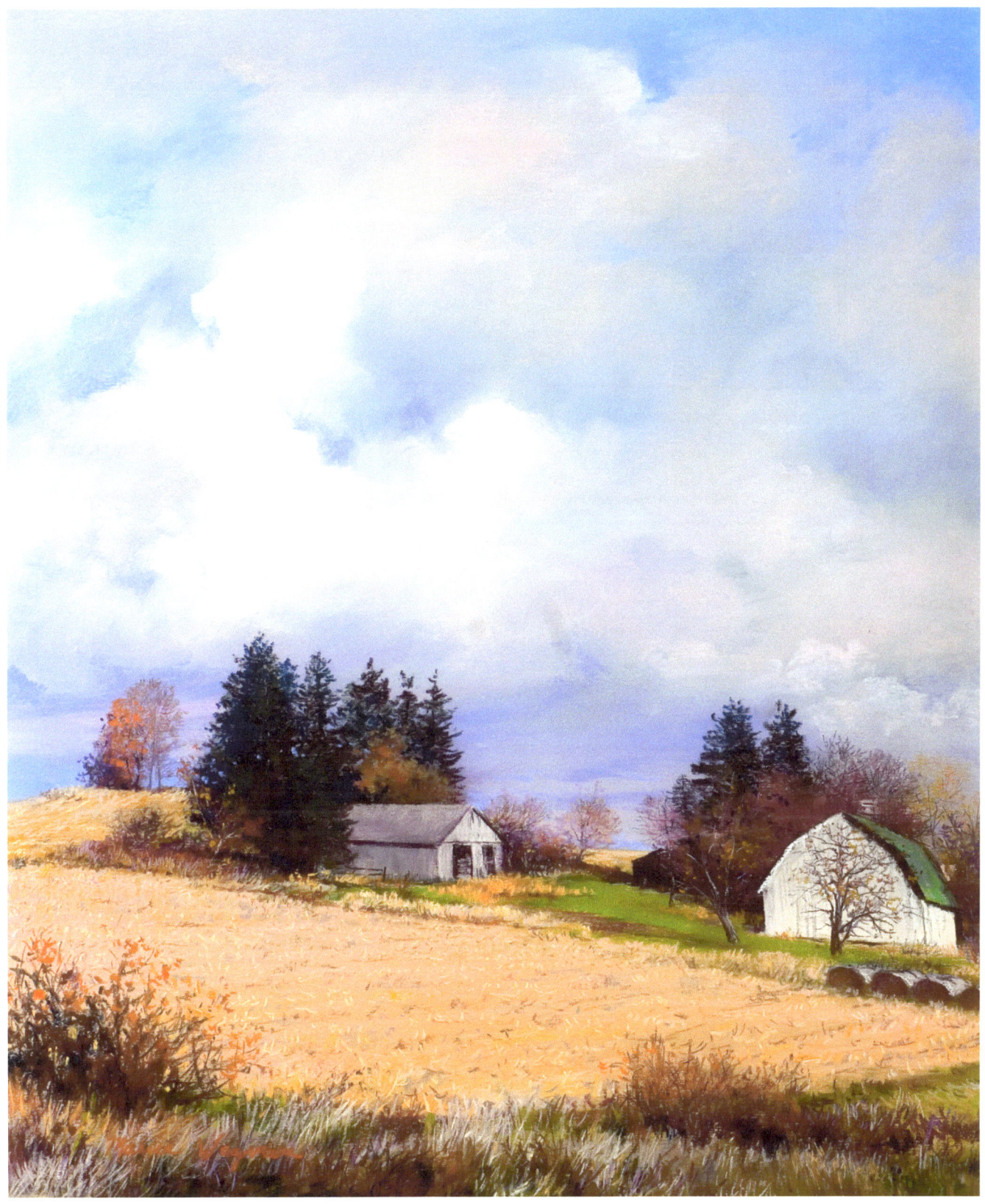

Hill Farm 21 x 18 in.

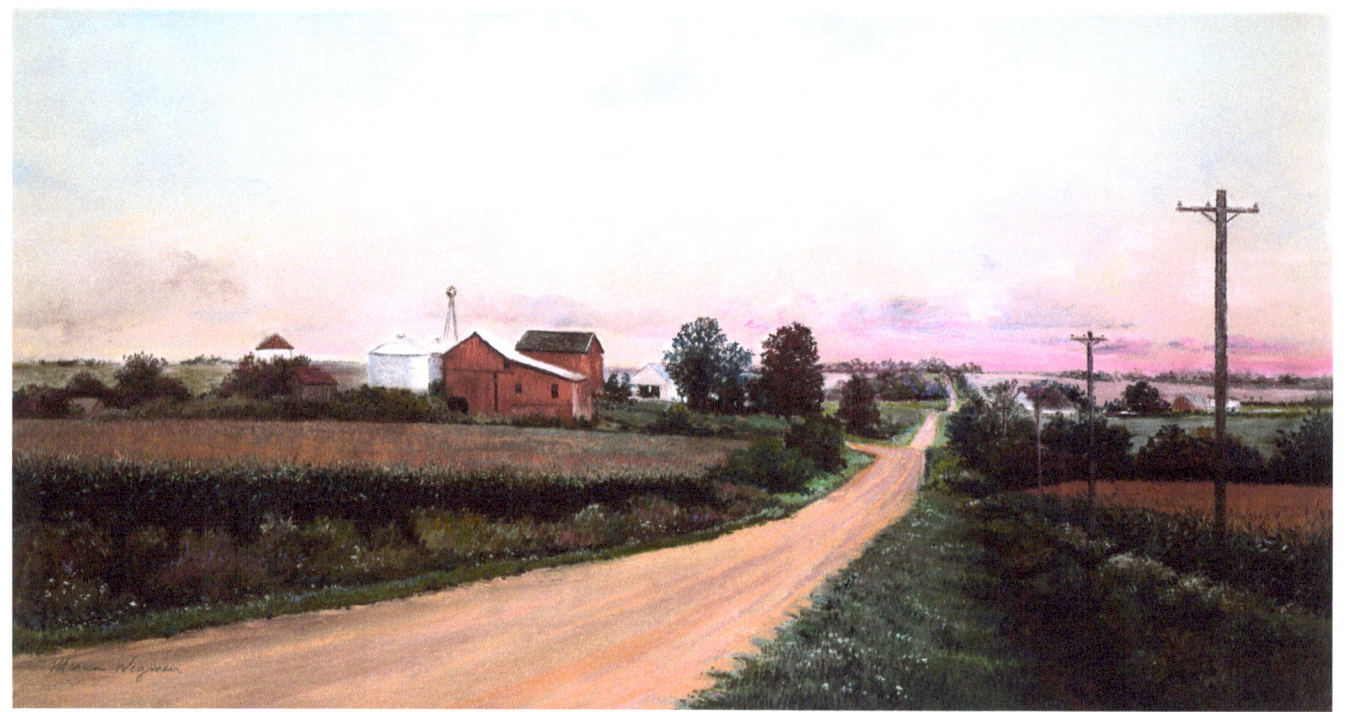

Farm Road 12 x 24 in.

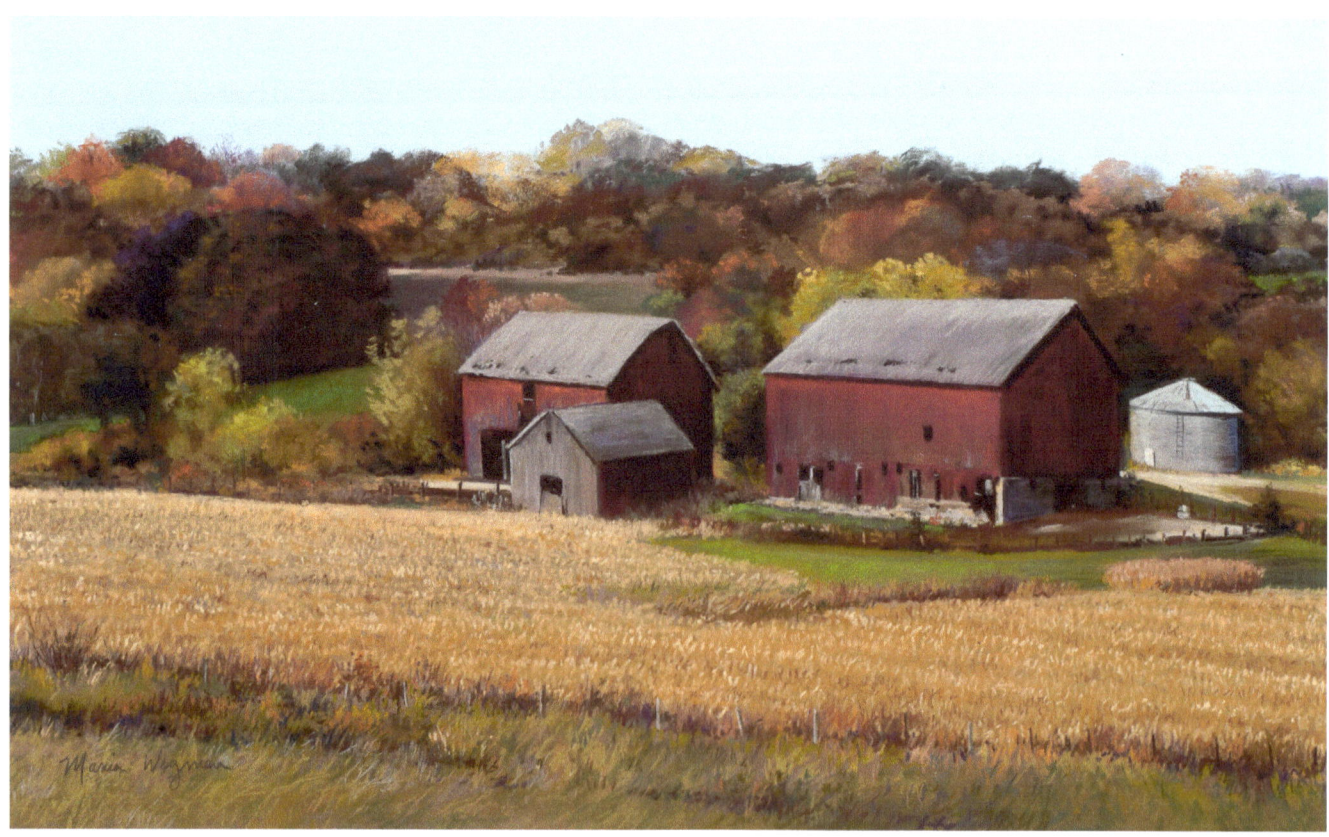

Northeast Iowa Farm 12 x 20 in.

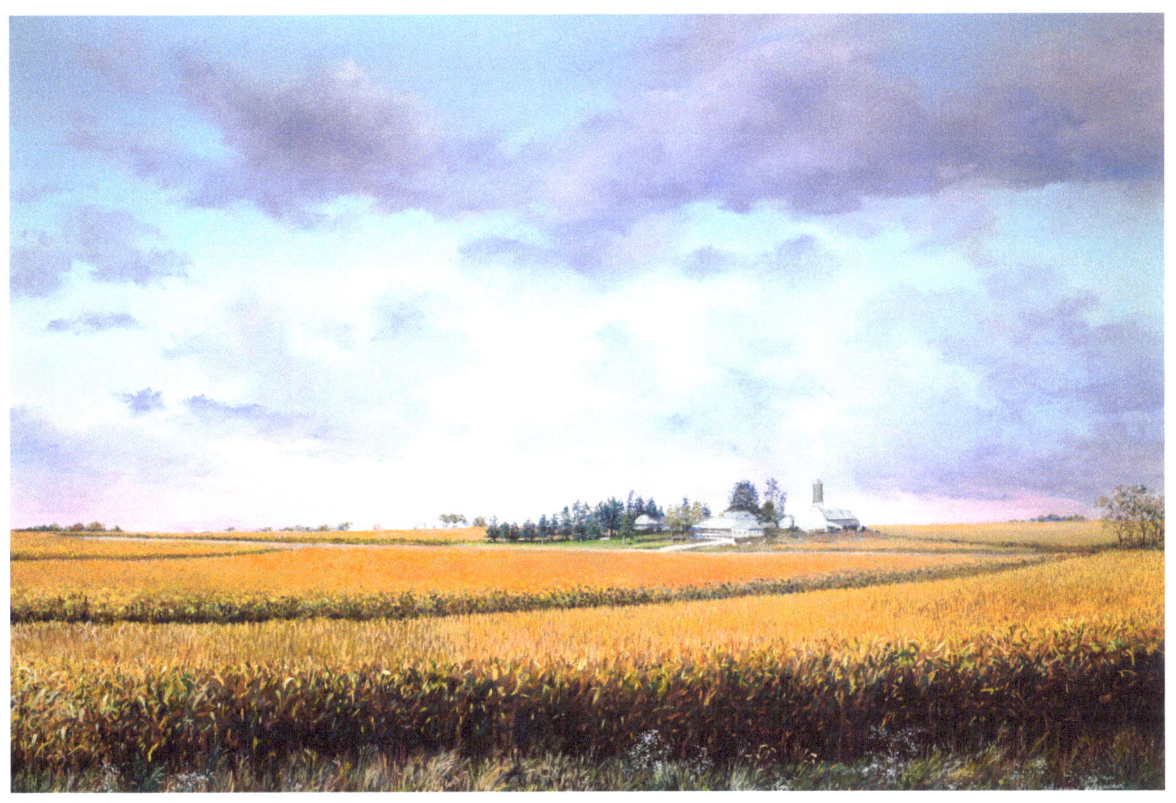

Niebuhr Farm 24 x 36 in.

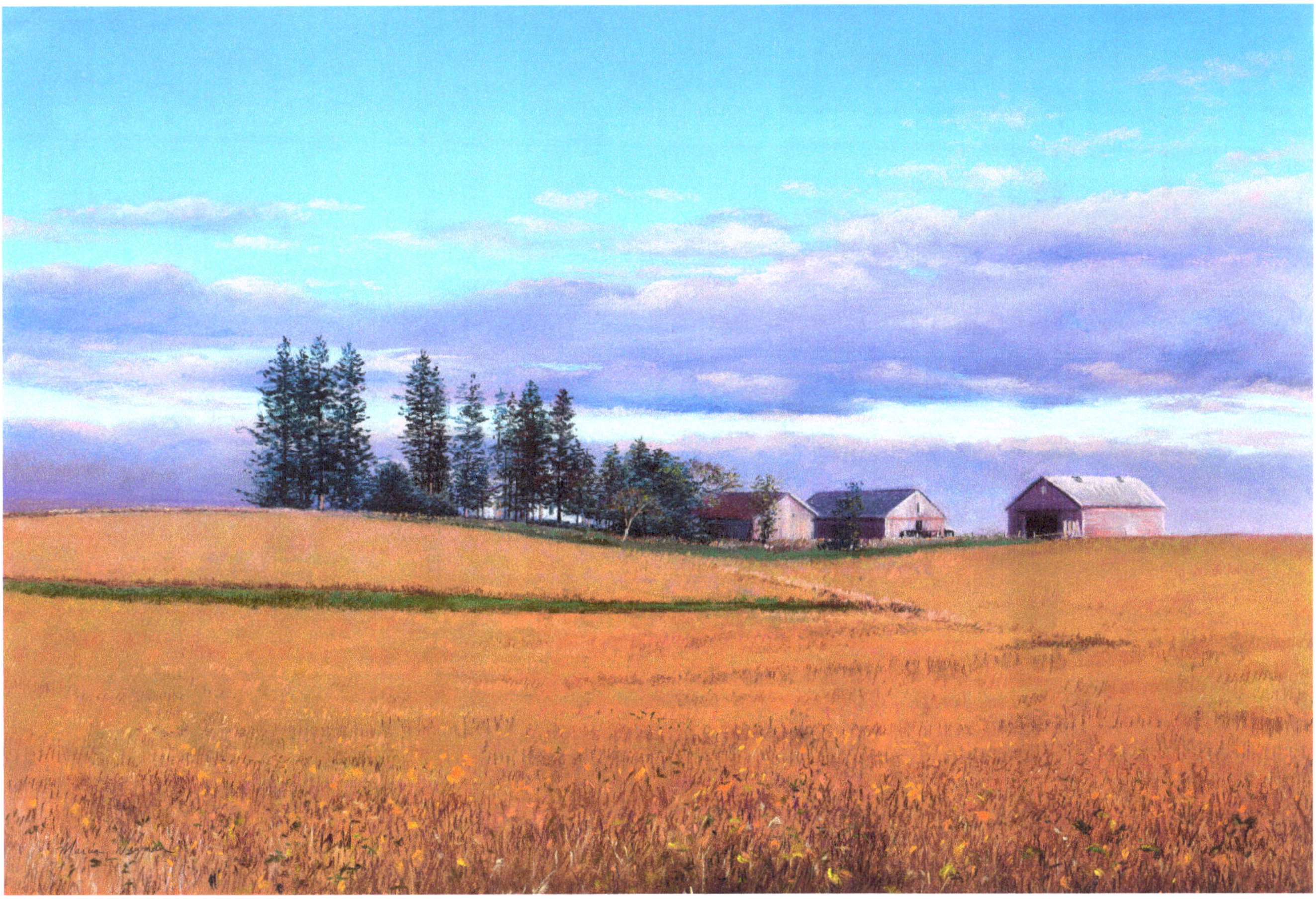

Soybean Field and Farm 24 x 36 in.

—23

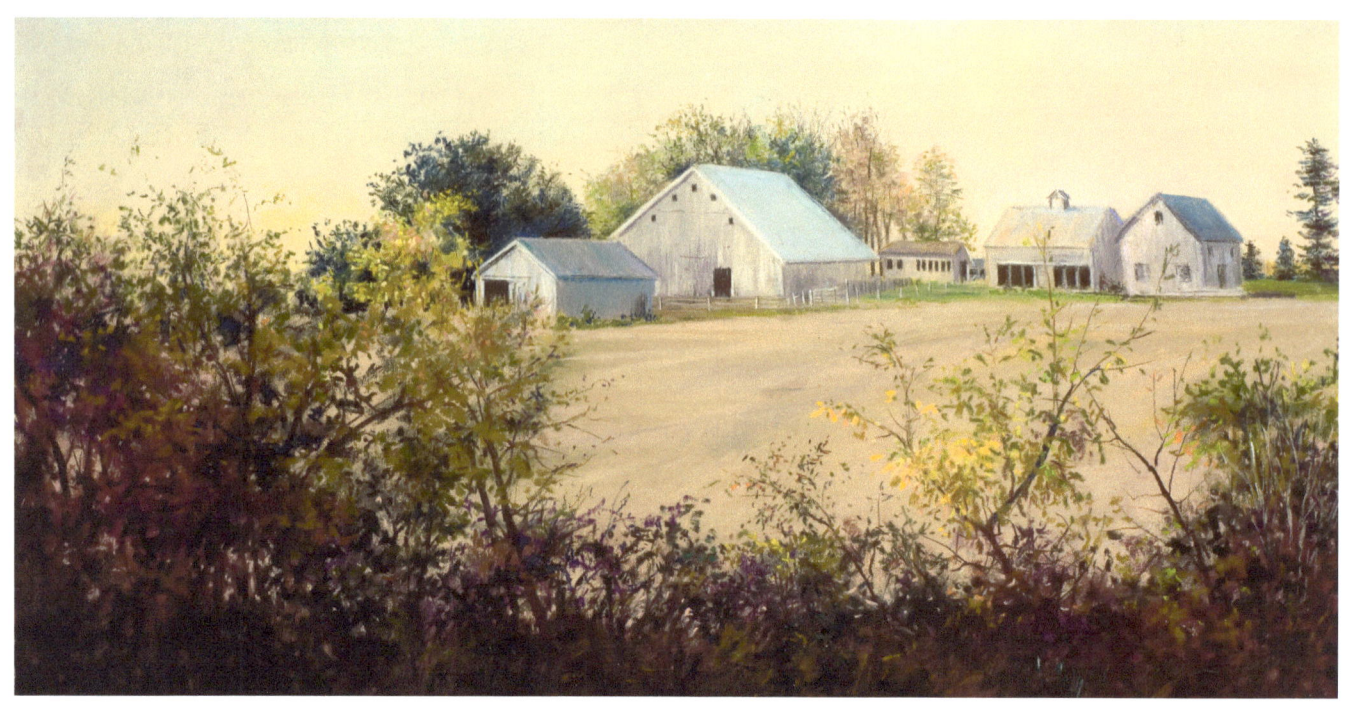

Morning Farm 12 x 24 in.

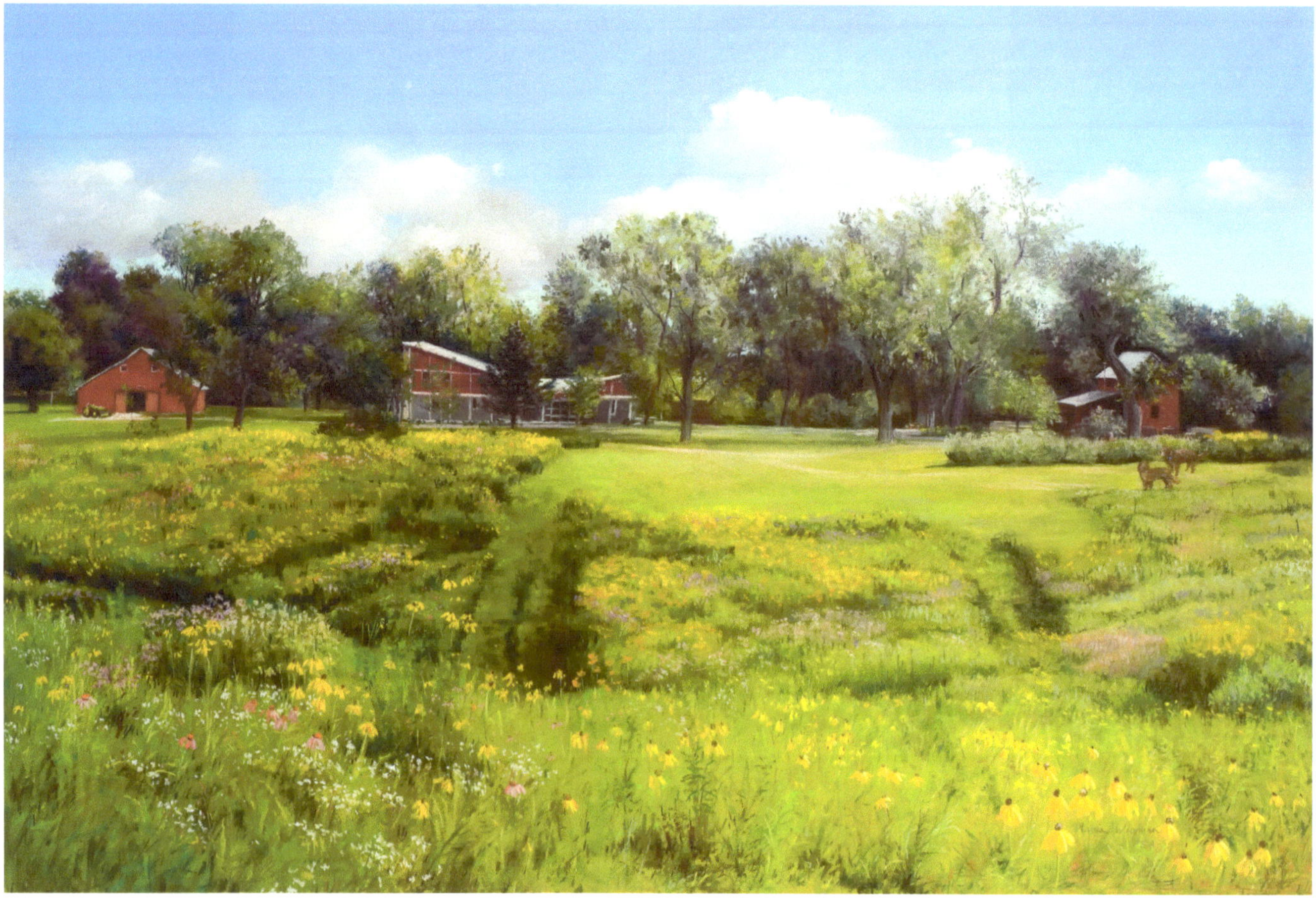

Zimmerman Farm 24 x 36 in.

Cattle

Cattle are very curious creatures. I love the way they come crowding over to the fence together to see me with my camera. I have the feeling they are saying, "Take my picture, take my picture," like a herd of children. So I do, and some interesting paintings featuring cattle have resulted.

I especially like the all-black variety of cattle, as they work well compositionally. Rendering legs is the most challenging part, figuring out which leg belongs to which animal.

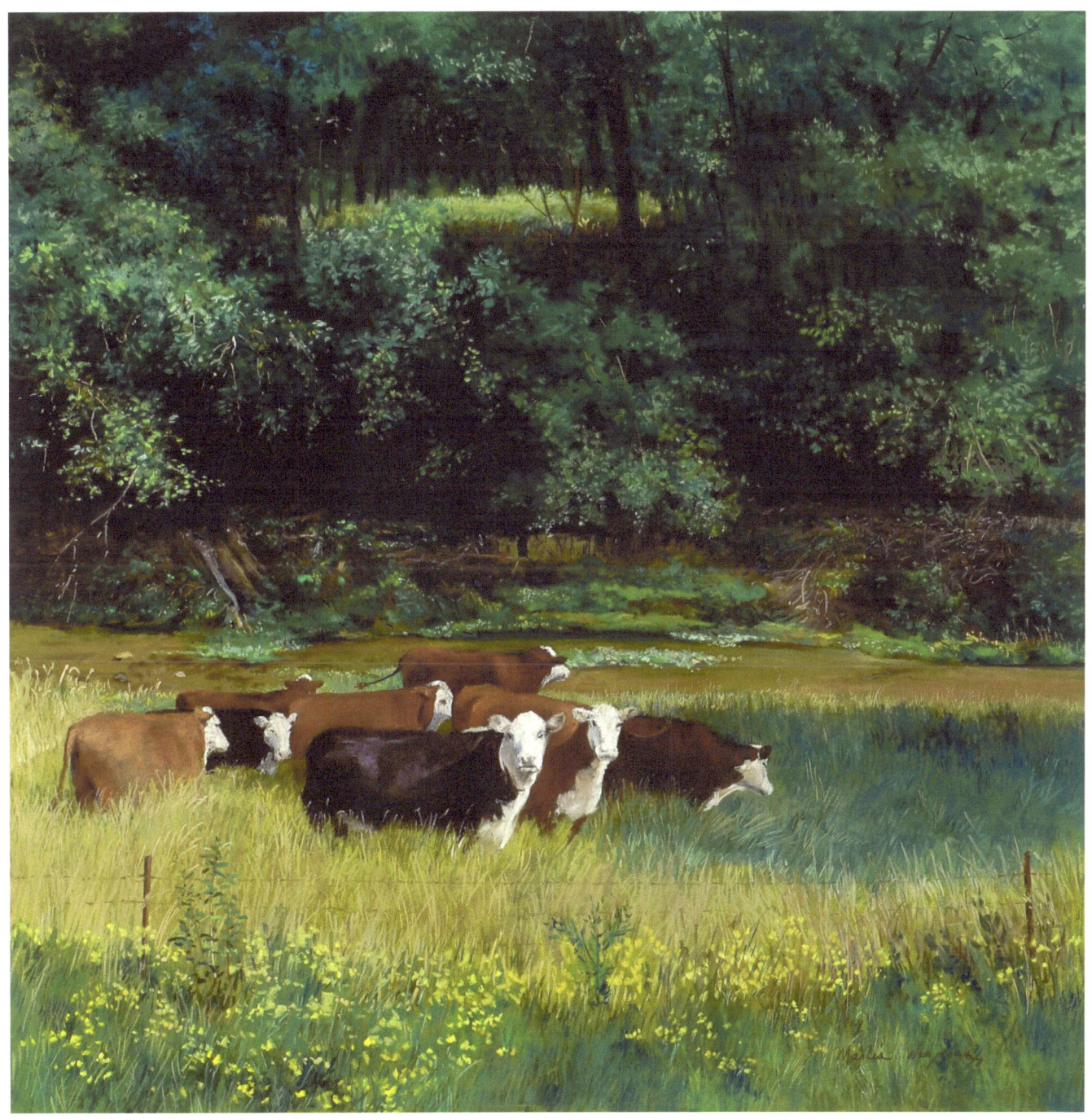

Cattle Haven 24 x 24 in.

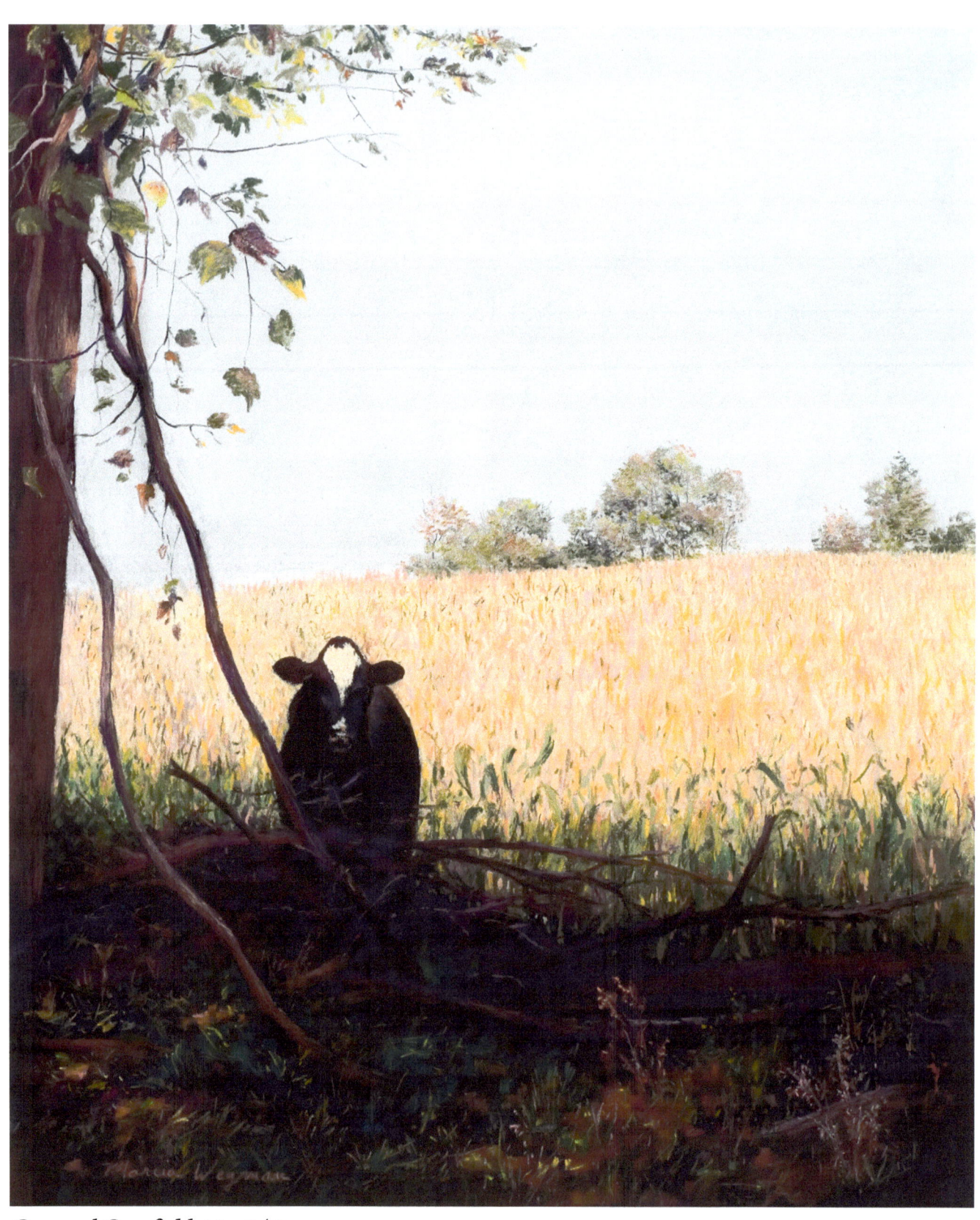

Cow and Cornfield 30 x 24 in.

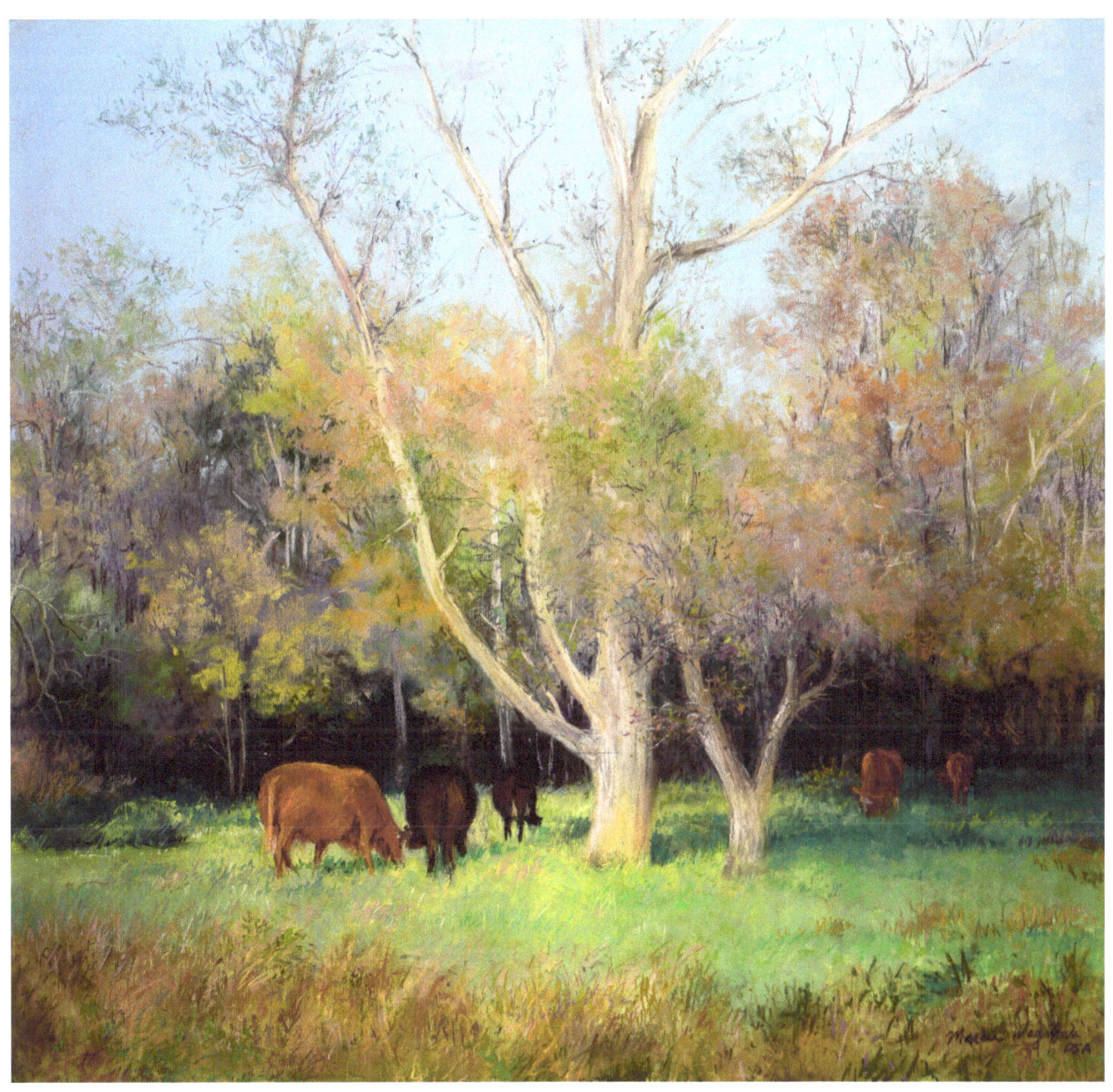

One Fall Day 24 x 27 in.

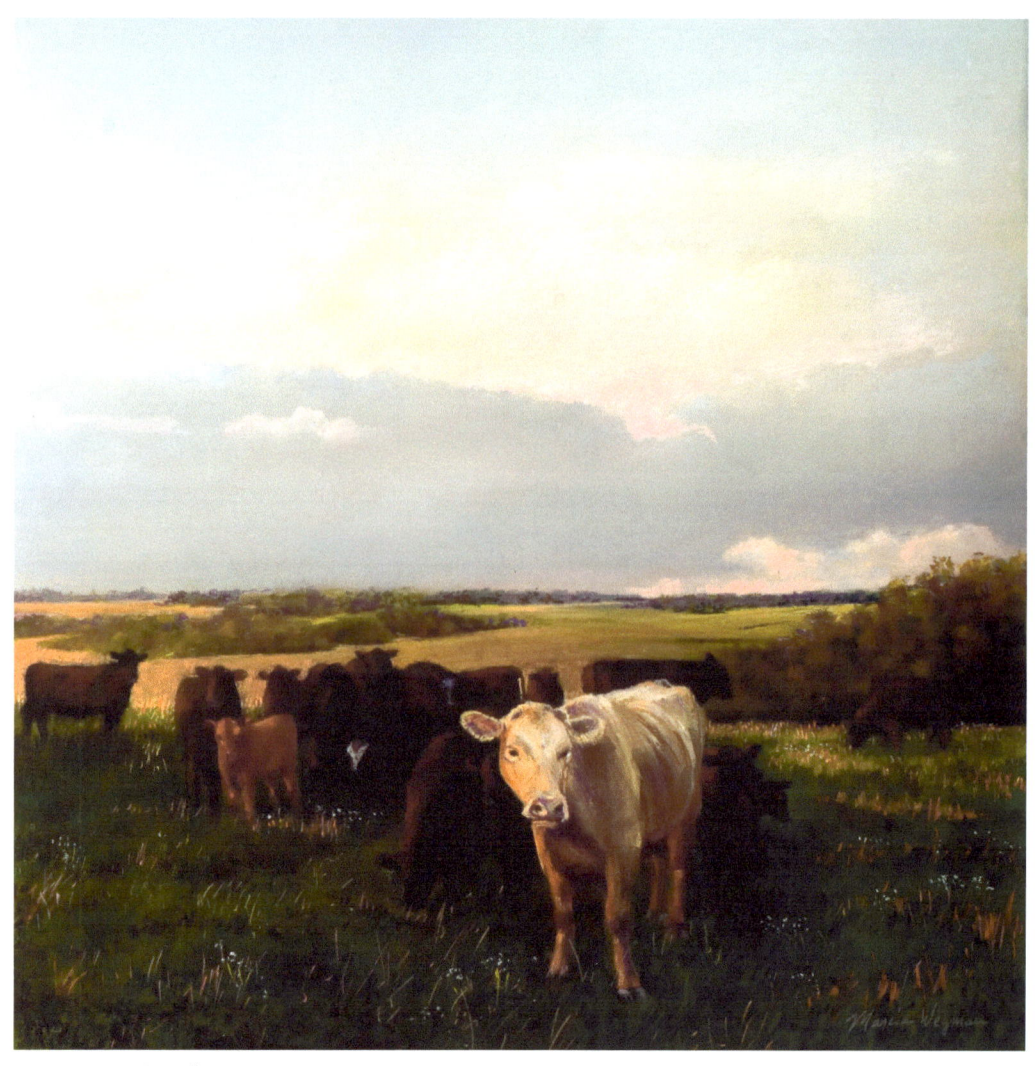

Evening Cattle 21 x 21 in.

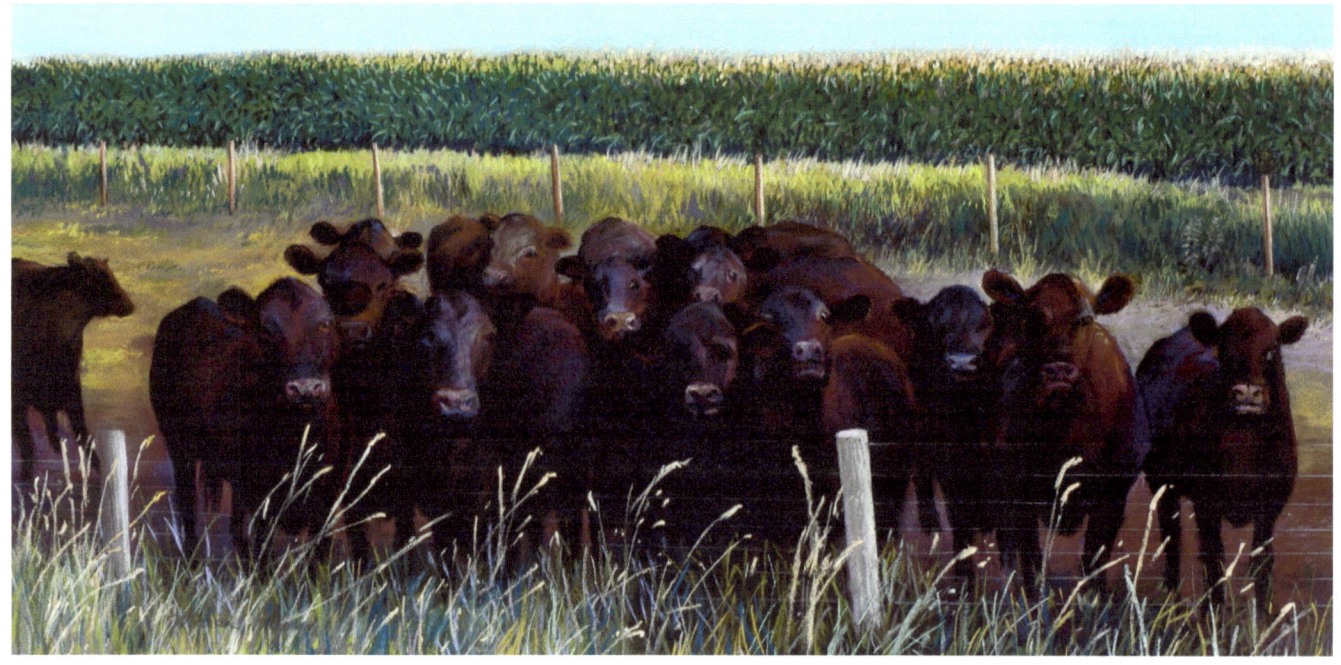

Cattle Lined Up 12 x 24 in.

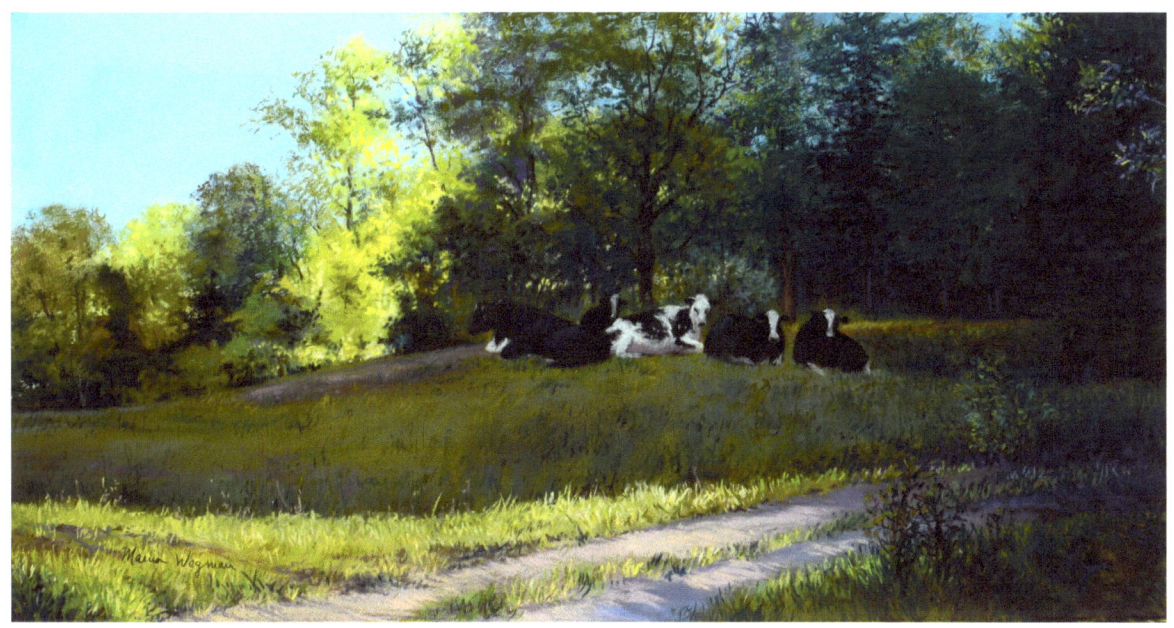

Resting Cattle 12 x 24 in.

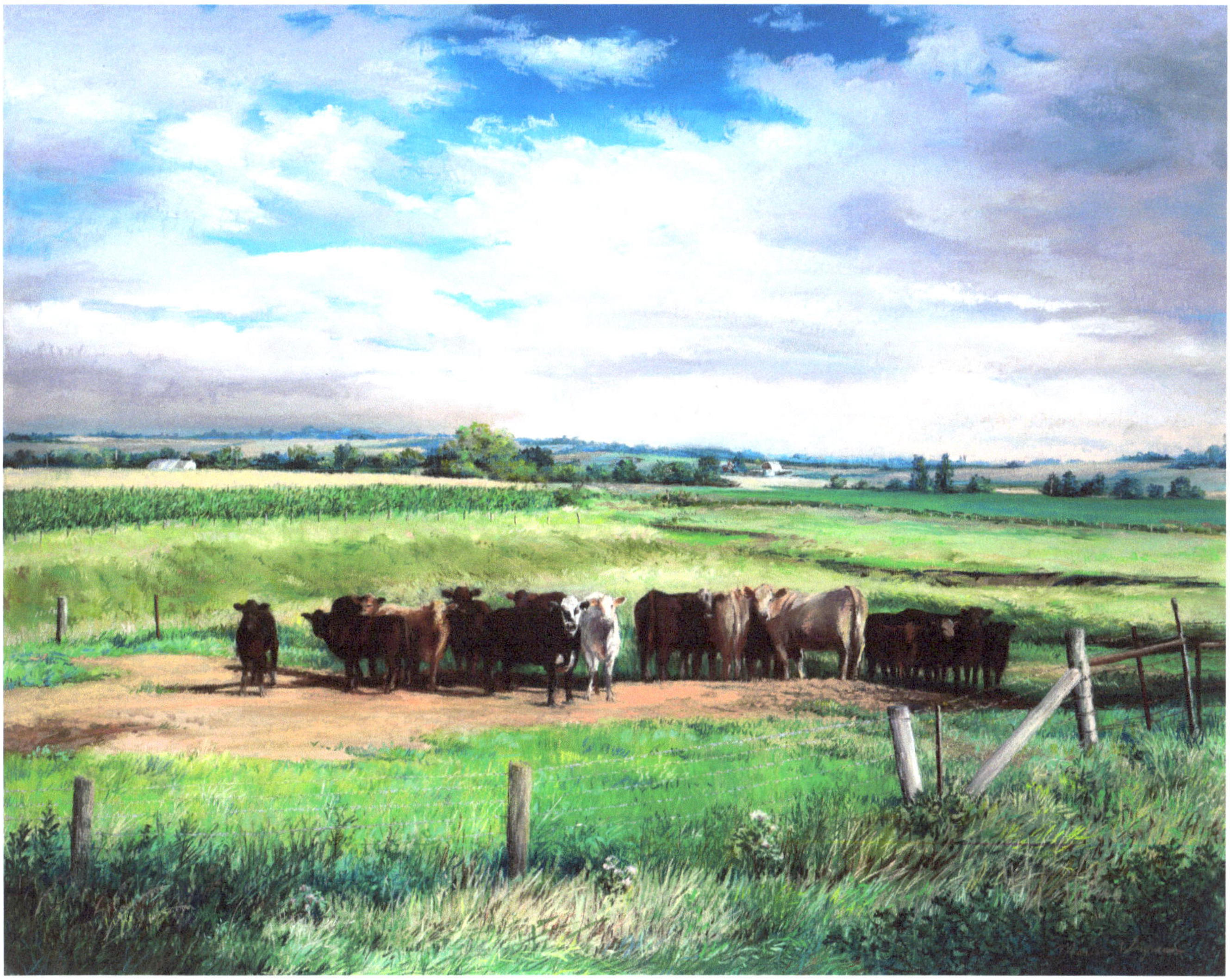

Herd 21 x 27 in.

—29

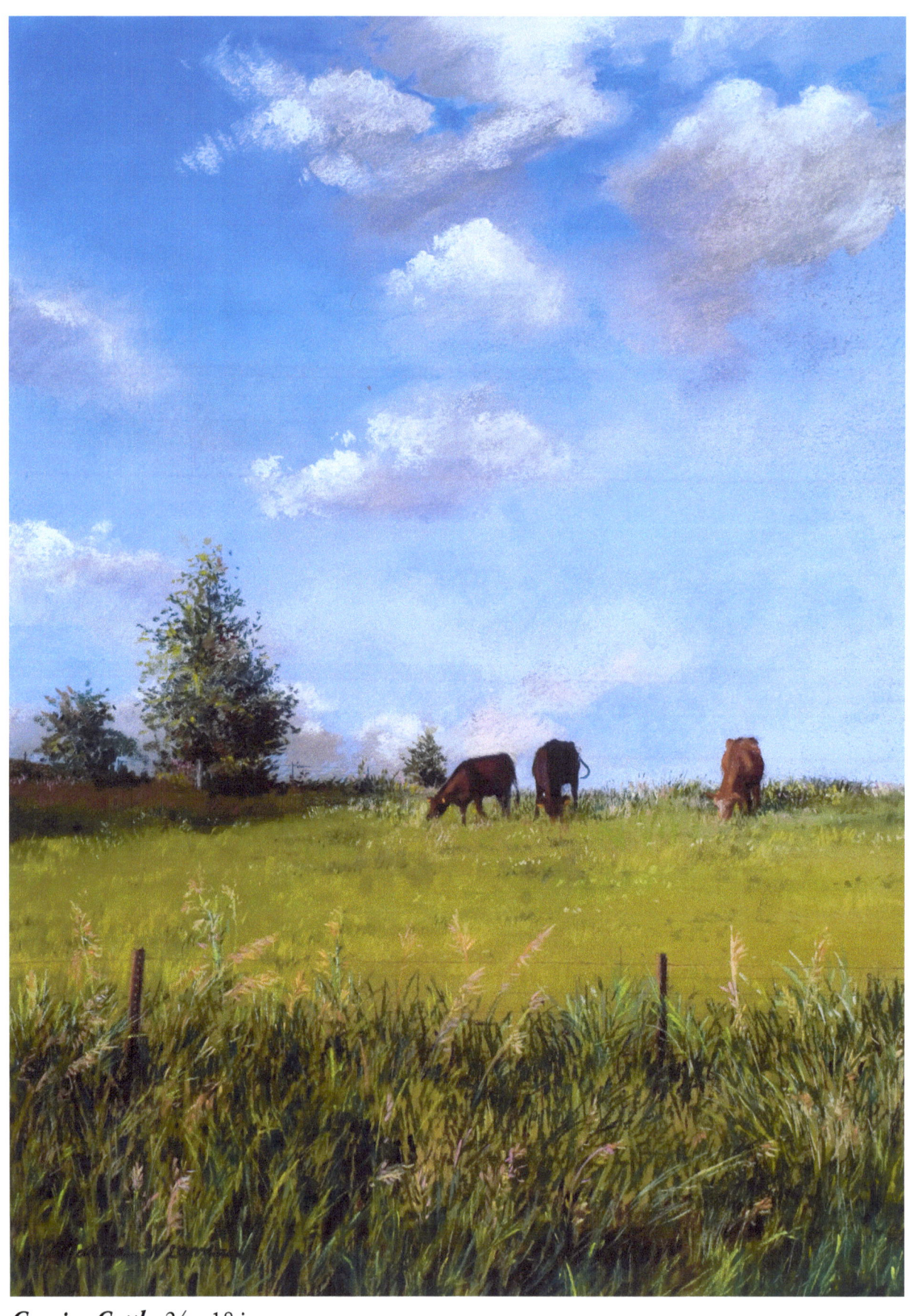

Grazing Cattle 24 x 18 in.

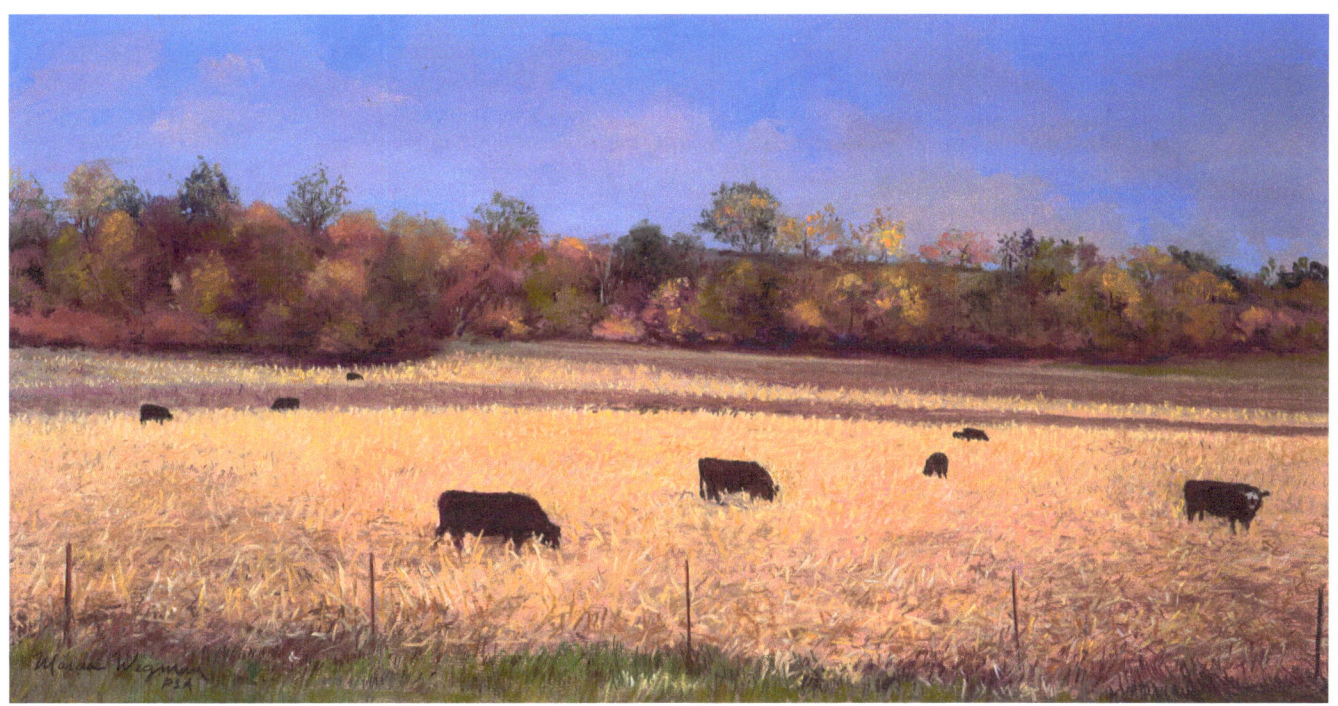

Cattle Grazing in Cornfield 12 x 24 in.

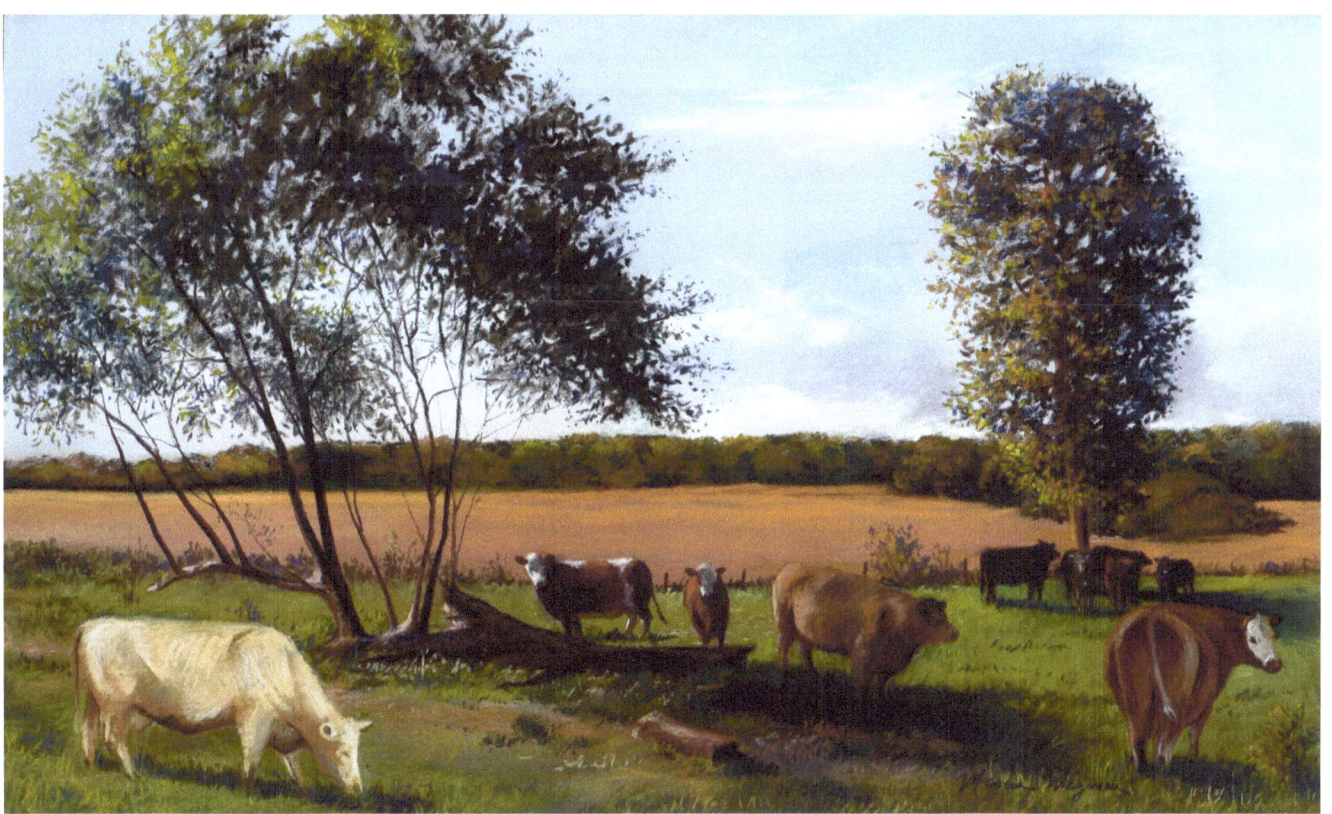

Cattle in Fall Pasture 12 x 20 in.

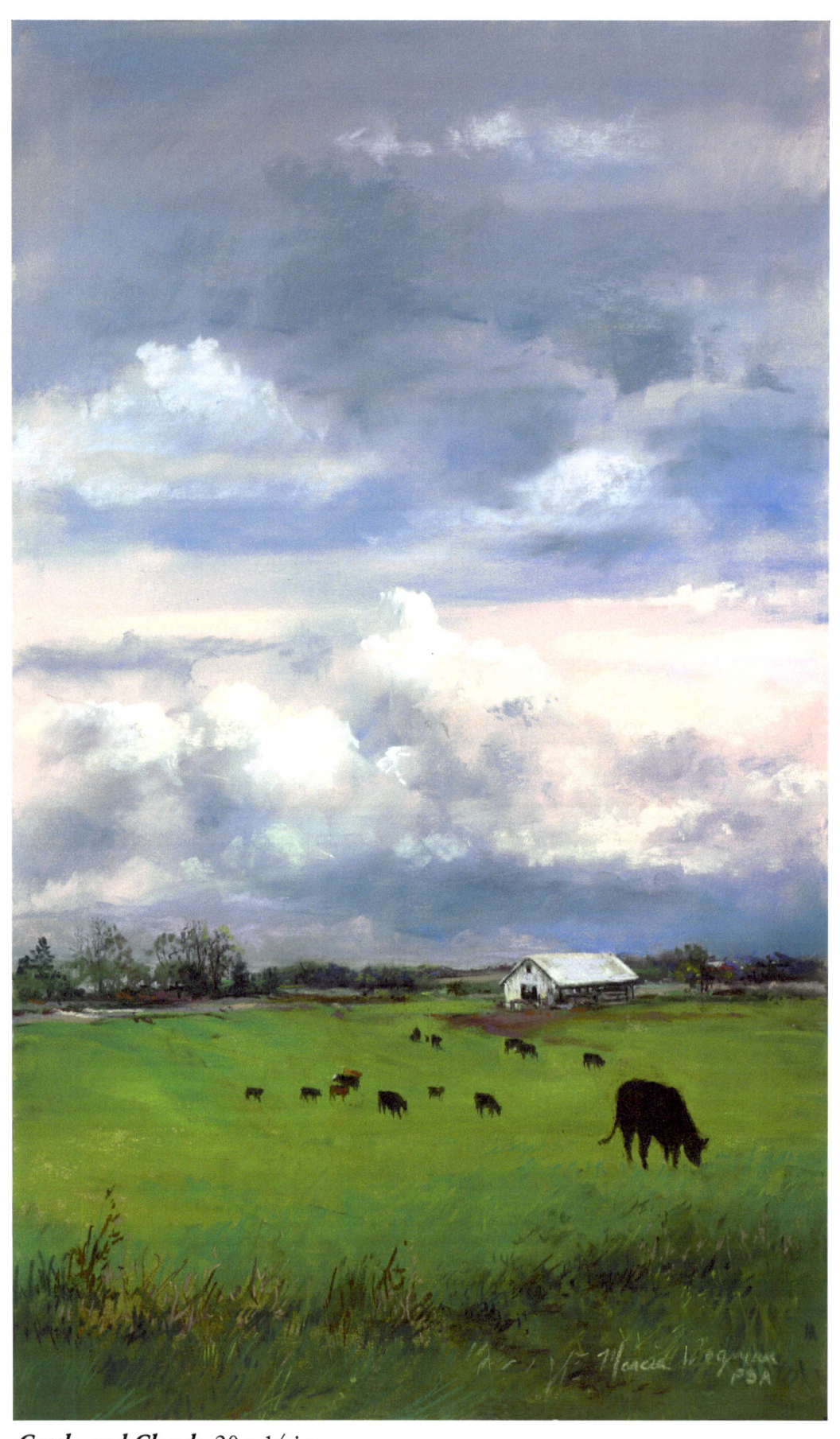

Cattle and Clouds 20 x 14 in.

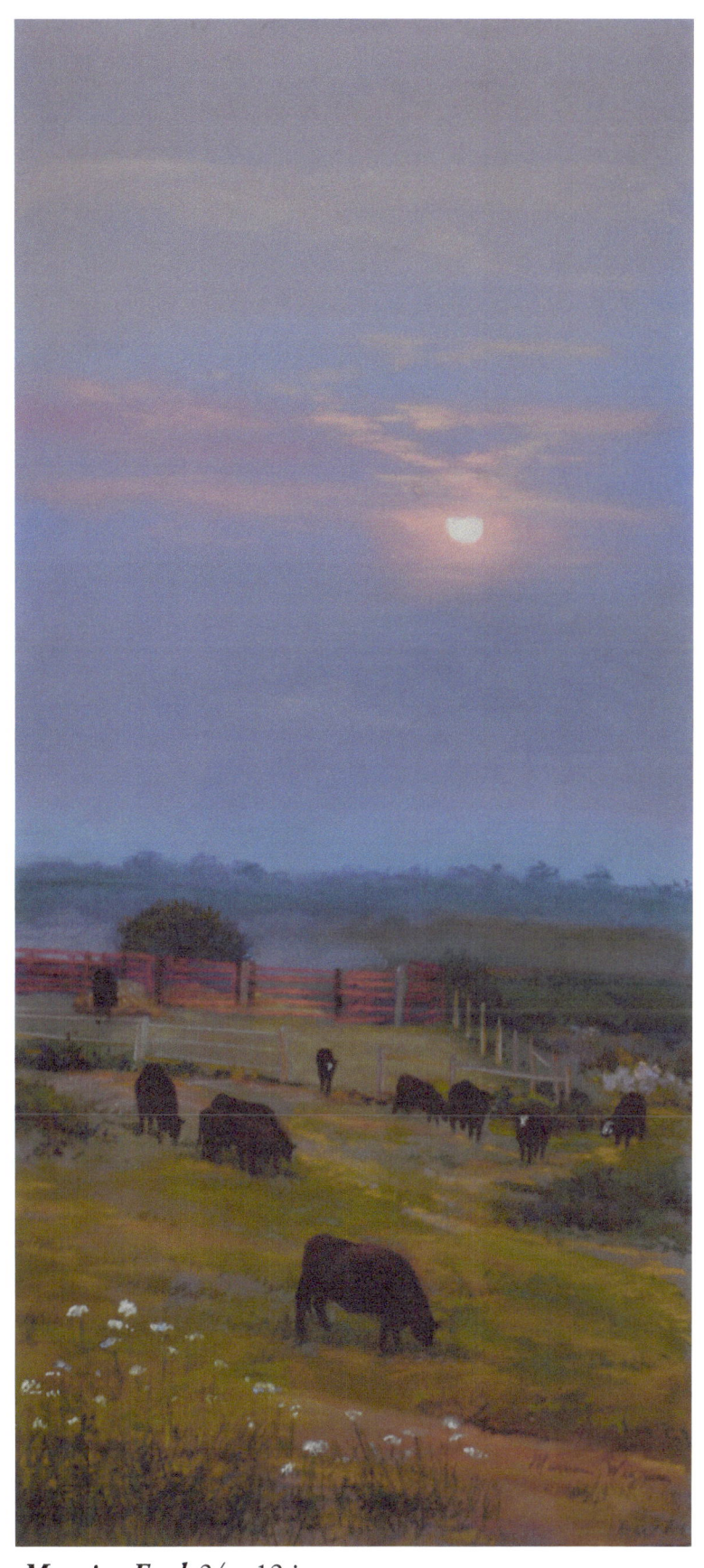

Morning Feed 24 x 12 in.

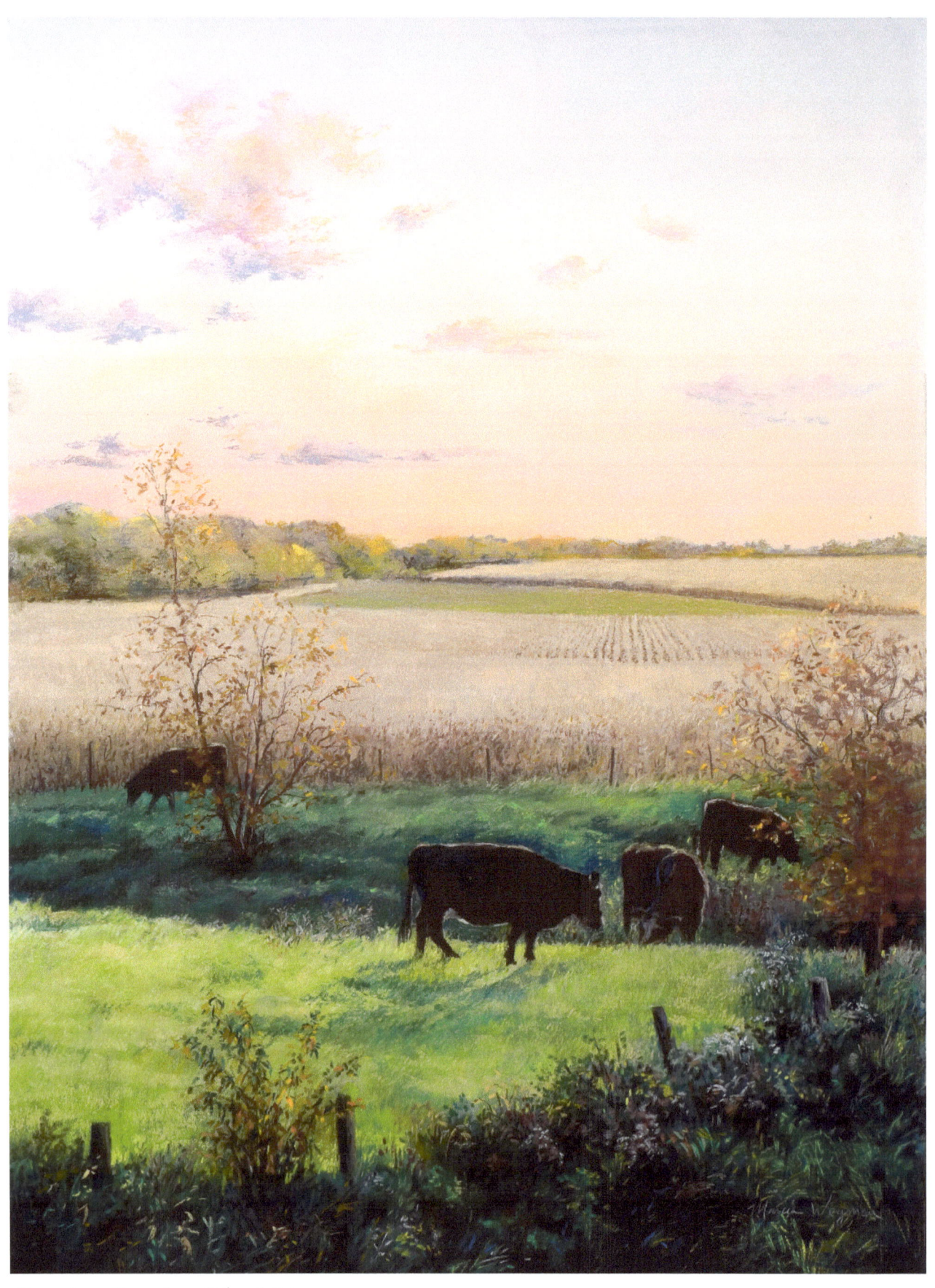

Evening Grazing 24 x 18 in.

Wild Flowers and Grass

Gardening is one of my passions. Spring through fall, I am always conflicted as to where to spend my time and energy each day, studio or garden. Because of my observation and knowledge of how things grow, the rendering of plant life along the roadsides, always accompanying the crop fields, is one of the most delightful parts of landscape painting for me.

At the beginning of the painting, I put down a quick, rough indication of the foreground plants but save the fun of the more refined painting of flowers and grasses for the very end. The best for the last!

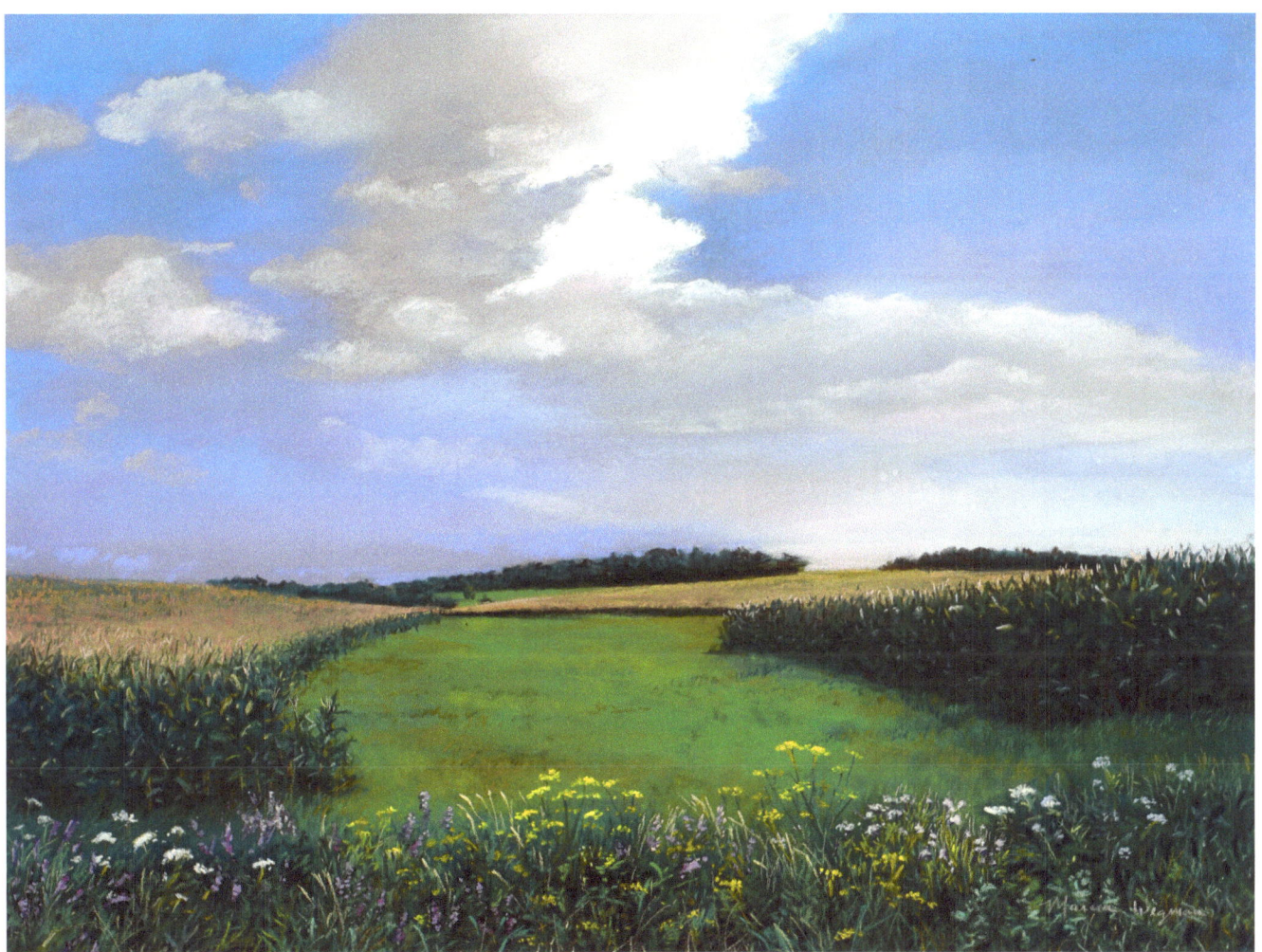

Summer Fields and Flowers 18 x 24 in.

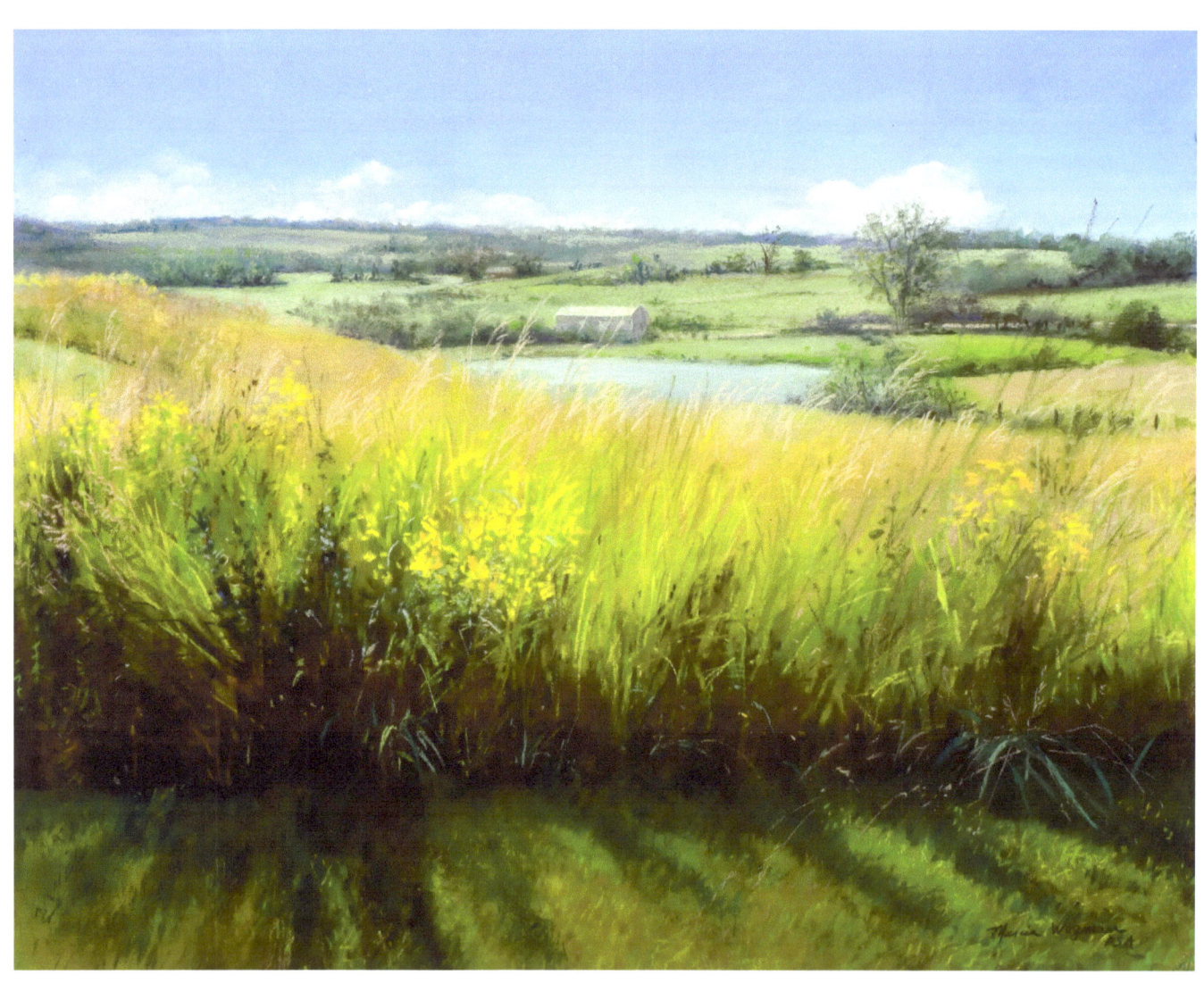

Shadowed Grass 24 x 36 in.

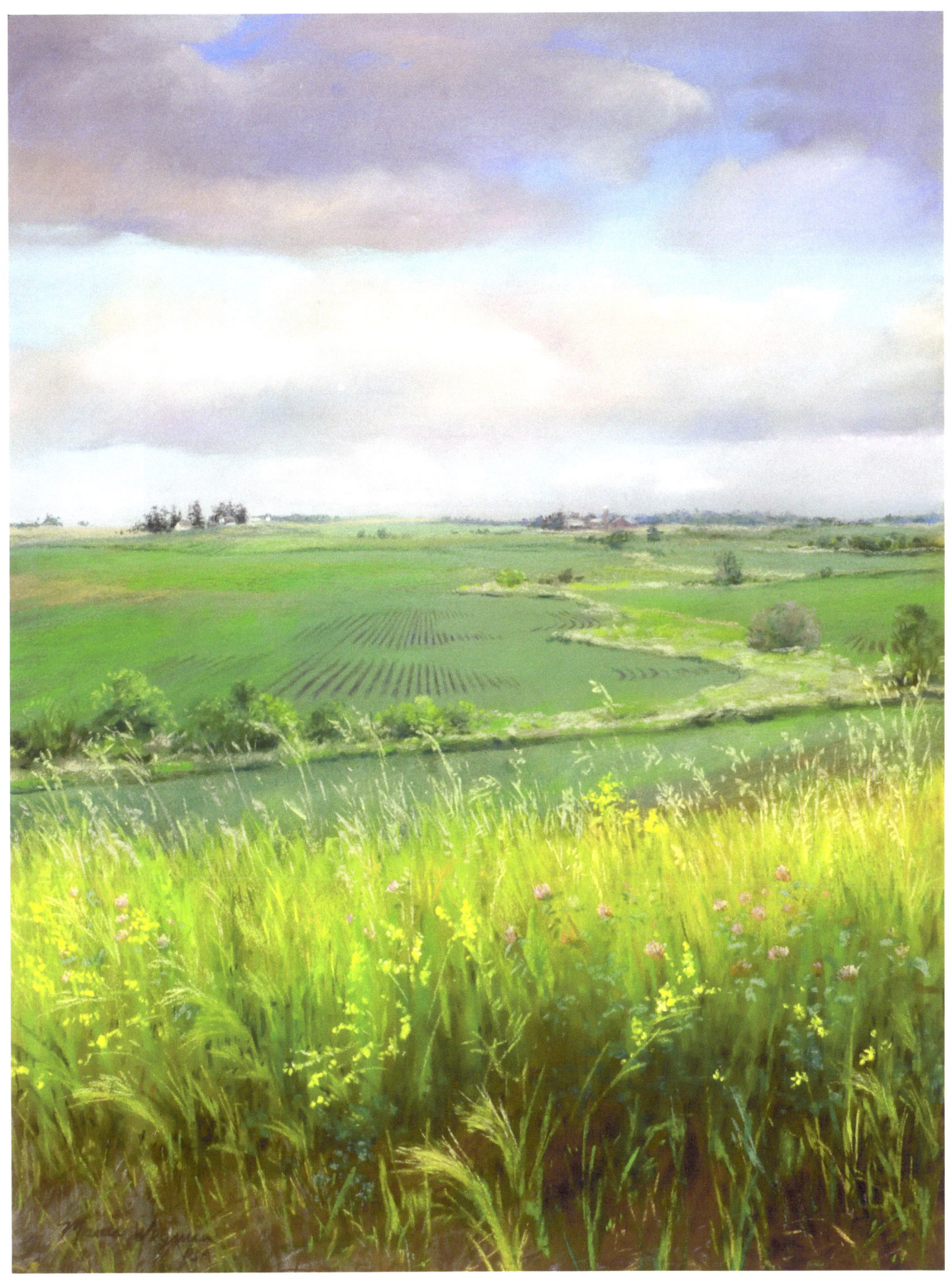

June Fields and Flowers 25 x 19 in.

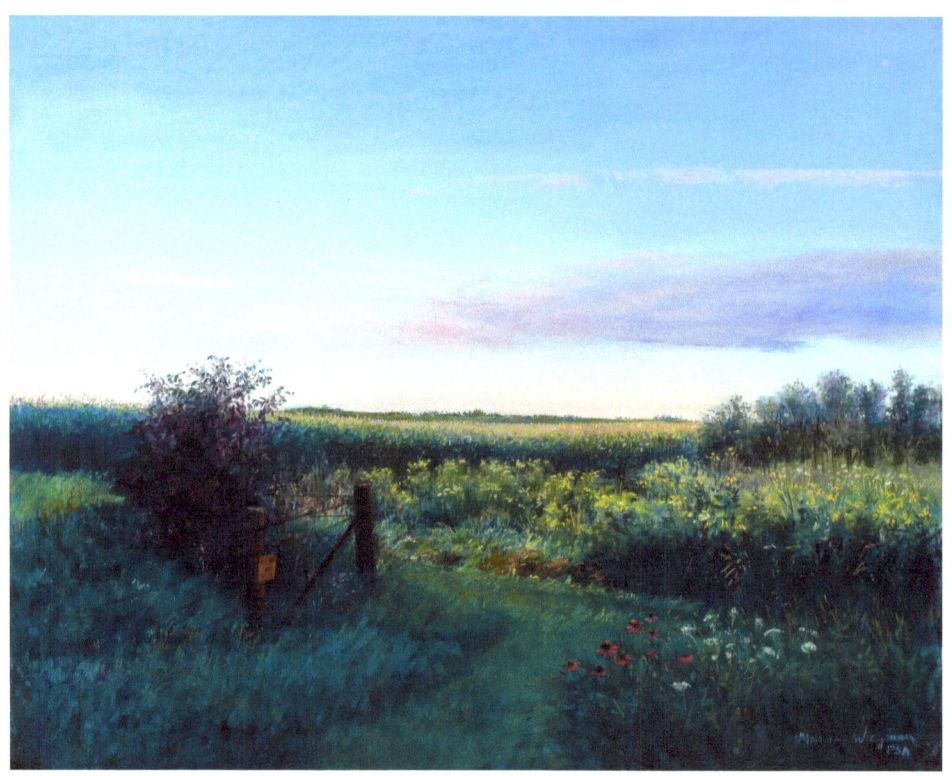

August Morning 21 x 27 in.

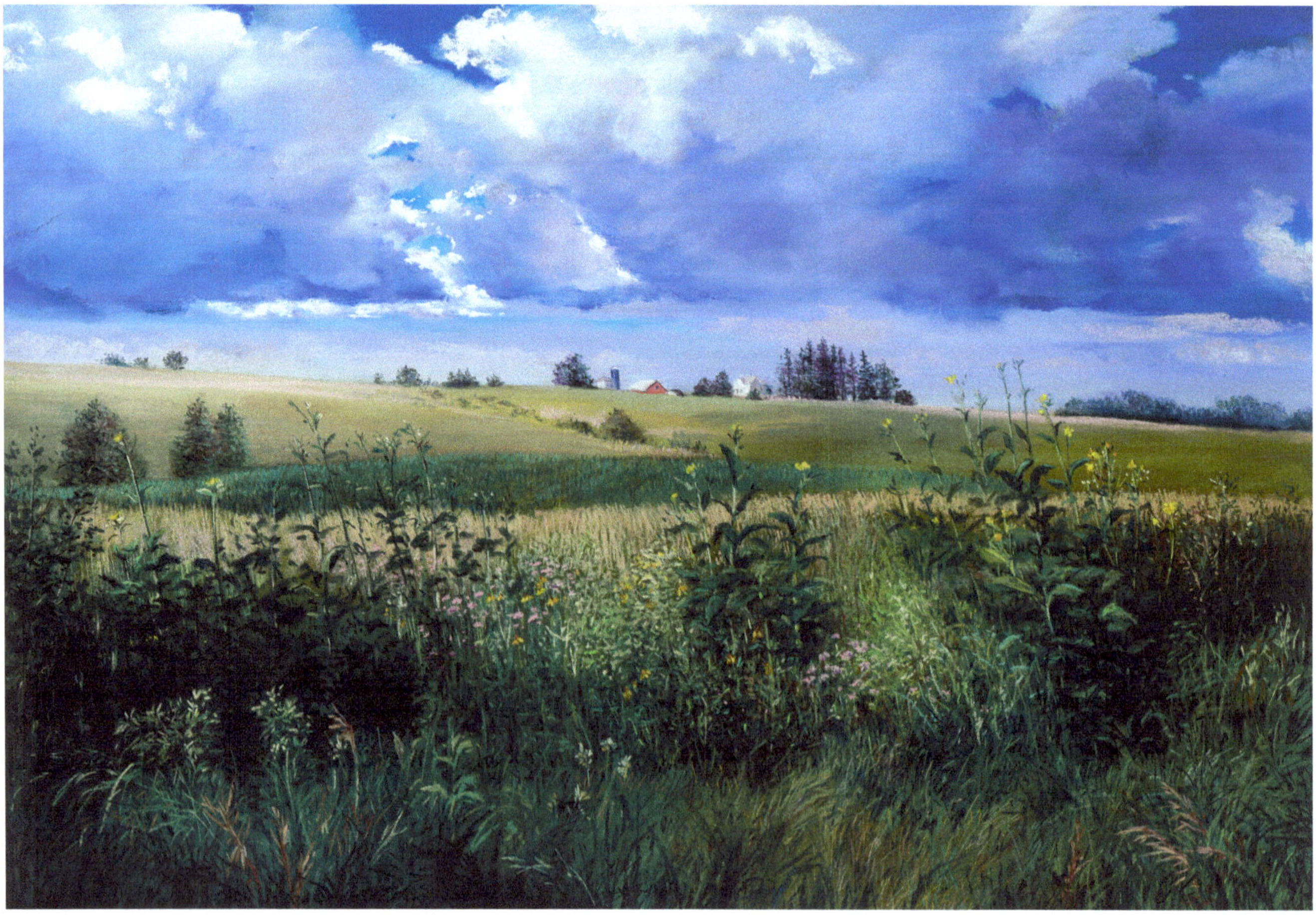

Roadside Grass and Flowers 24 x 36 in.

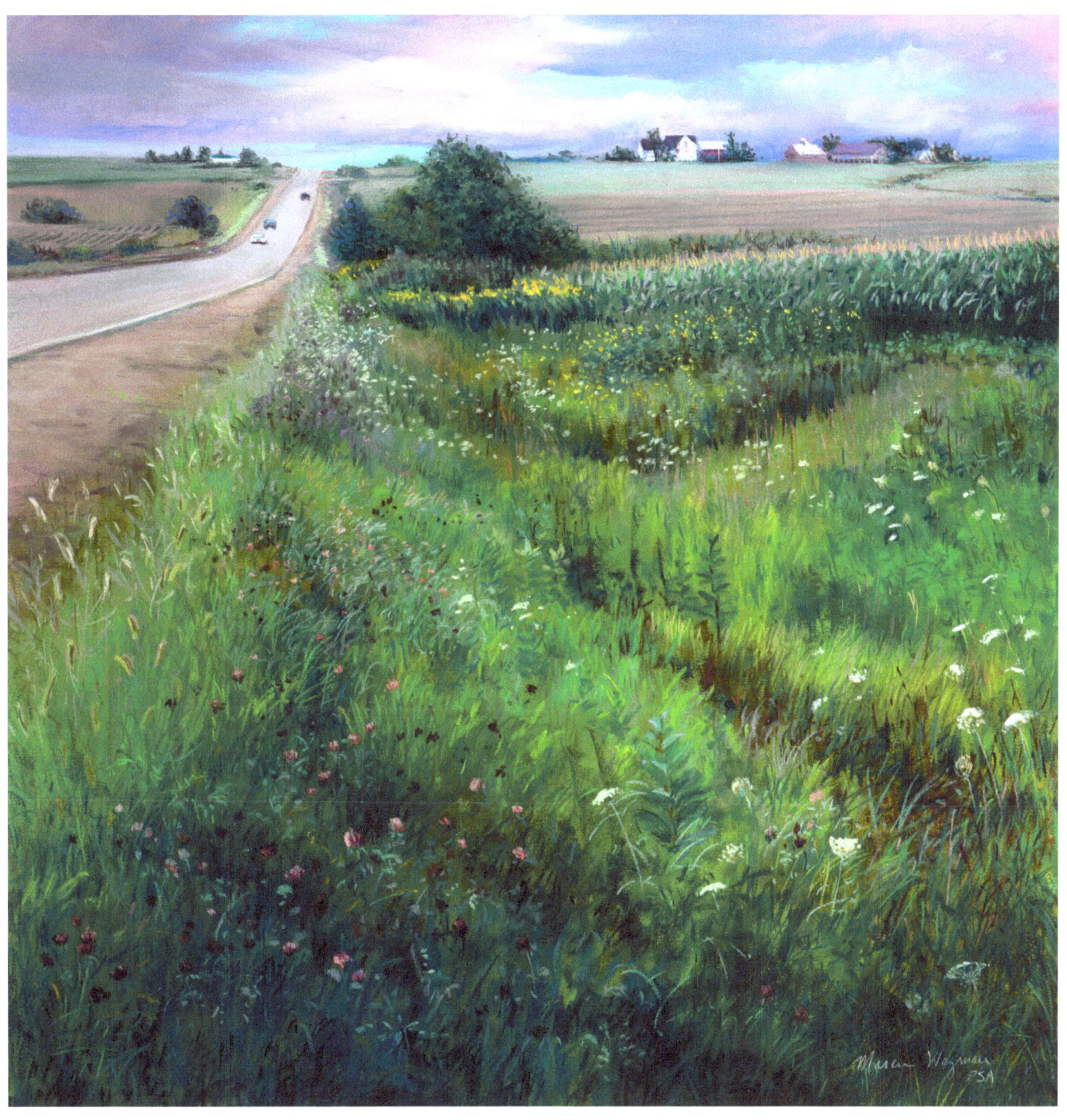

Roadside 21 x 21 in.

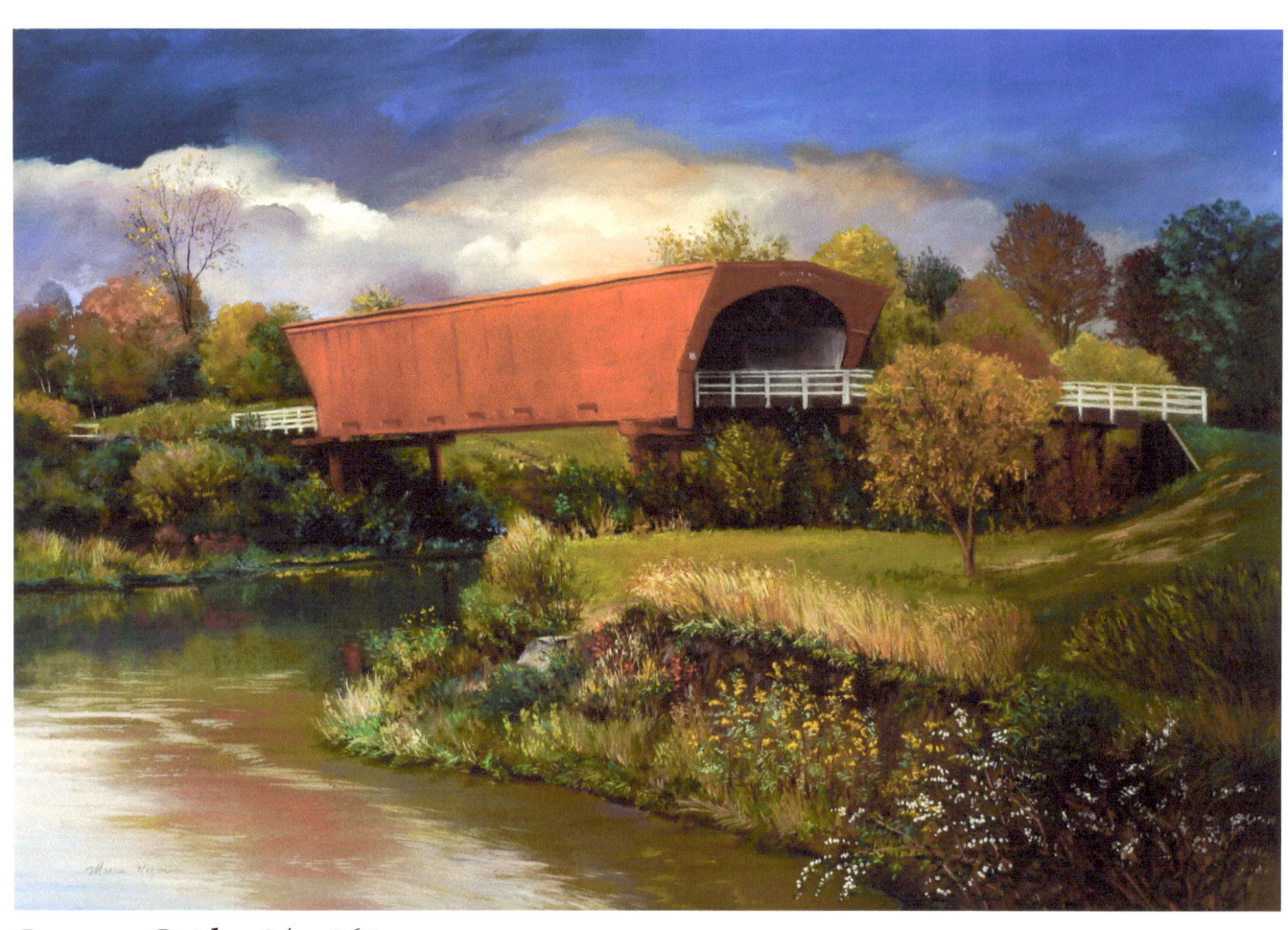

Roseman Bridge 24 x 36 in.

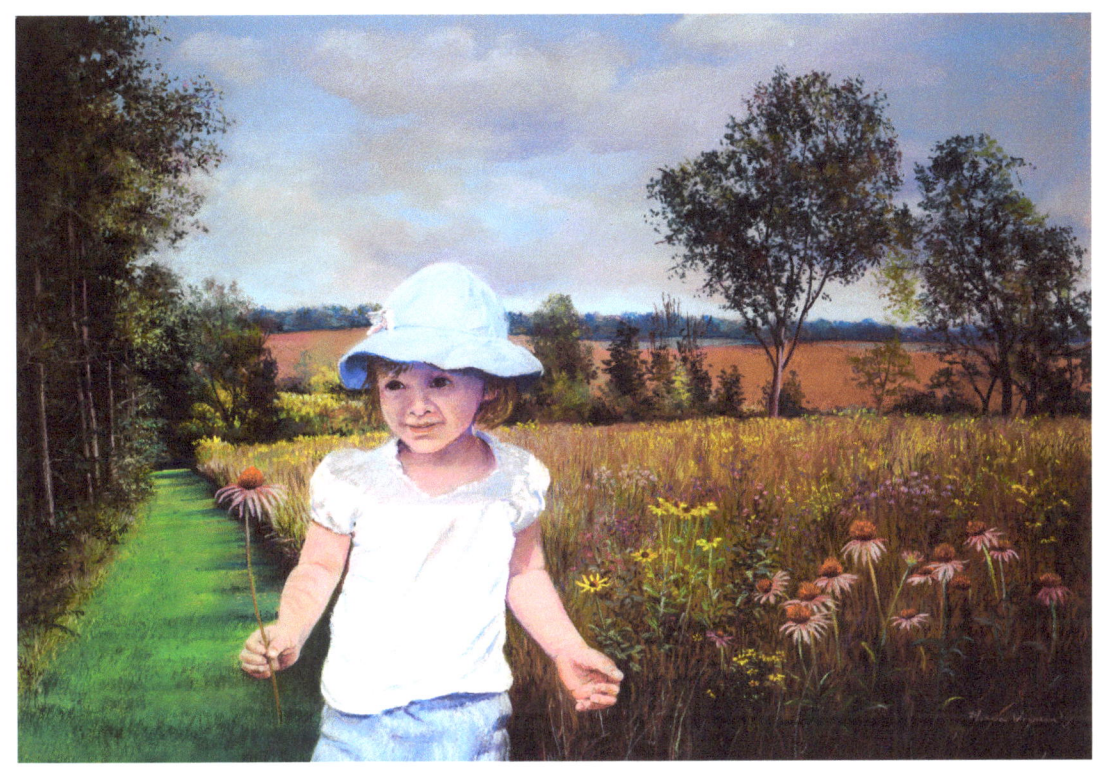

Prairie Child 24 x 36 in.

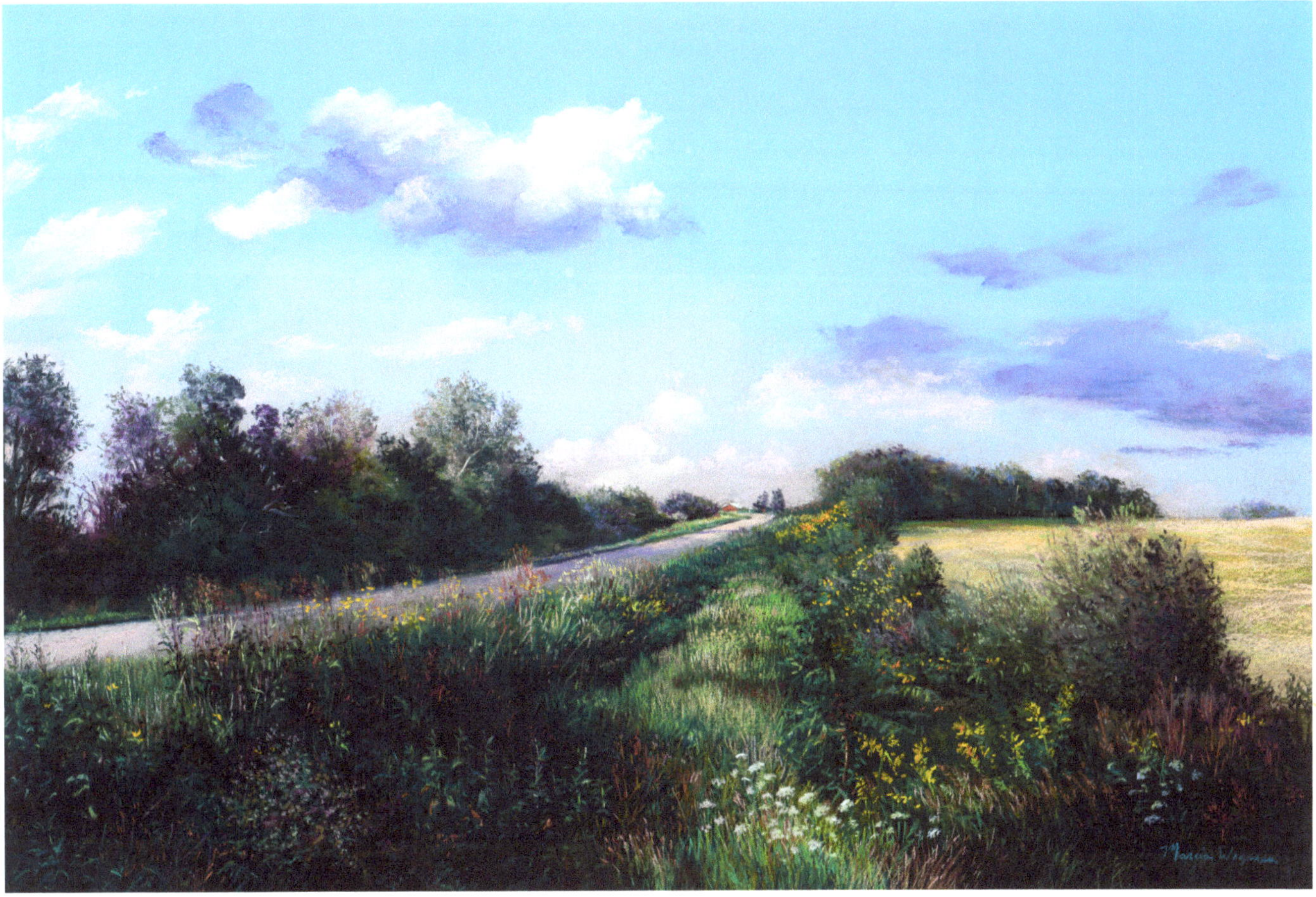

Prairie du Chien Road 24 x 36 in.

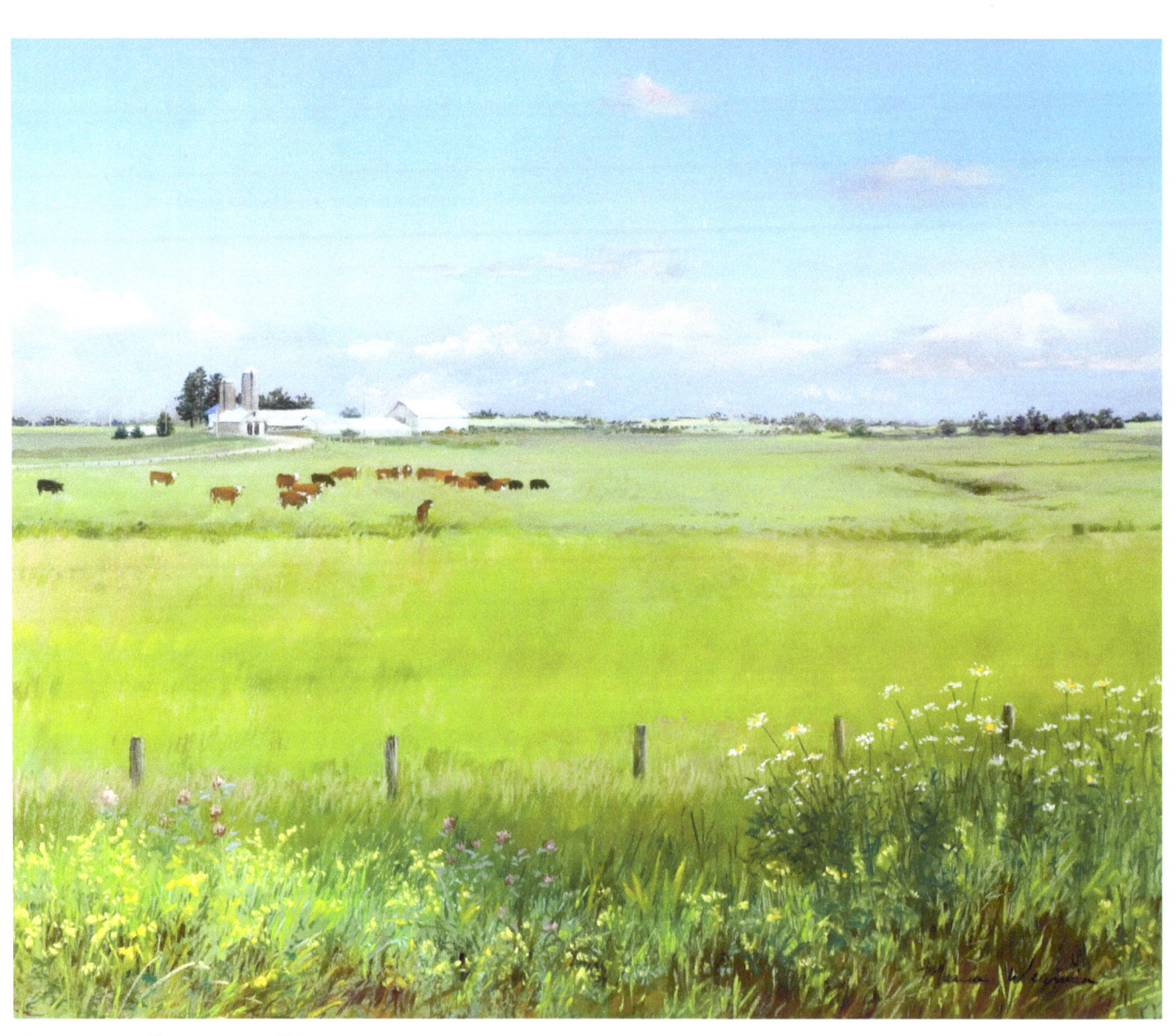

Summer Flowers and Pasture 18 x 22 in.

Sky

The sky is often my most favorite part of the picture to paint. Although I always use a photo reference, I have much more freedom to play with shapes, colors, and patterns with the sky part of the composition.

The challenge is in working with edges in cloud formations. Some are soft and amorphous, and some are quite hard-edged, as in a white cumulus cloud against a bright blue sky.

Morning and evening skies are always the most interesting because of the varied, rich colors. I keep a camera in my car and always have one eye on the sky.

I have taken some very inspiring sky photos through the windshield of my car while waiting at a stoplight.

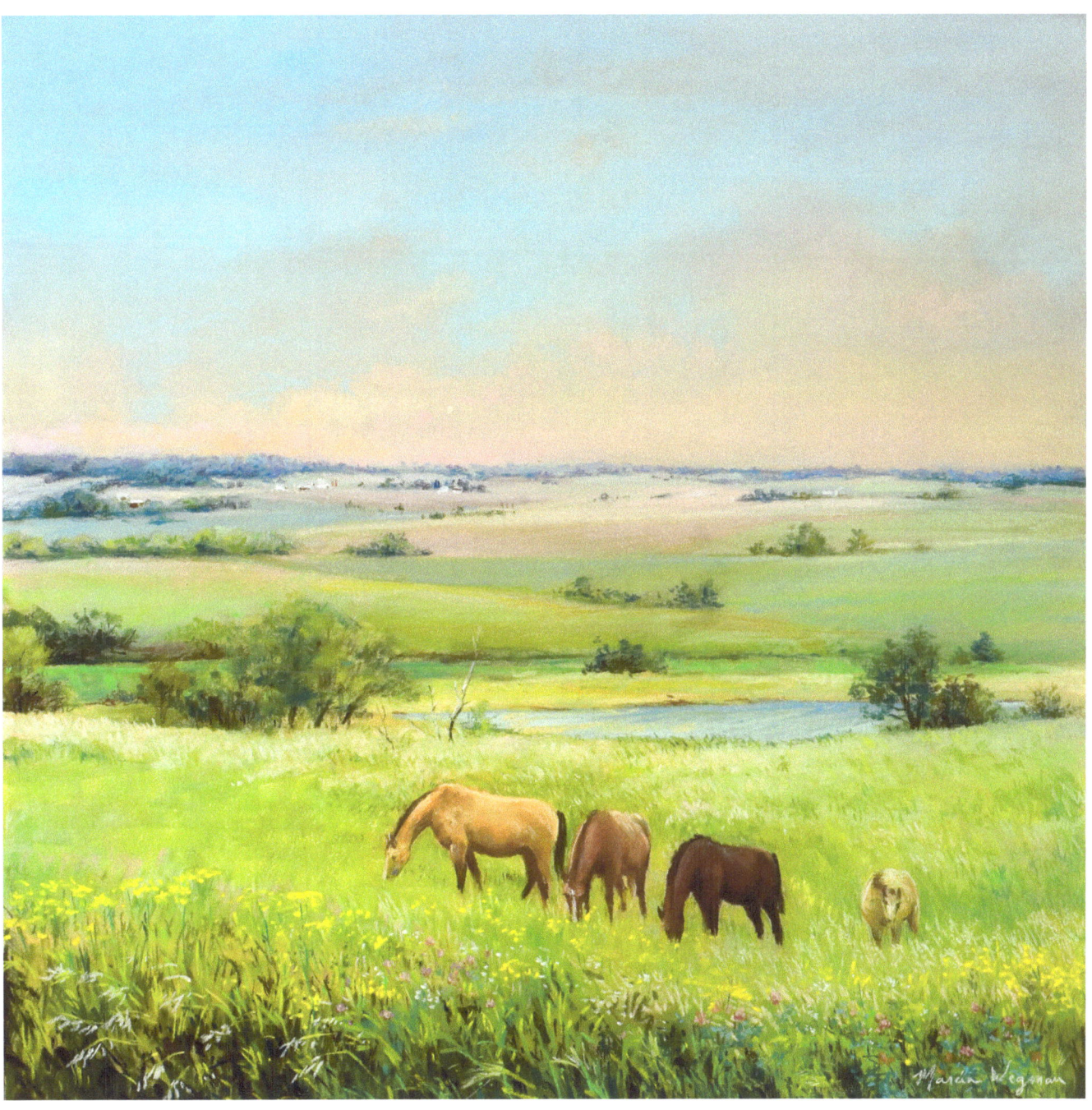

Grazing Horses 21 x 21 in.

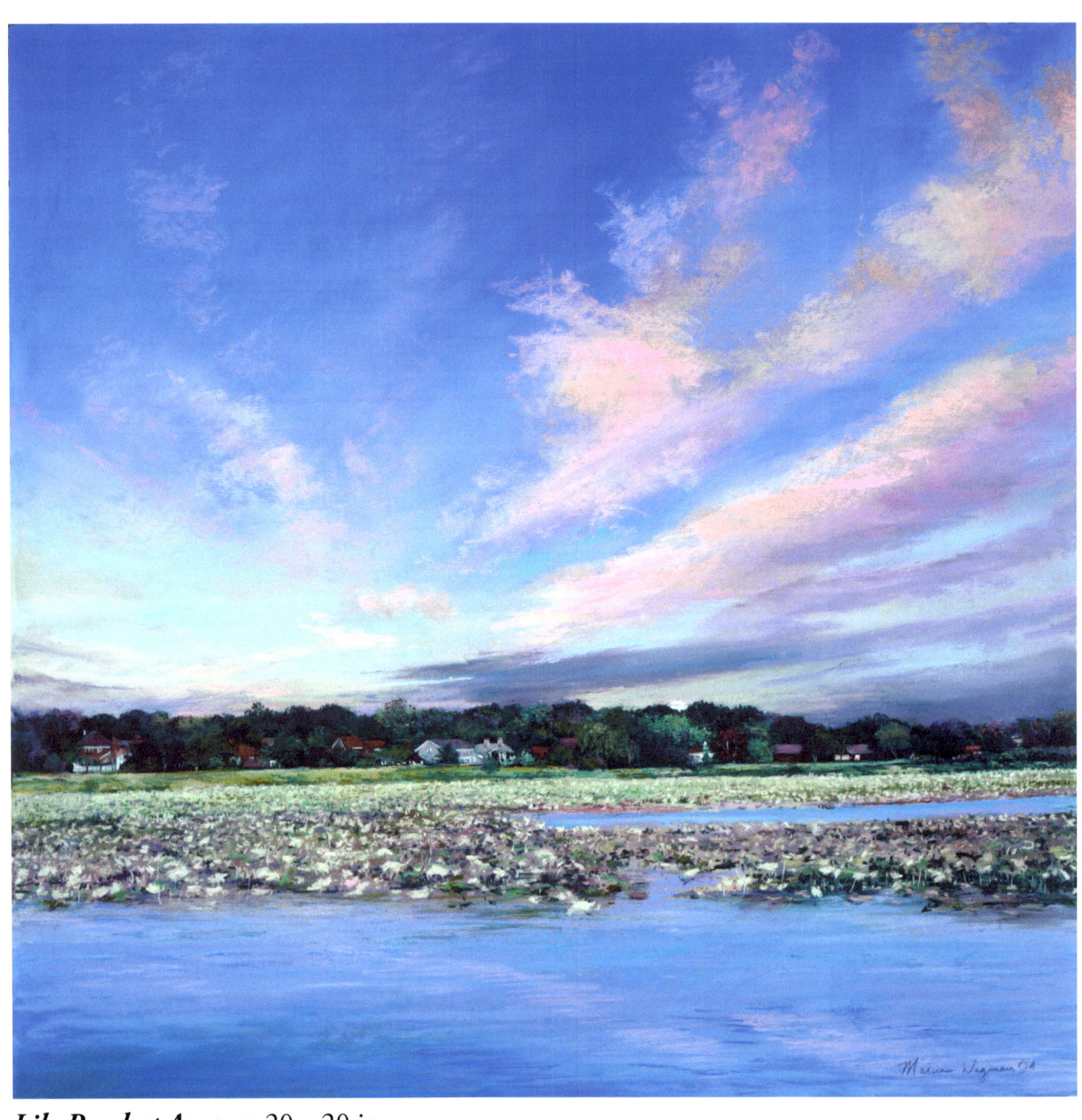

Lily Pond at Amana 20 x 20 in.

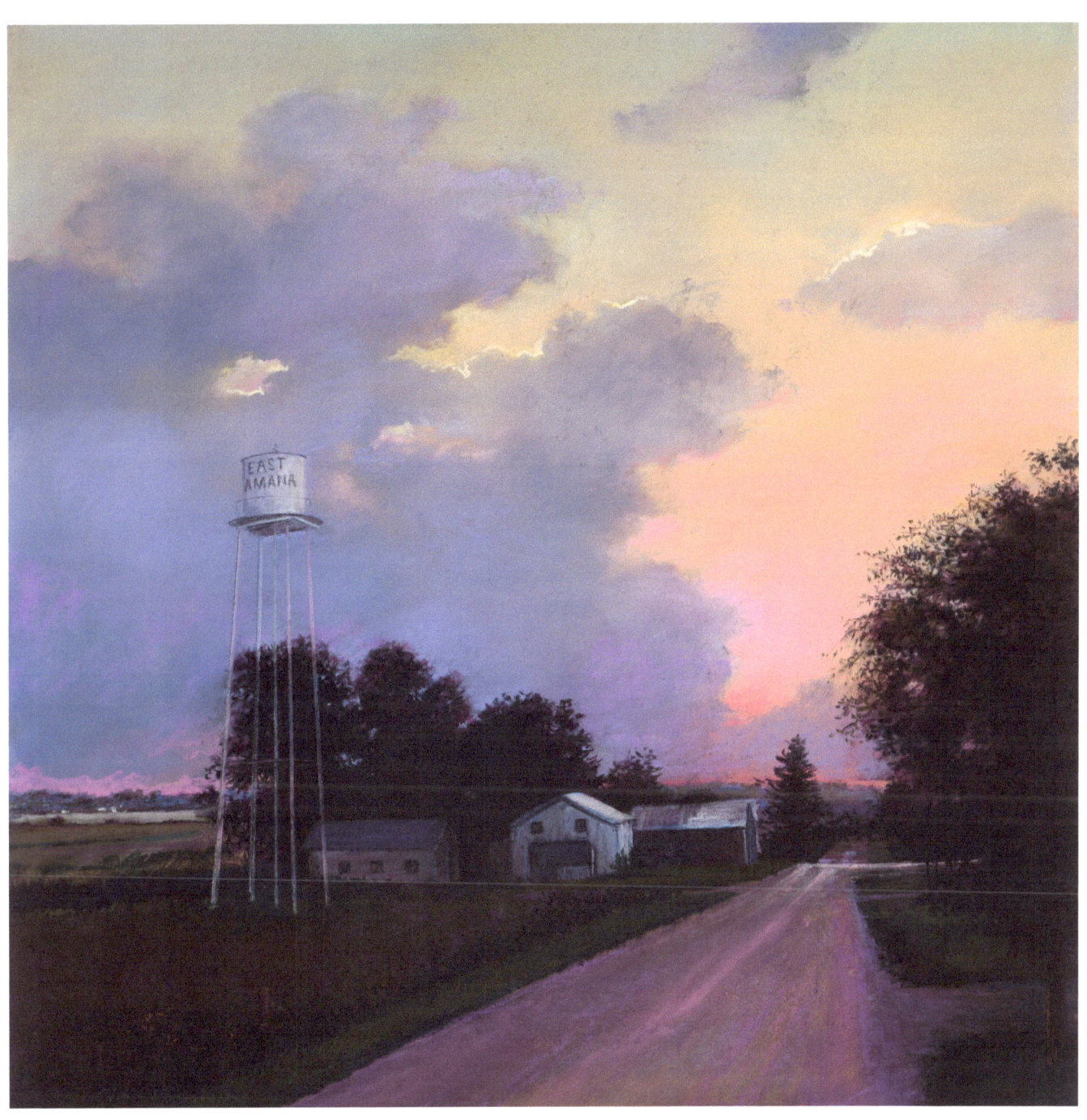

Sunset at East Amana 20 x 20 in.

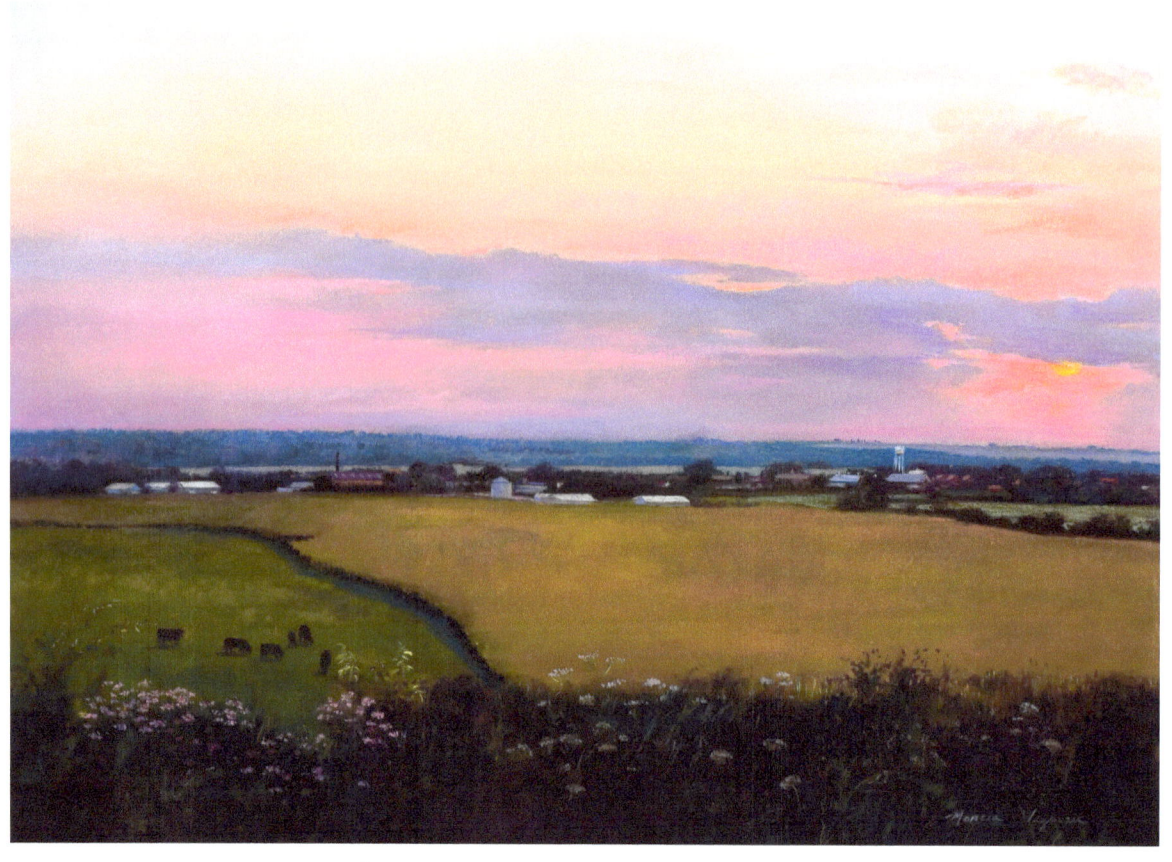

Amana Evening 18 x 24 in.

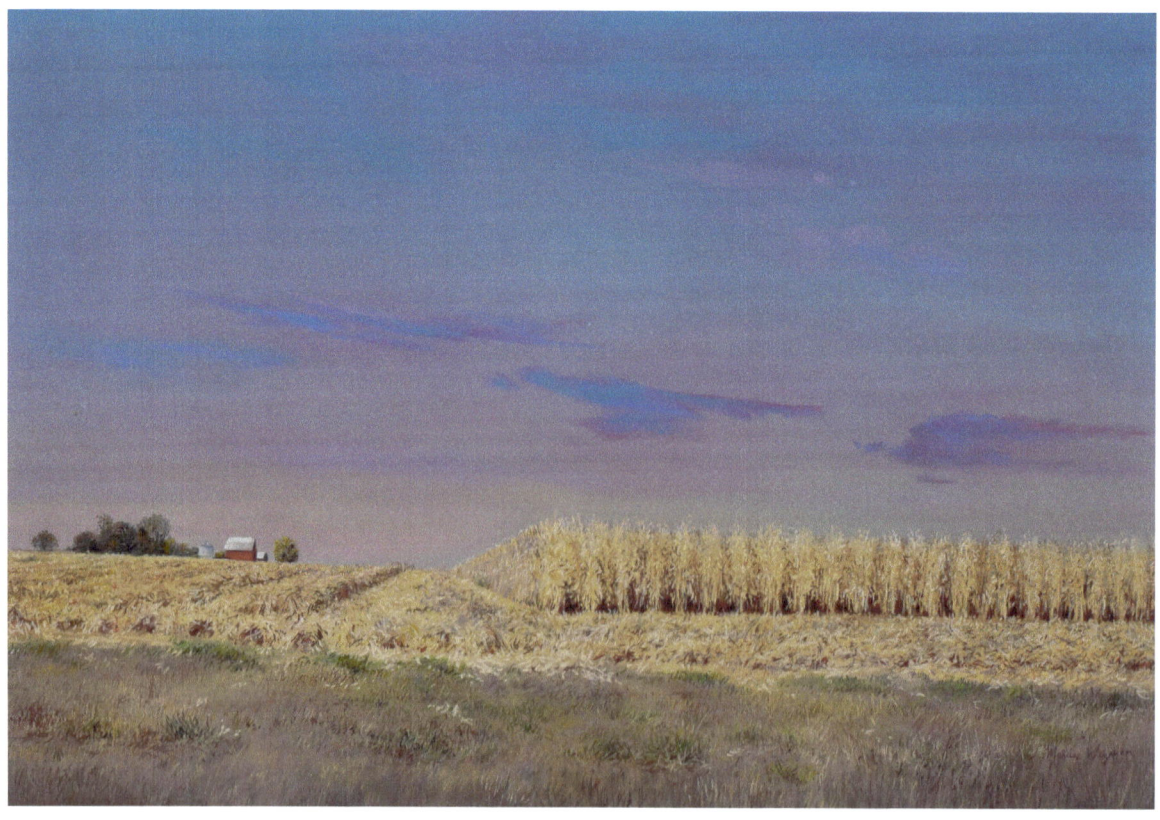

Corn Harvest 24 x 36 in.

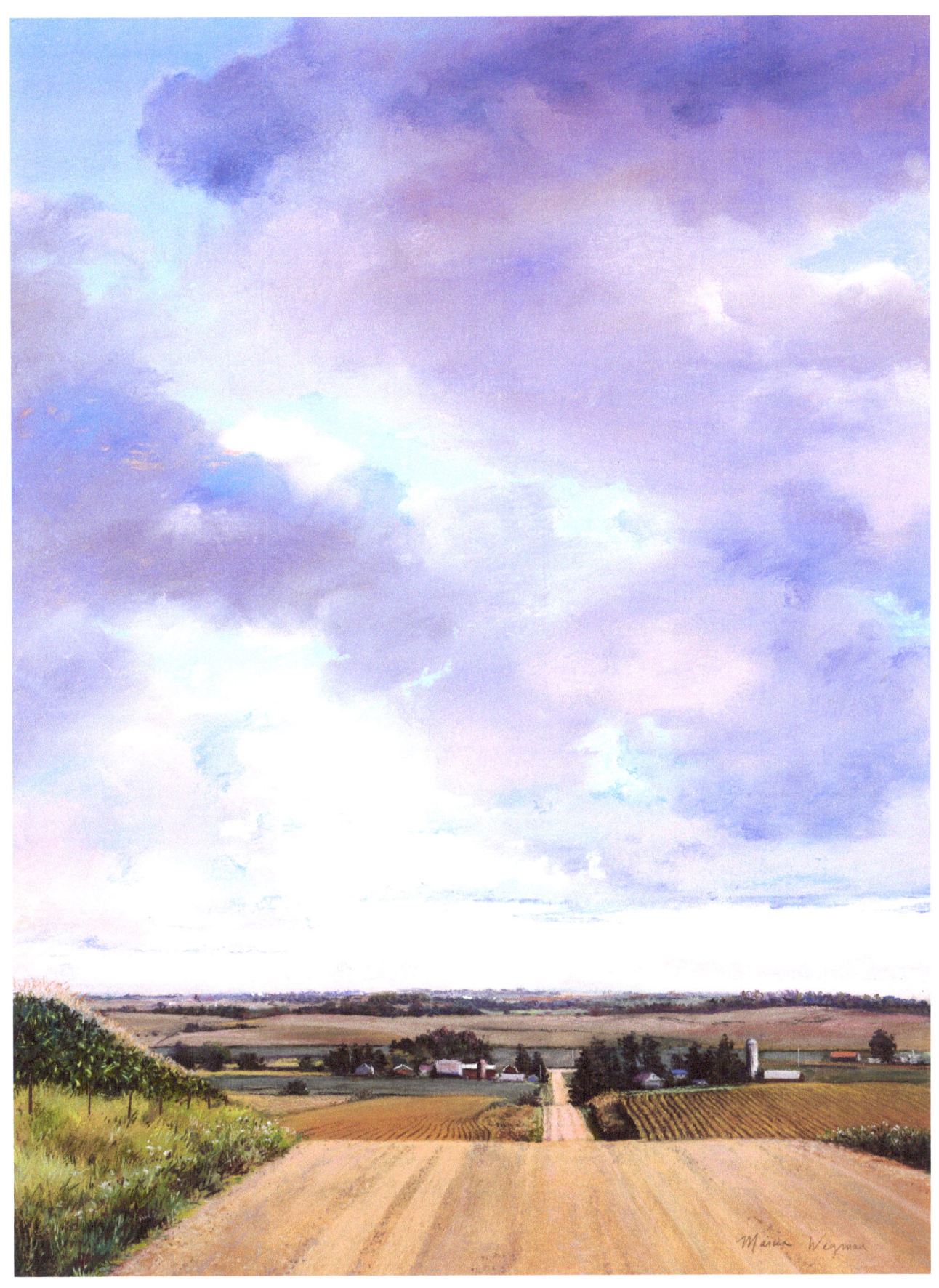
Country Road Near Maquoketa 24 x 18 in.

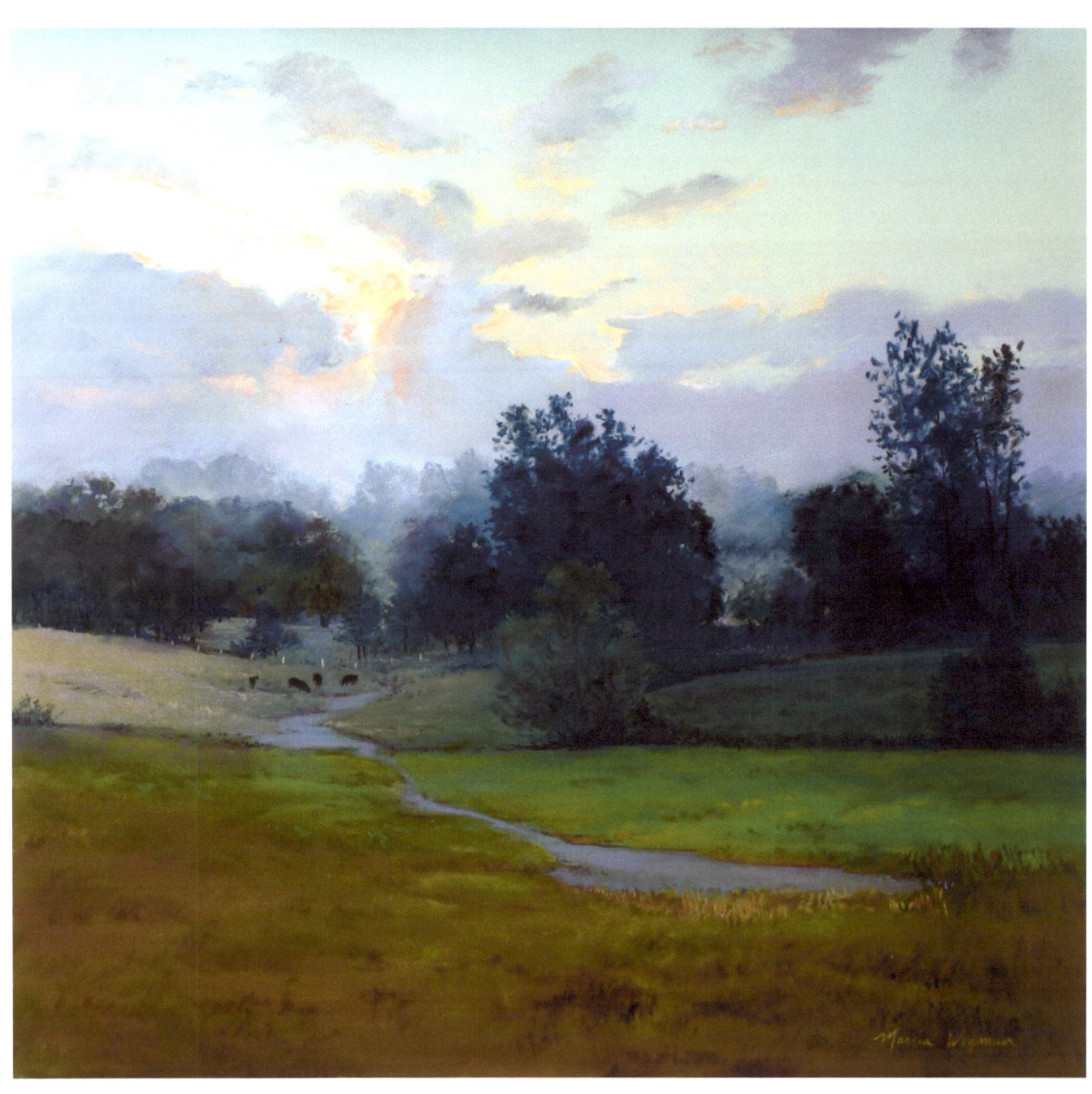

Cattle Pasture 25 x 25 in.

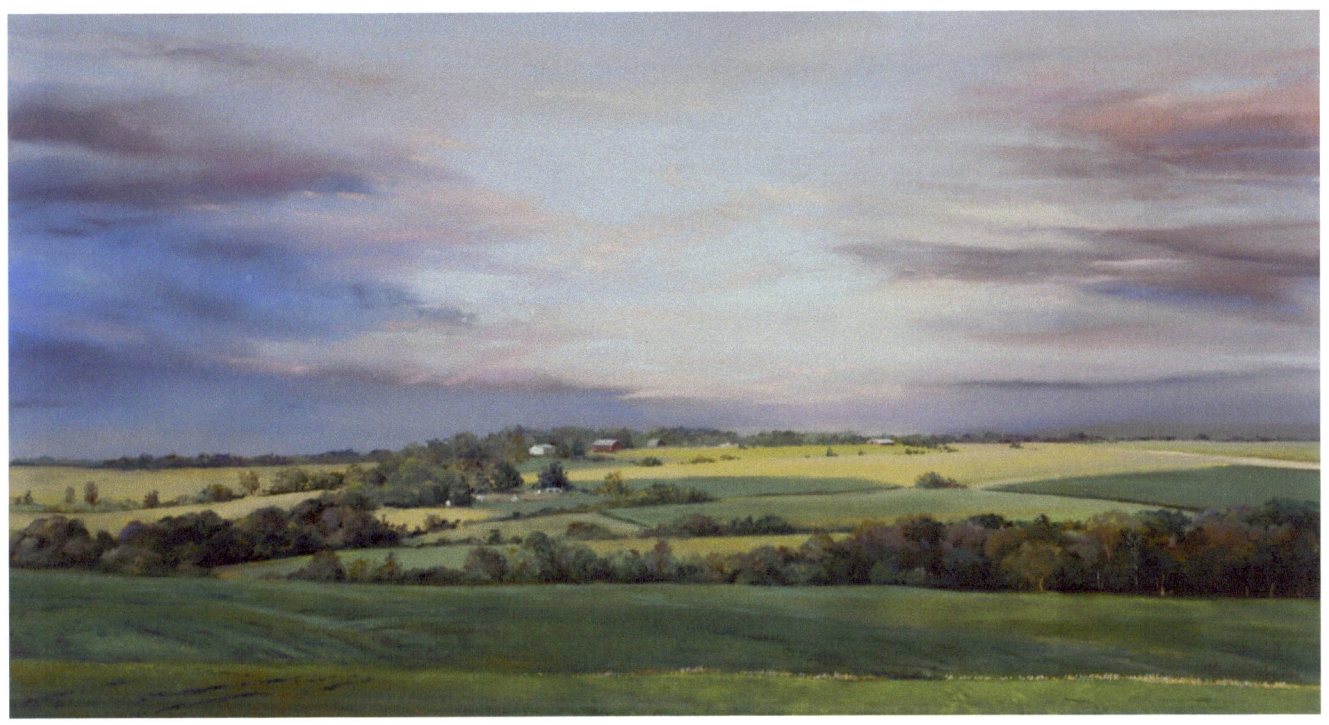

Evening Light Over the Land 18 x 36 in.

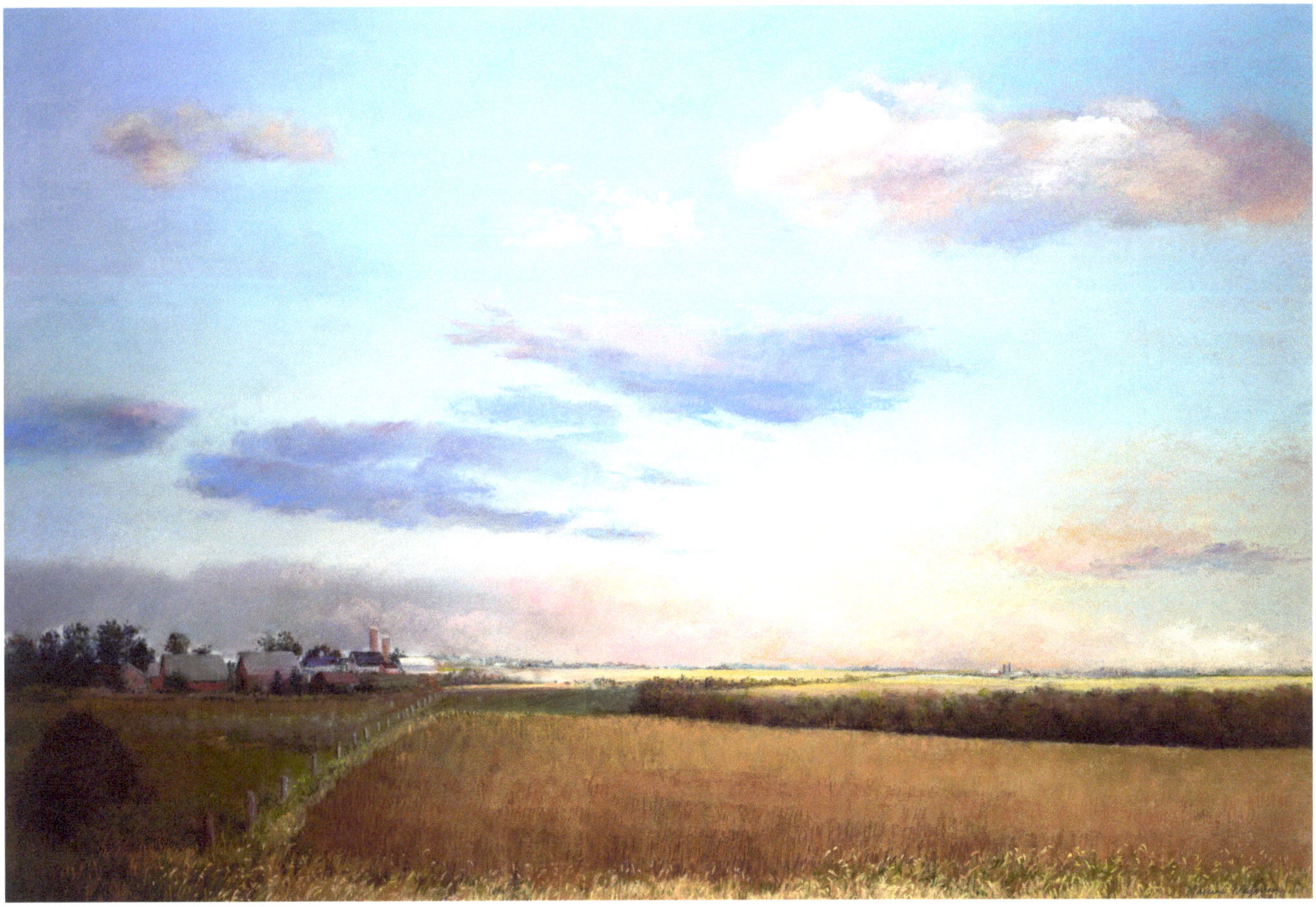

Dawn Fields 27 x 40 in.

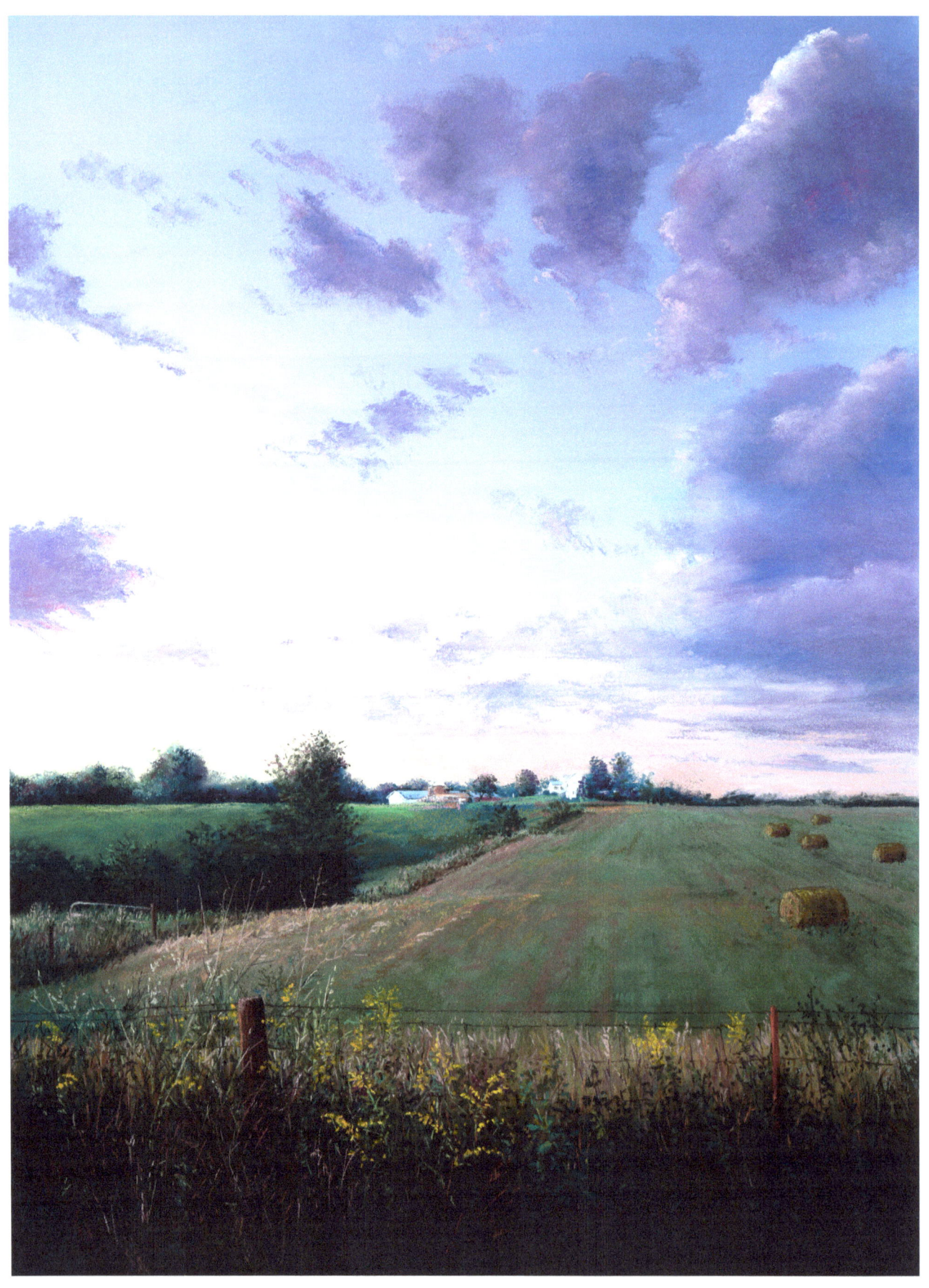

Late Summer Evening 32 x 24 in.

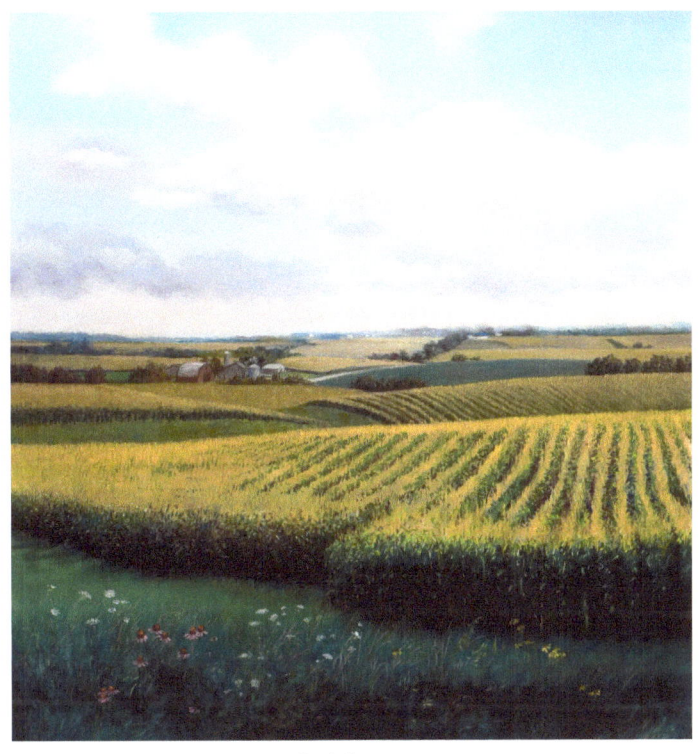

Late Summer Cornfields 28 x 28 in.

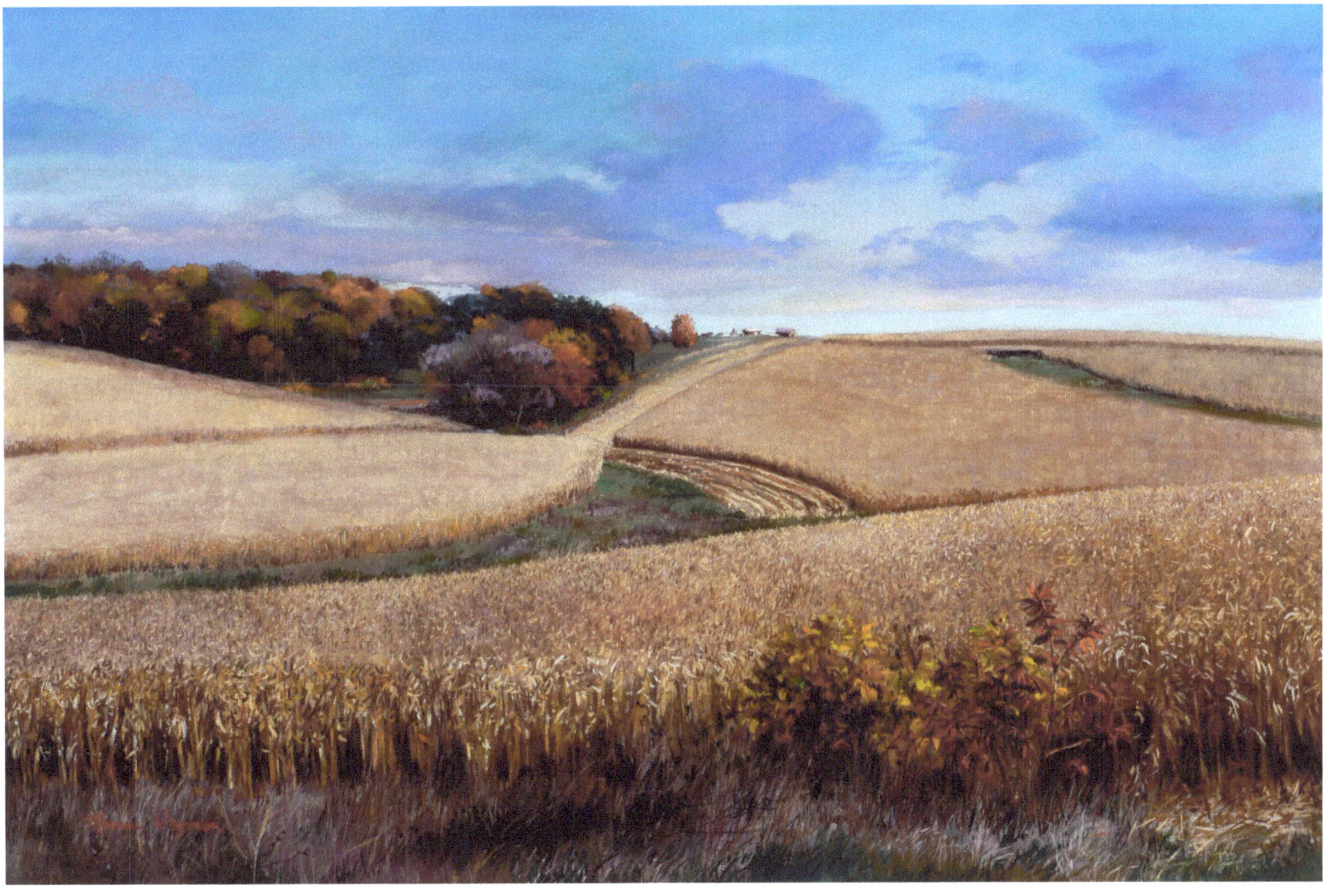

October Cornfields 25 x 40 in.

—51

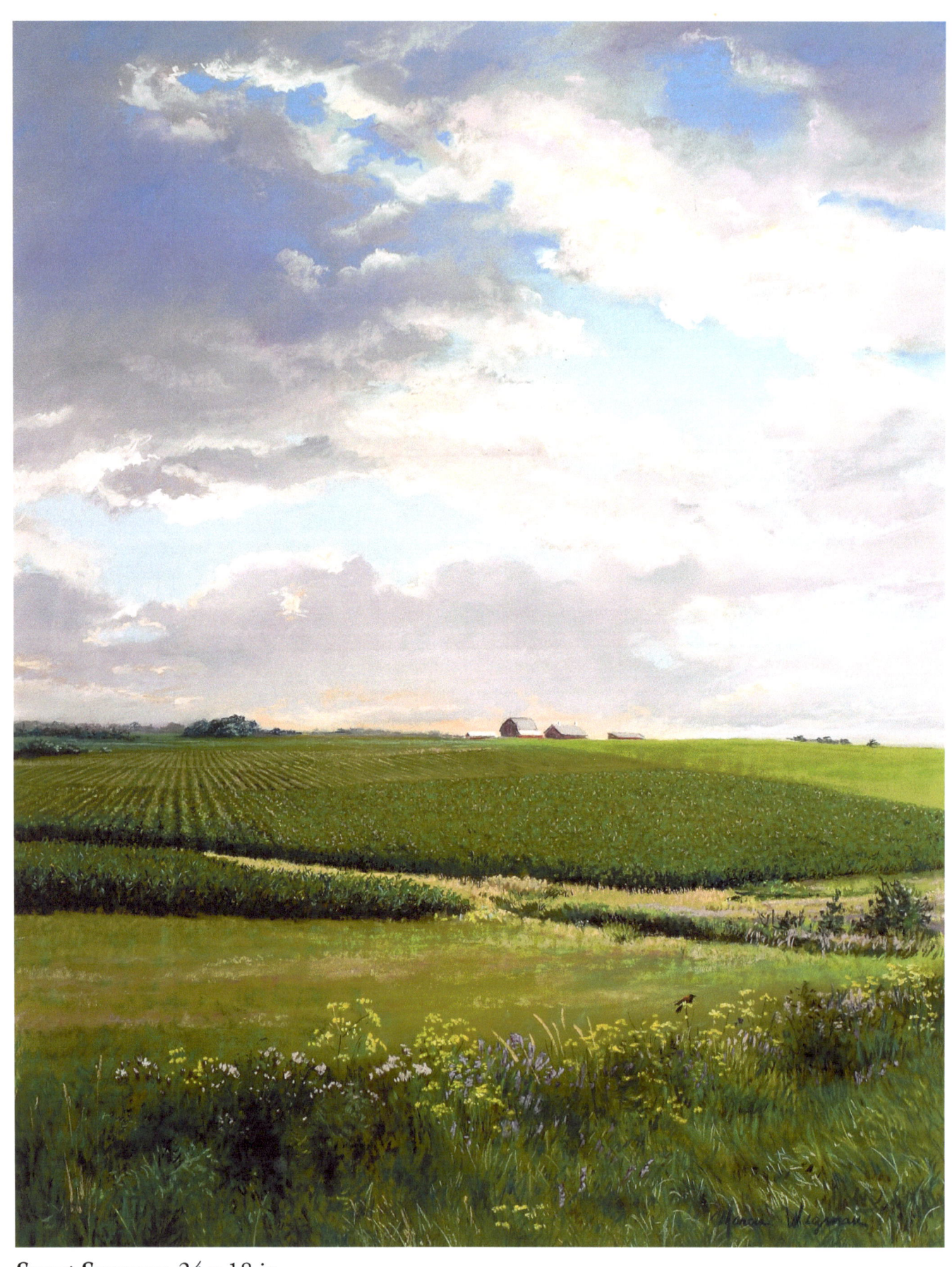

Sweet Summer 24 x 18 in.

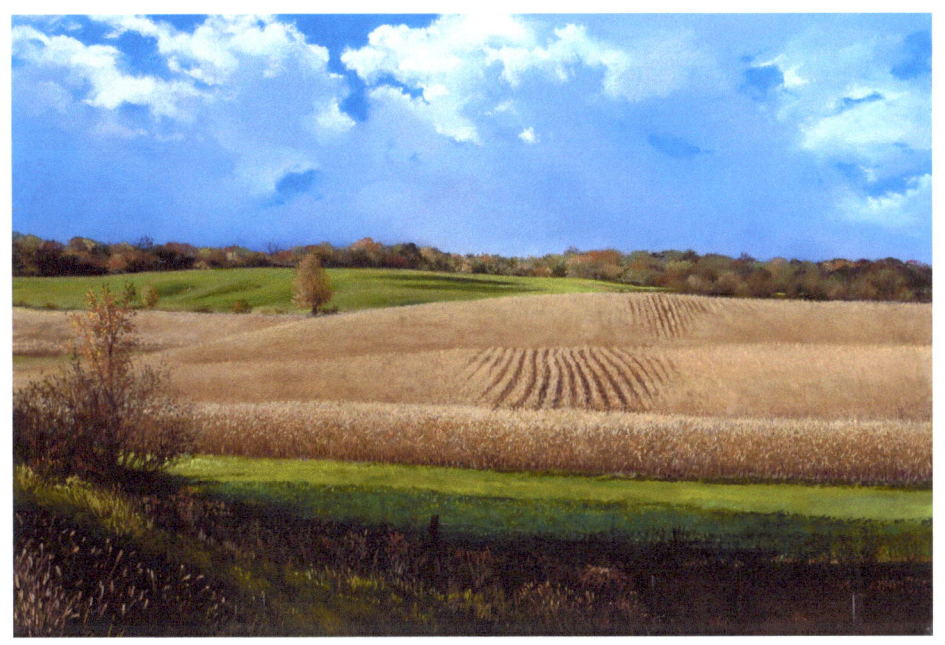

Iowa Fall Corn 24 x 36 in.

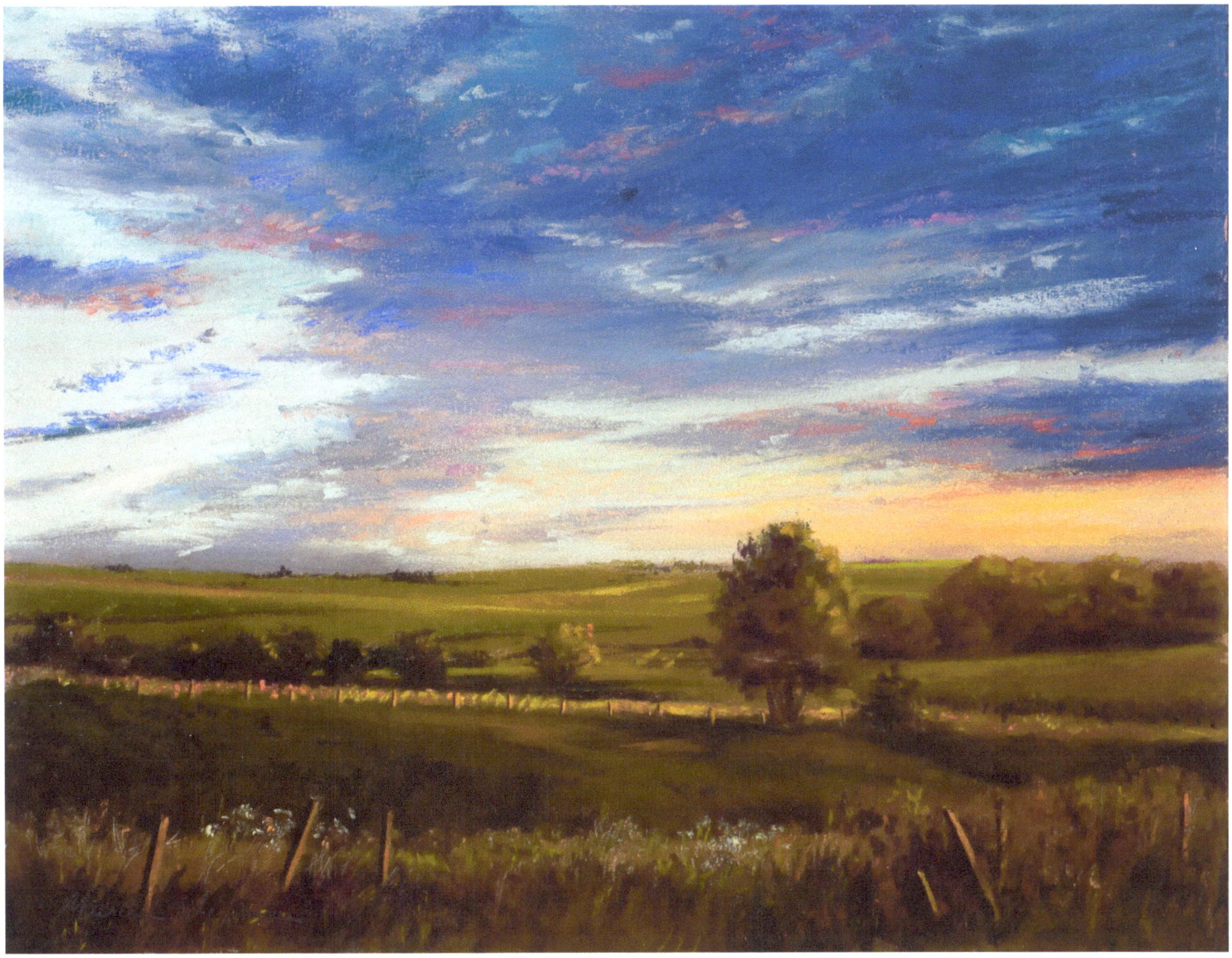

Evening Colors in August 9 x 12 in.

—53

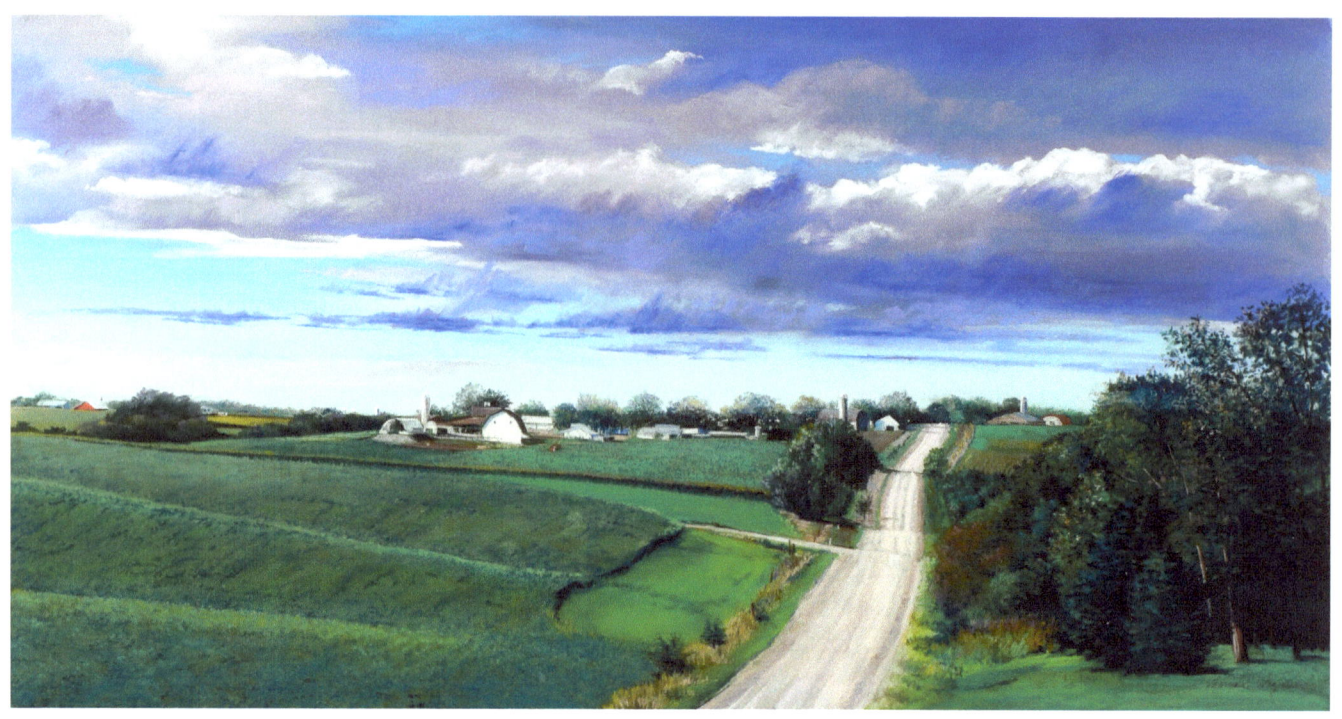

Near Kalona 20 x 20 in.

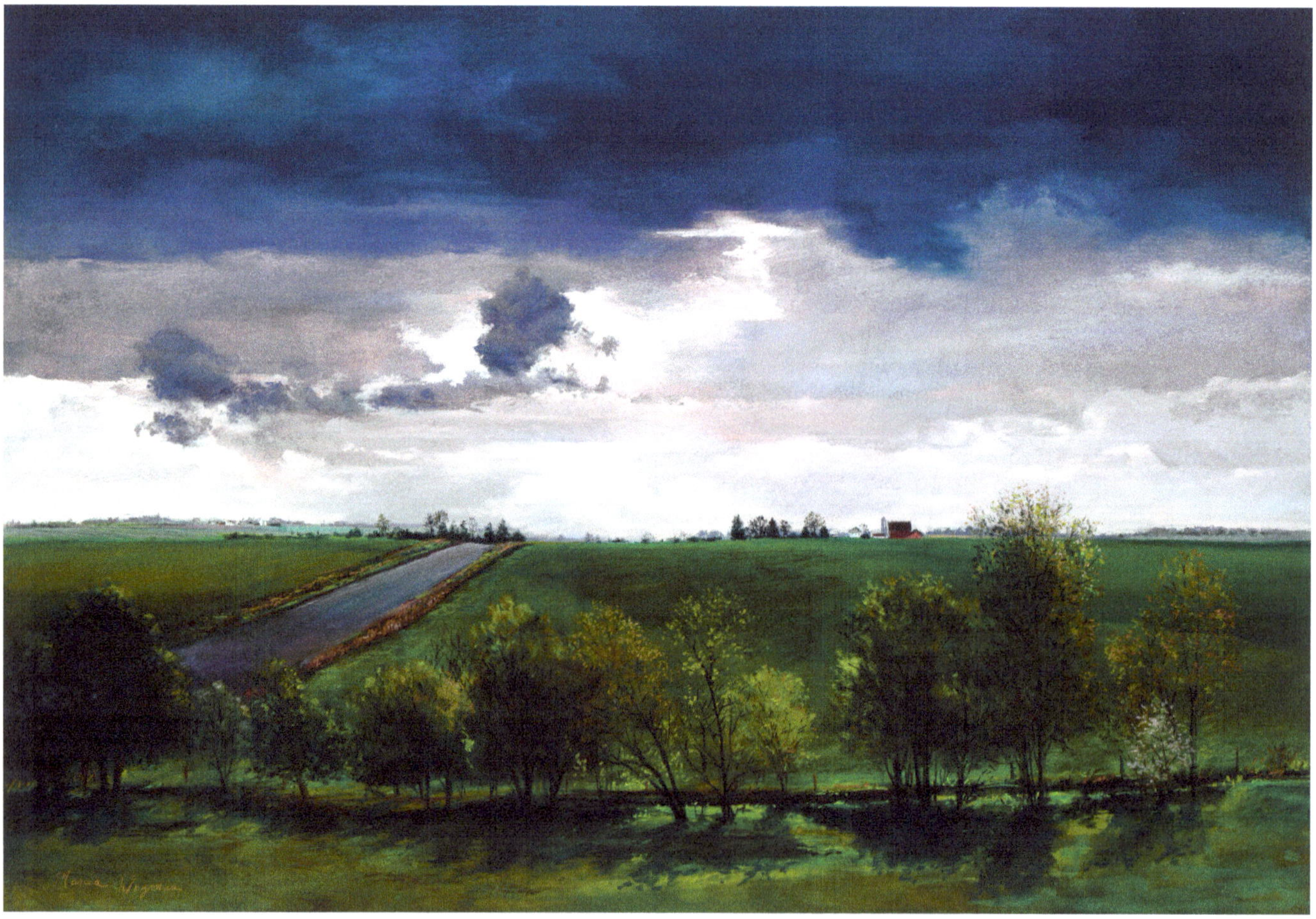

Threatening Spring Storm 24 x 36 in.

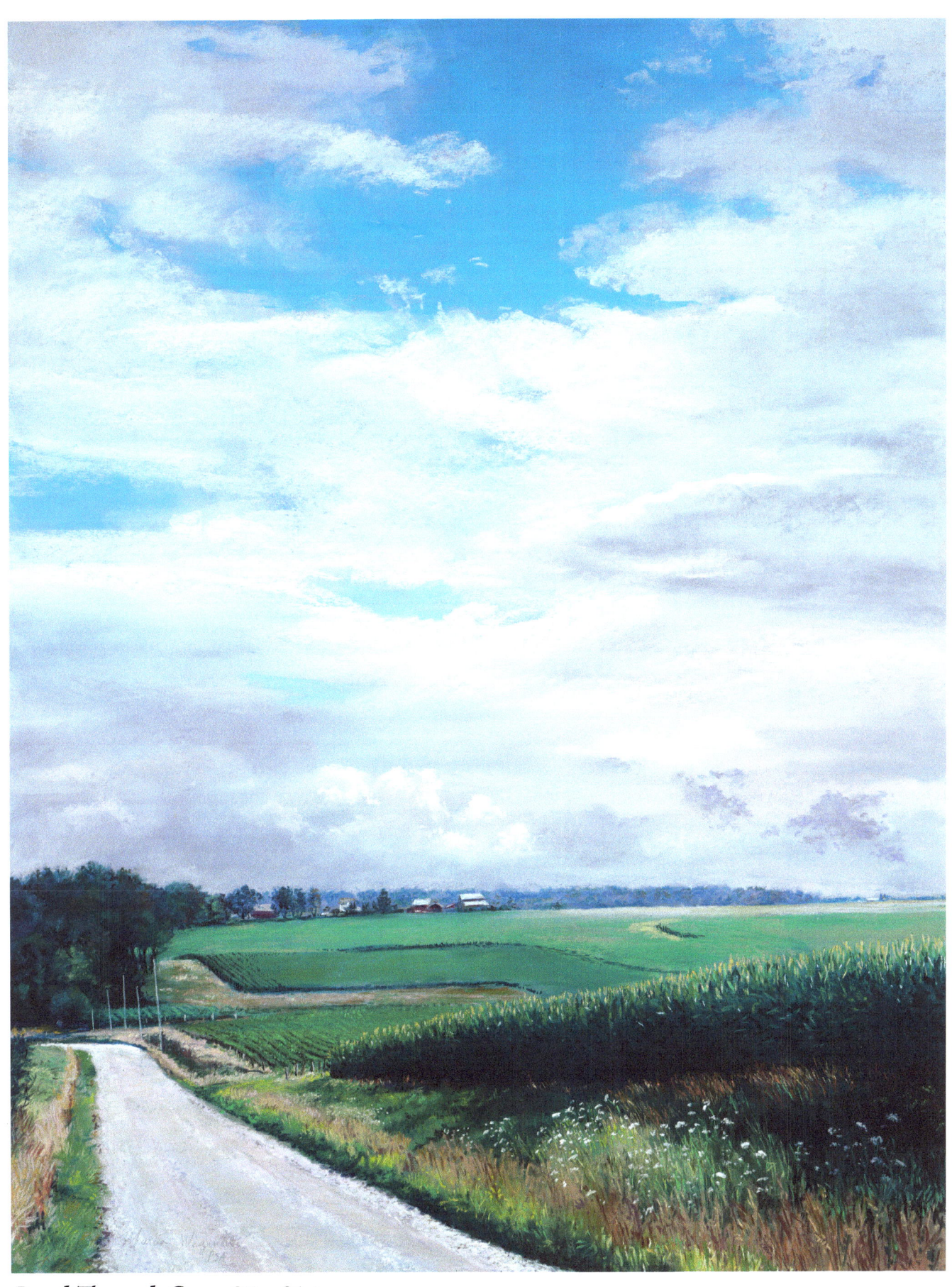

Road Through Corn 27 x 21 in.

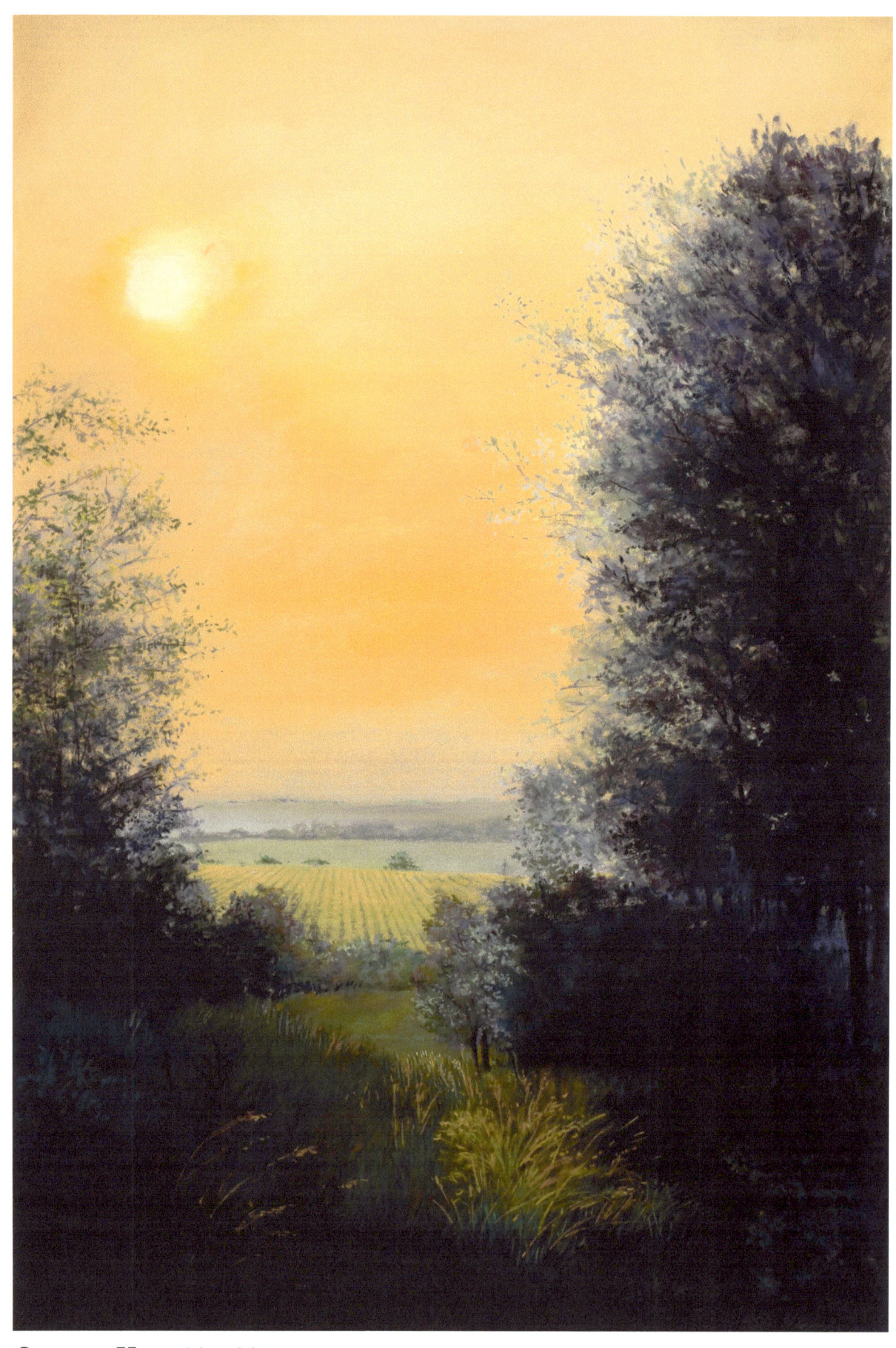

Summer Haze 30 x 20 in.

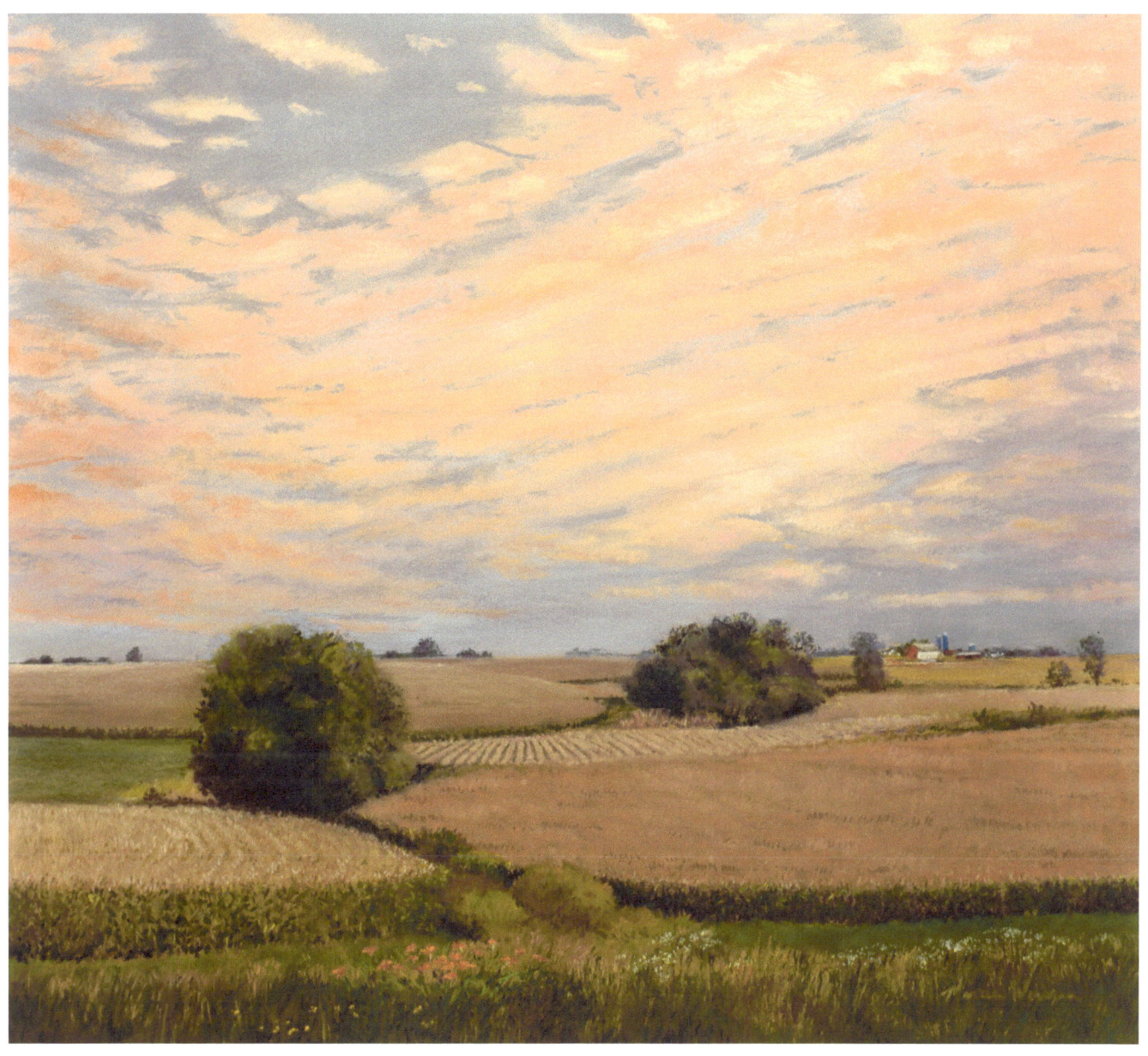

Summer Morning 21 x 24 in.

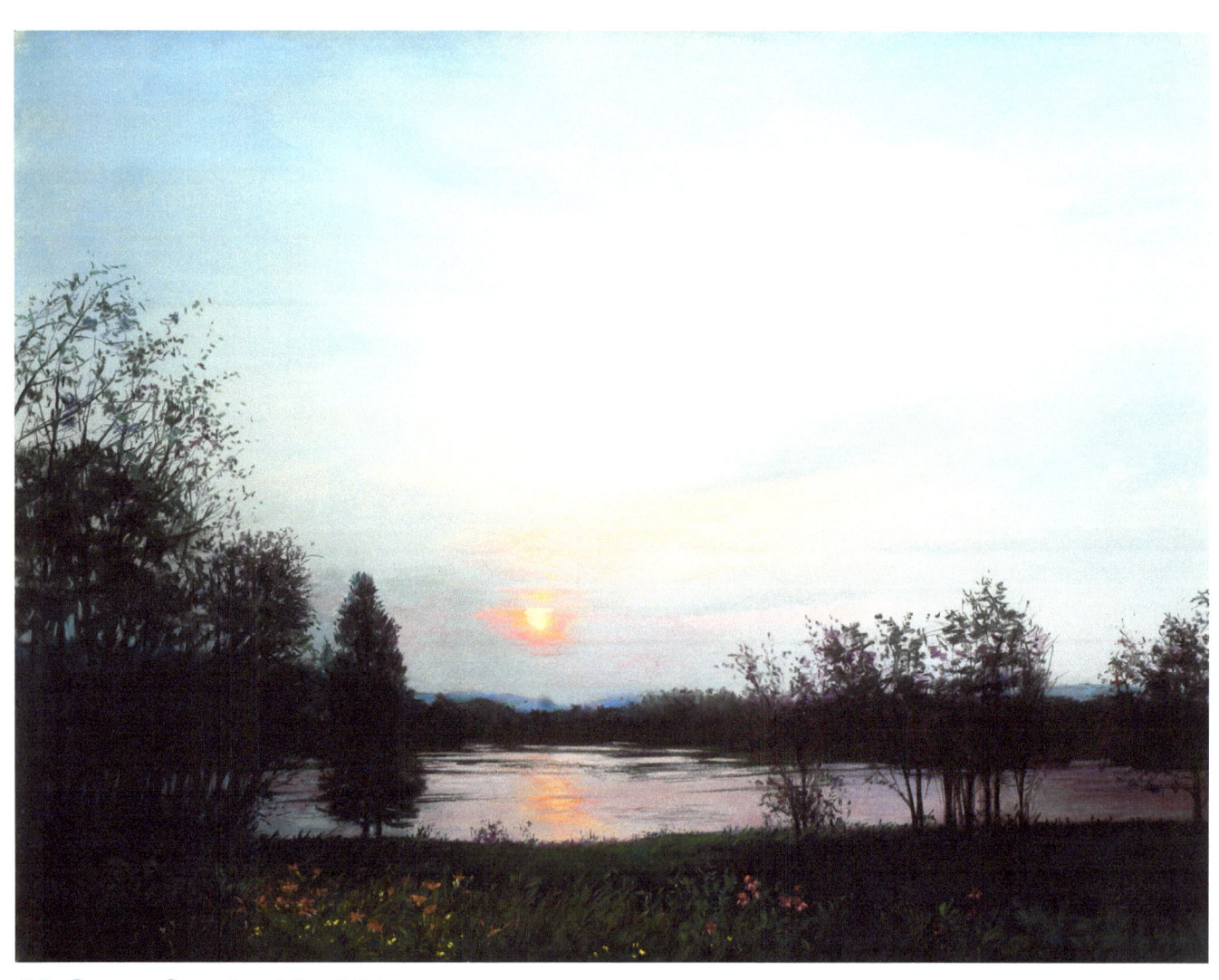

McGregor Sunrise 22 x 29 in.

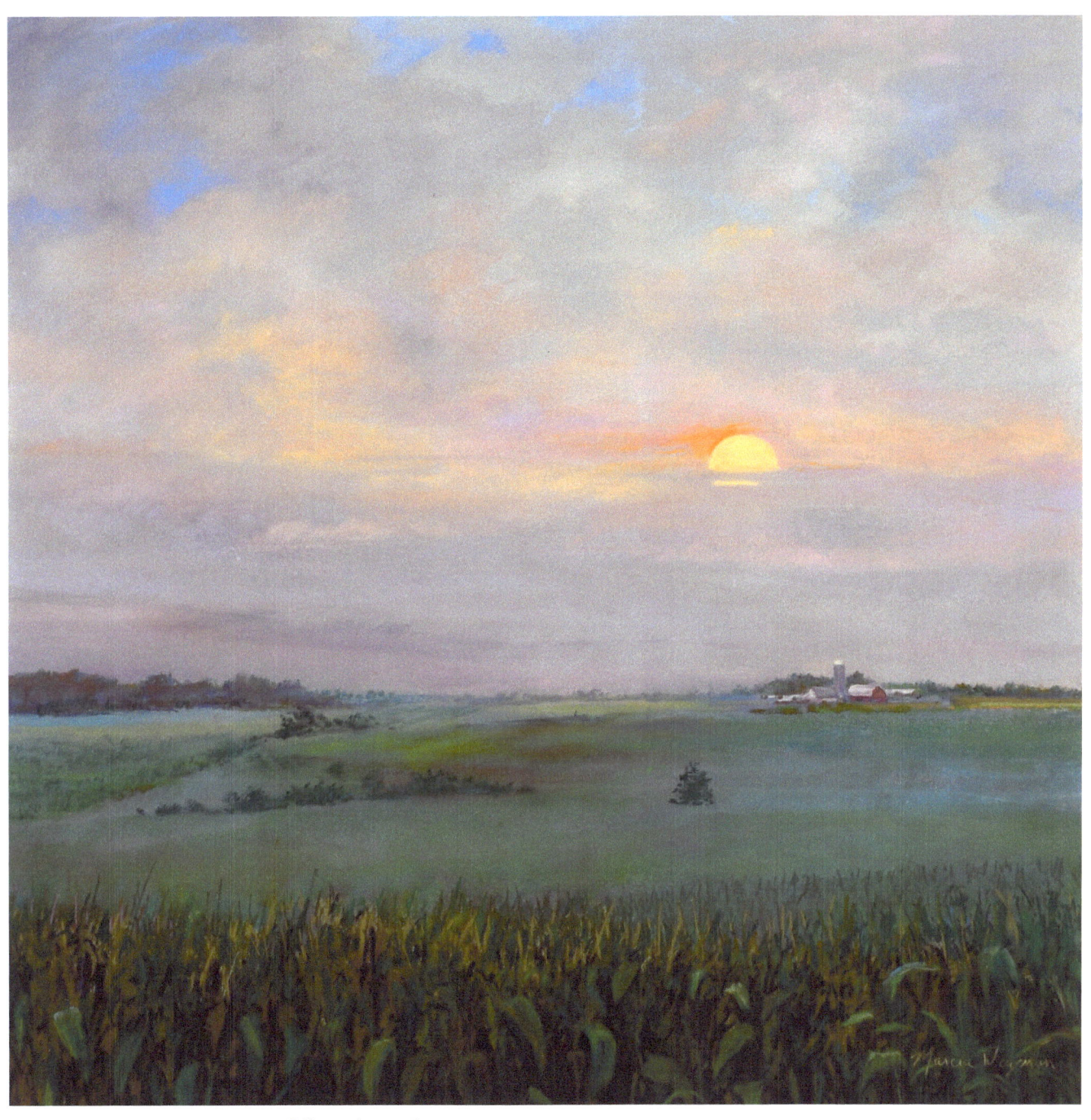

Mist Over Morning Fields 24 x 24 in.

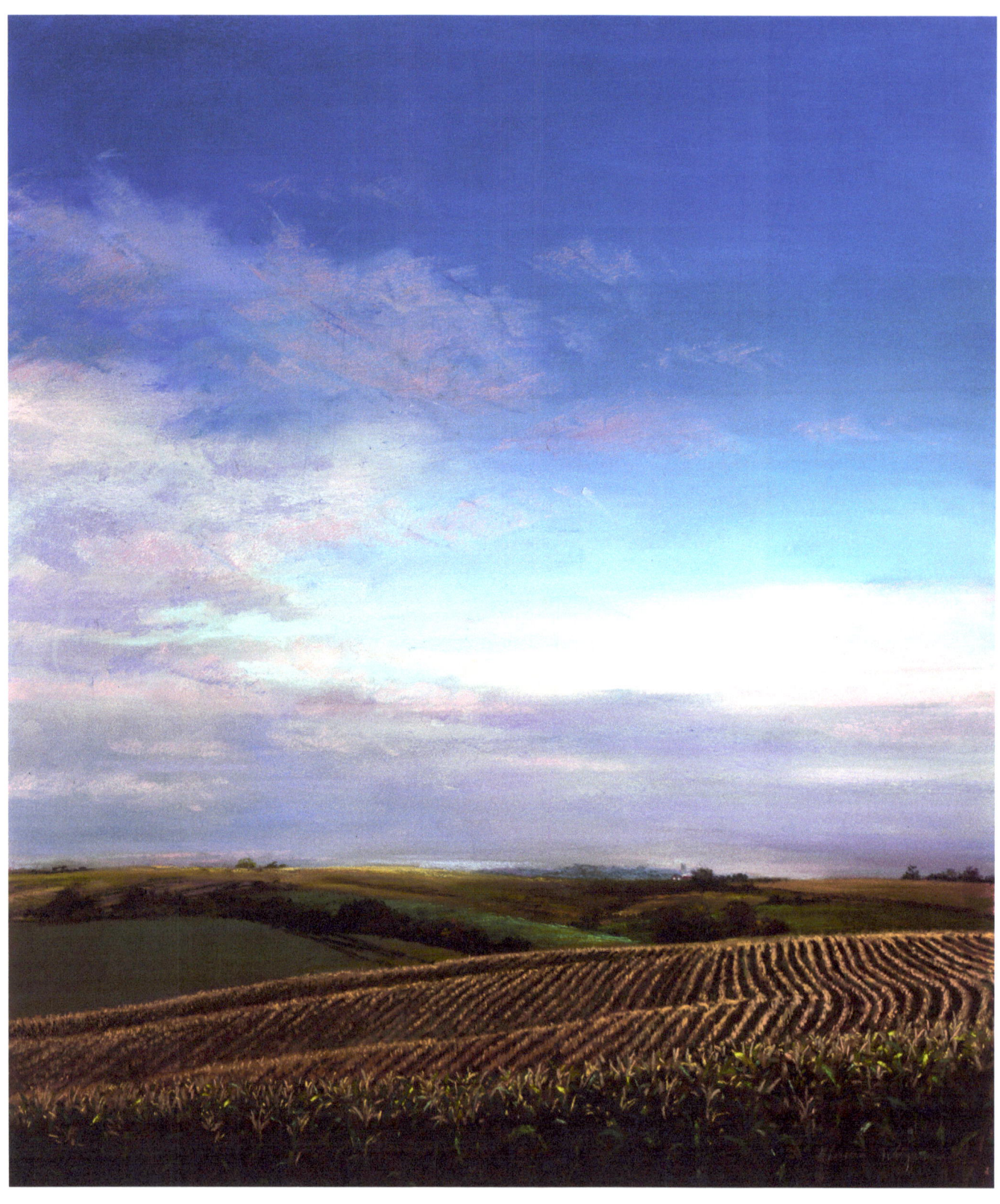

Corn Rows 21 x 18 in.

Rivers, Lakes, and Creeks

Water is quite an interesting challenge to paint. It takes very keen observation to see the colors, movement, and patterns in the water. The way clouds and land forms are reflected in the water is what makes it so interesting to observe and utilize compositionally.

All bodies of water can make for a wonderful addition to a landscape painting, whether it is a farm pond creating an unexpected note or the powerful Mississippi River.

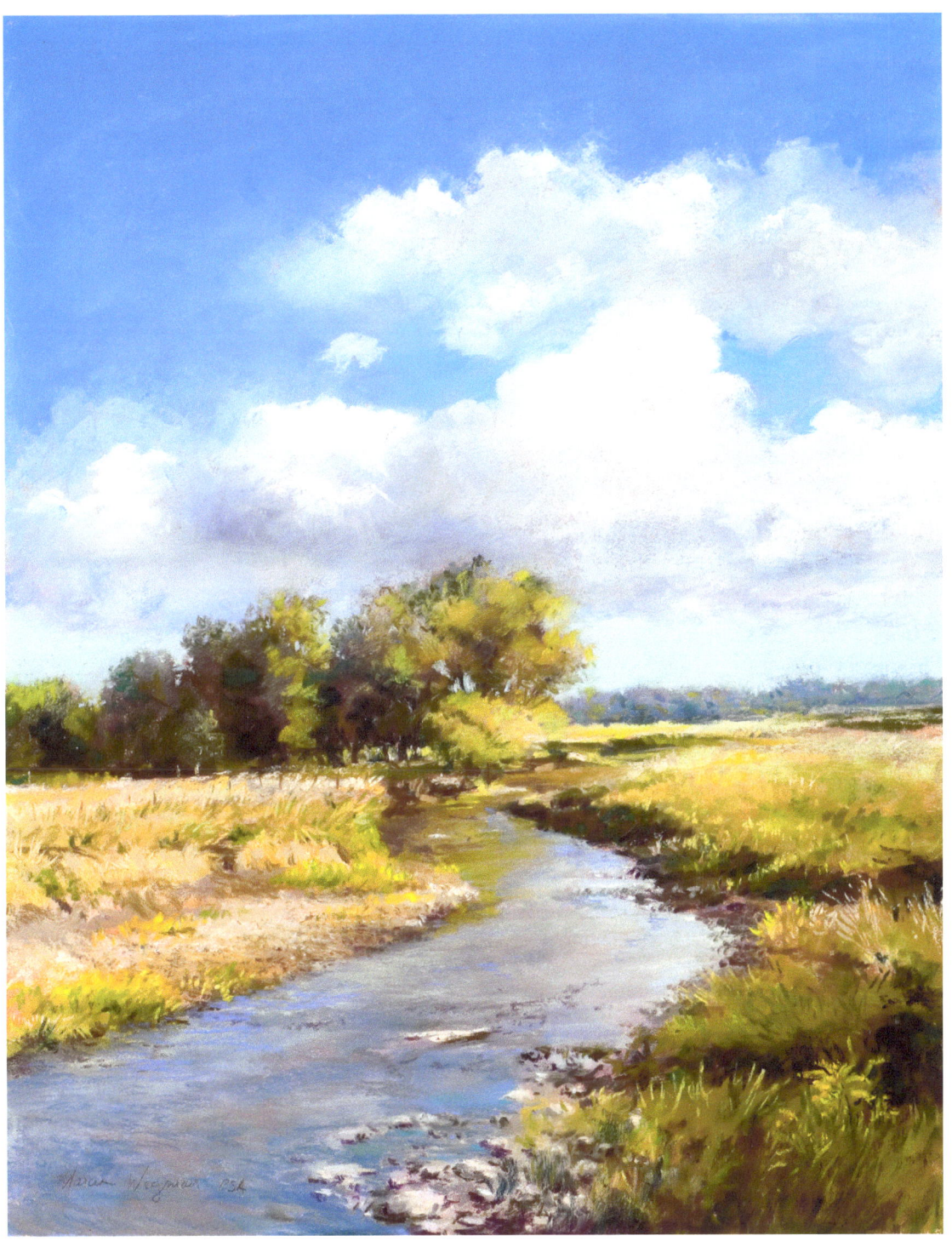

Farm Creek 17 x 13 in.

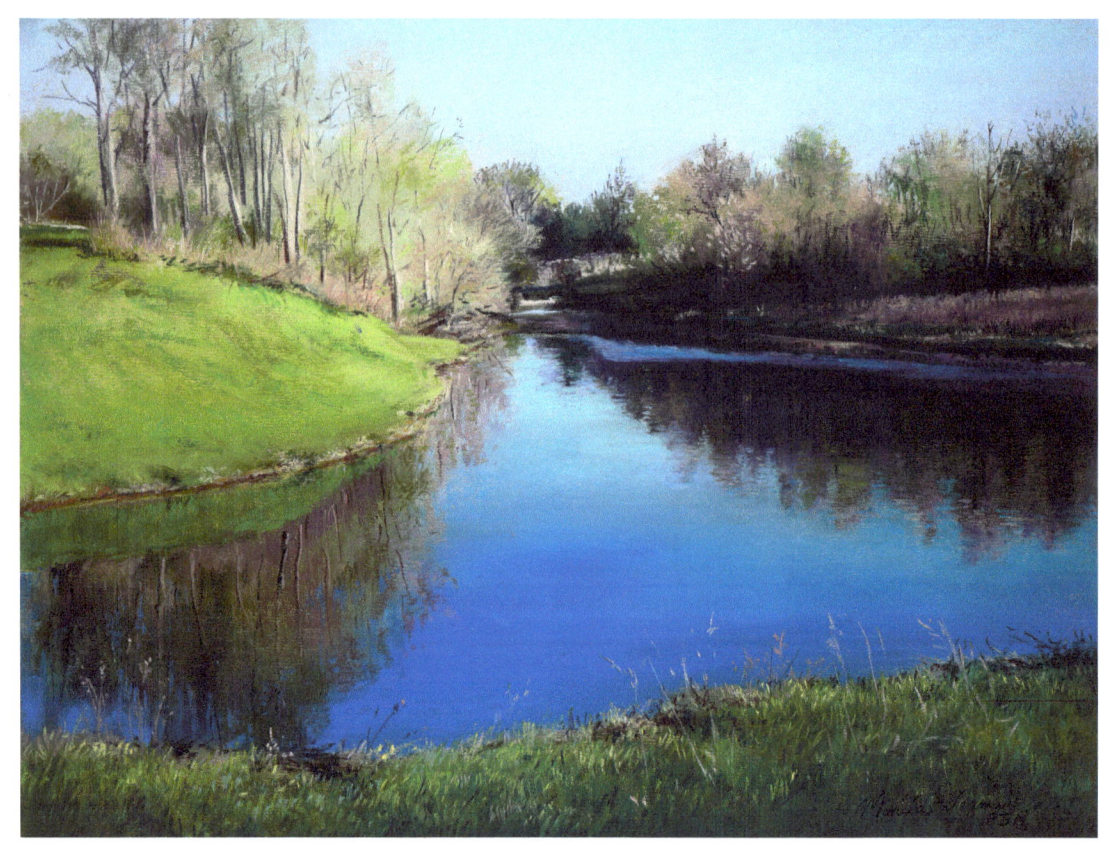

A Walk at Kent Park 15 x 20 in.

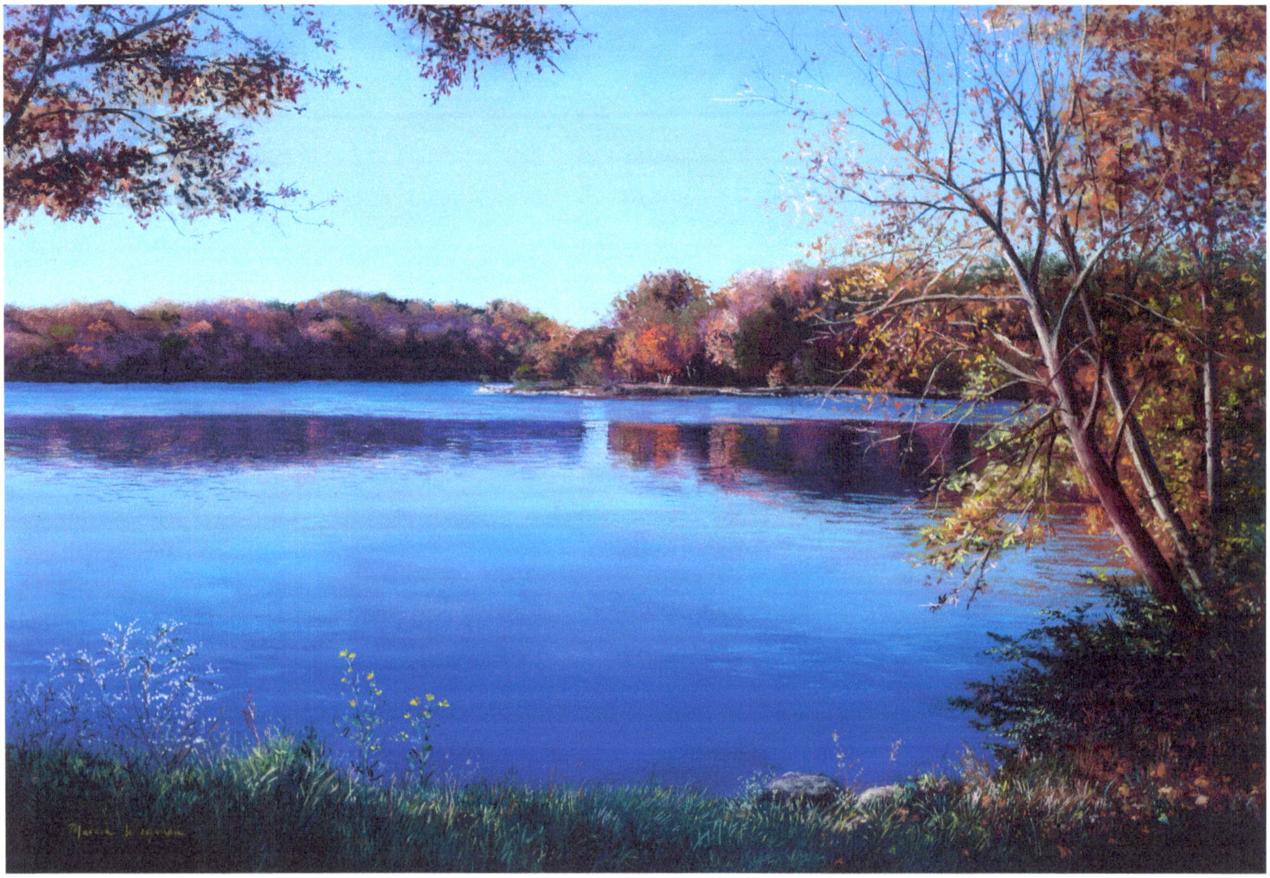

Lake Macbride 24 x 36 in.

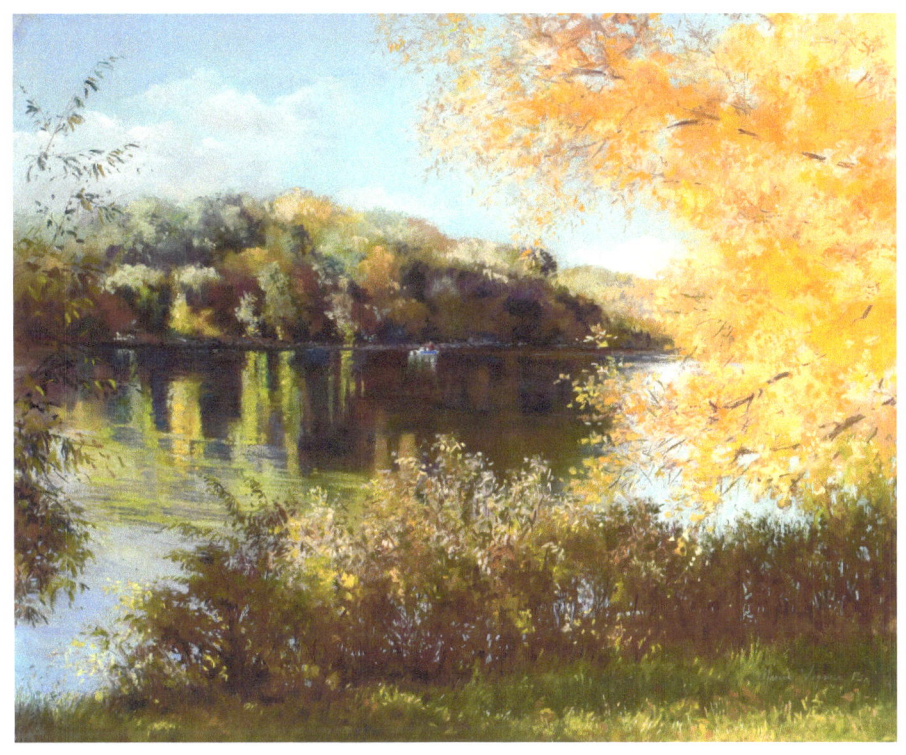

Macbride Fisherman 21 x 27 in.

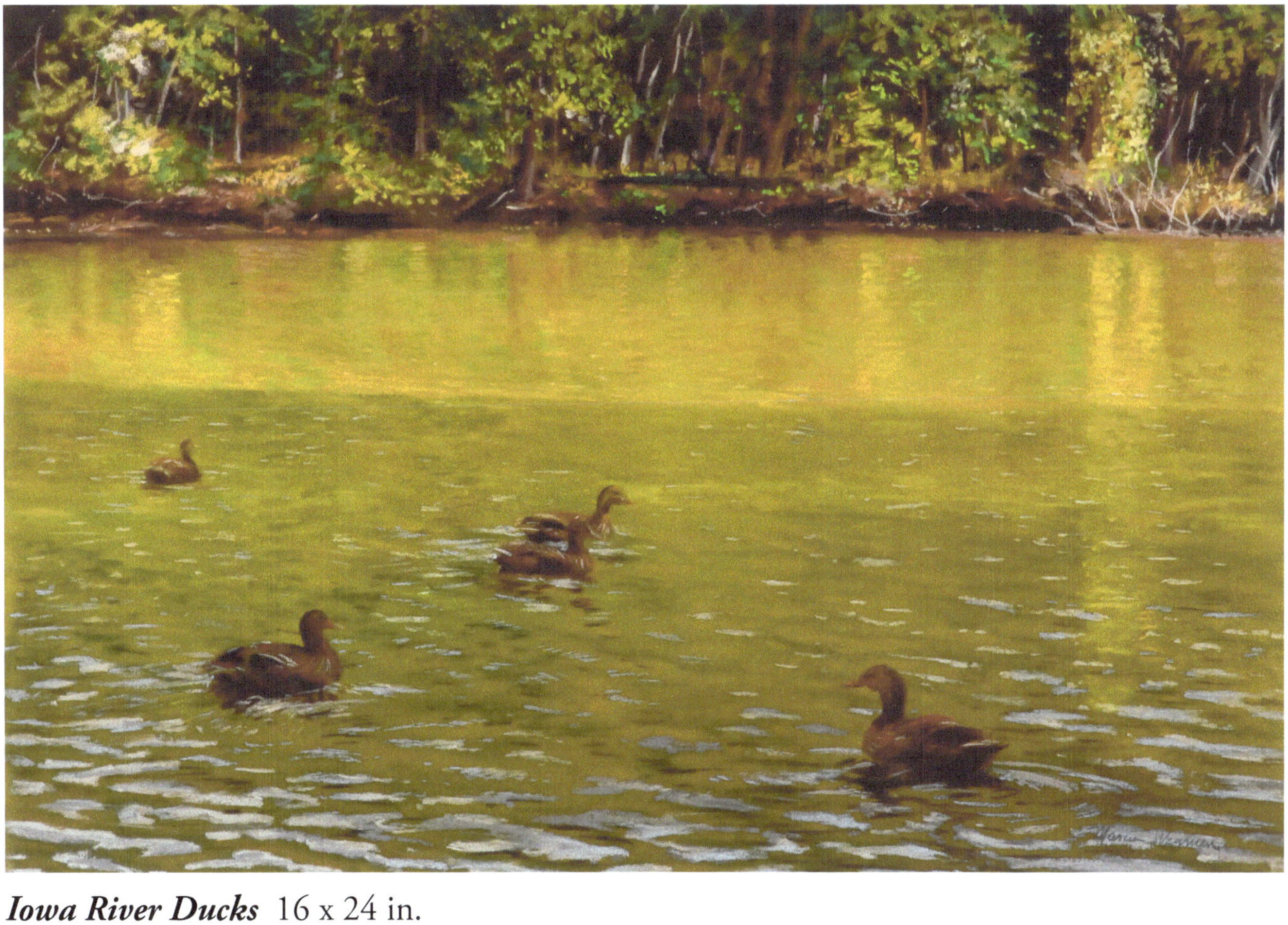

Iowa River Ducks 16 x 24 in.

—63

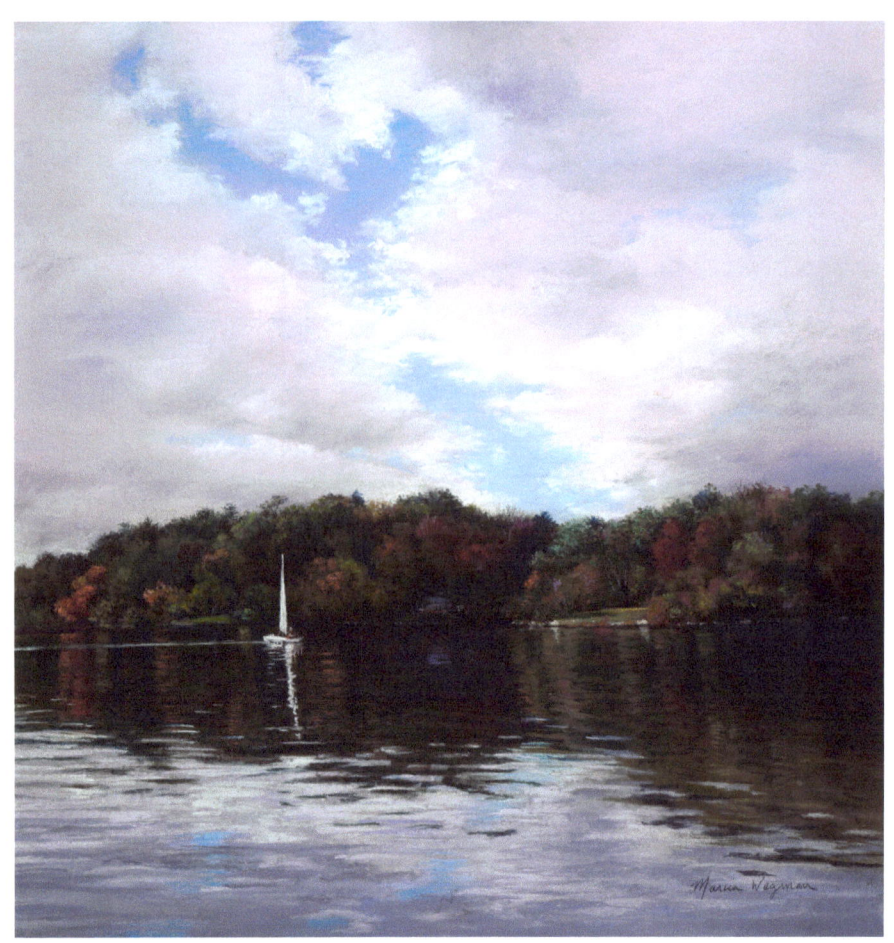
Afternoon on Lake Macbride 21 x 21 in.

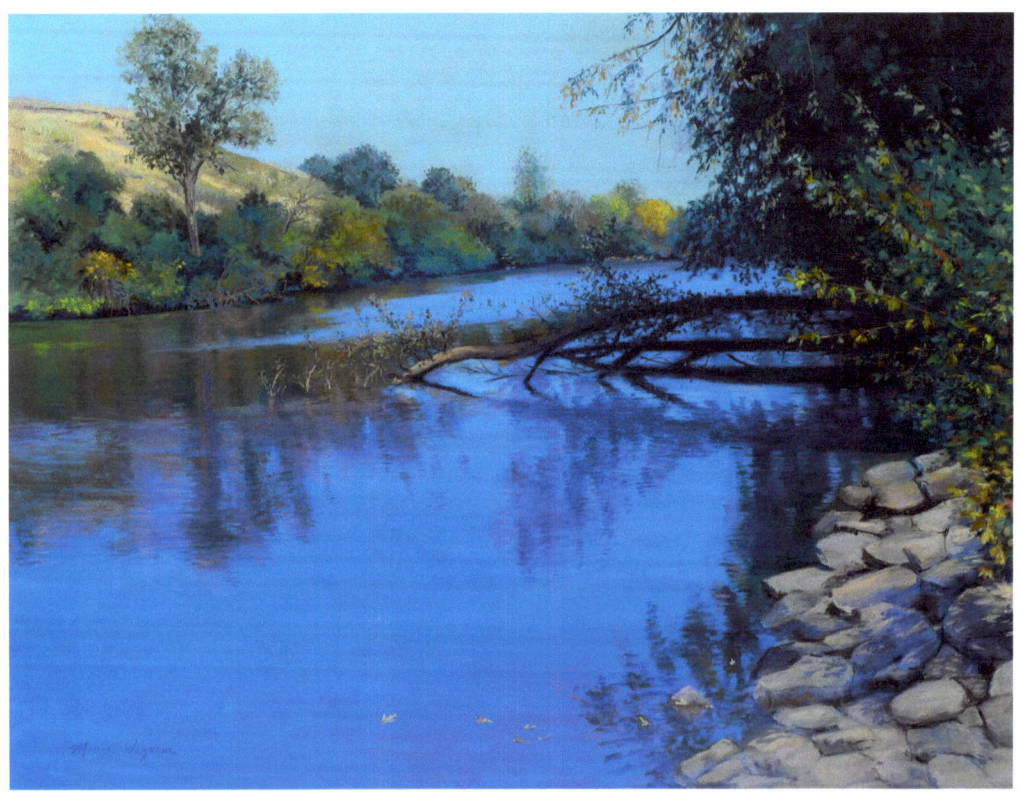
Iowa River at Waterworks Park 24 x 32 in.

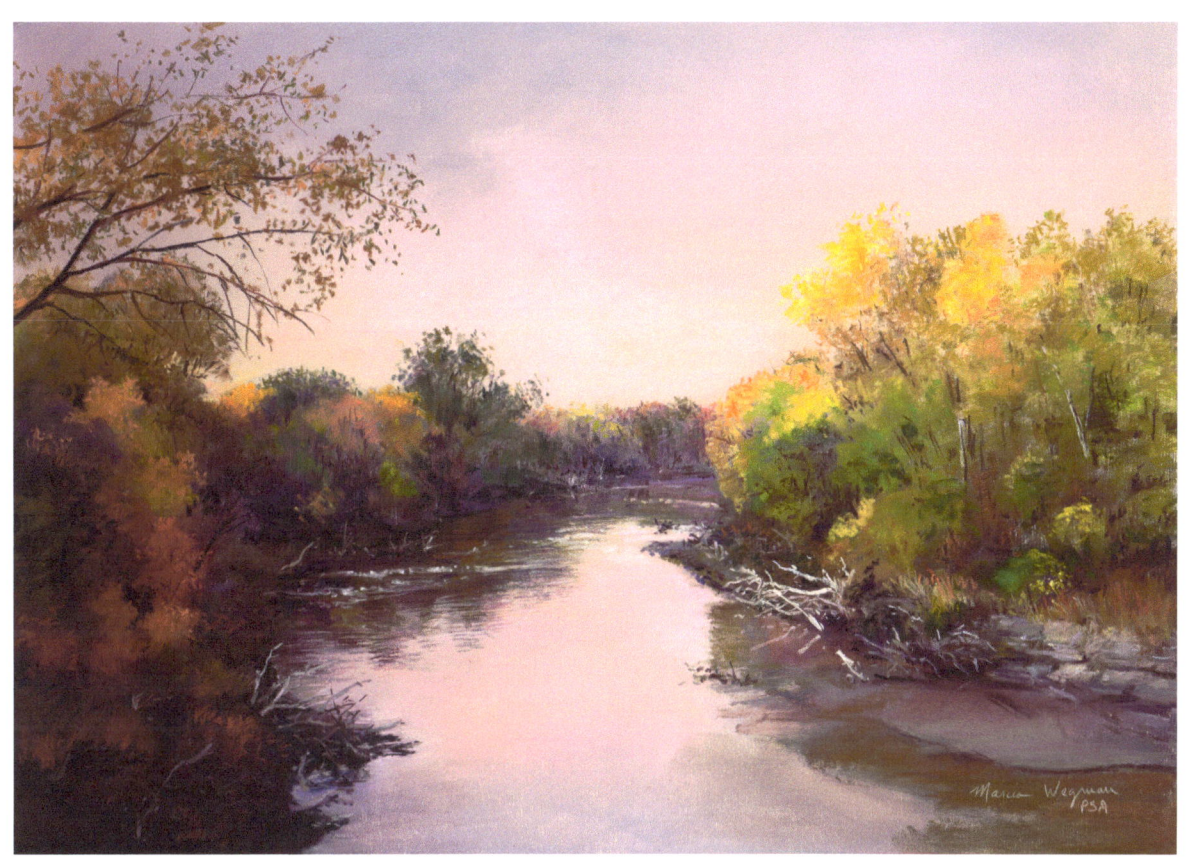
Early Morning River 17 x 24 in.

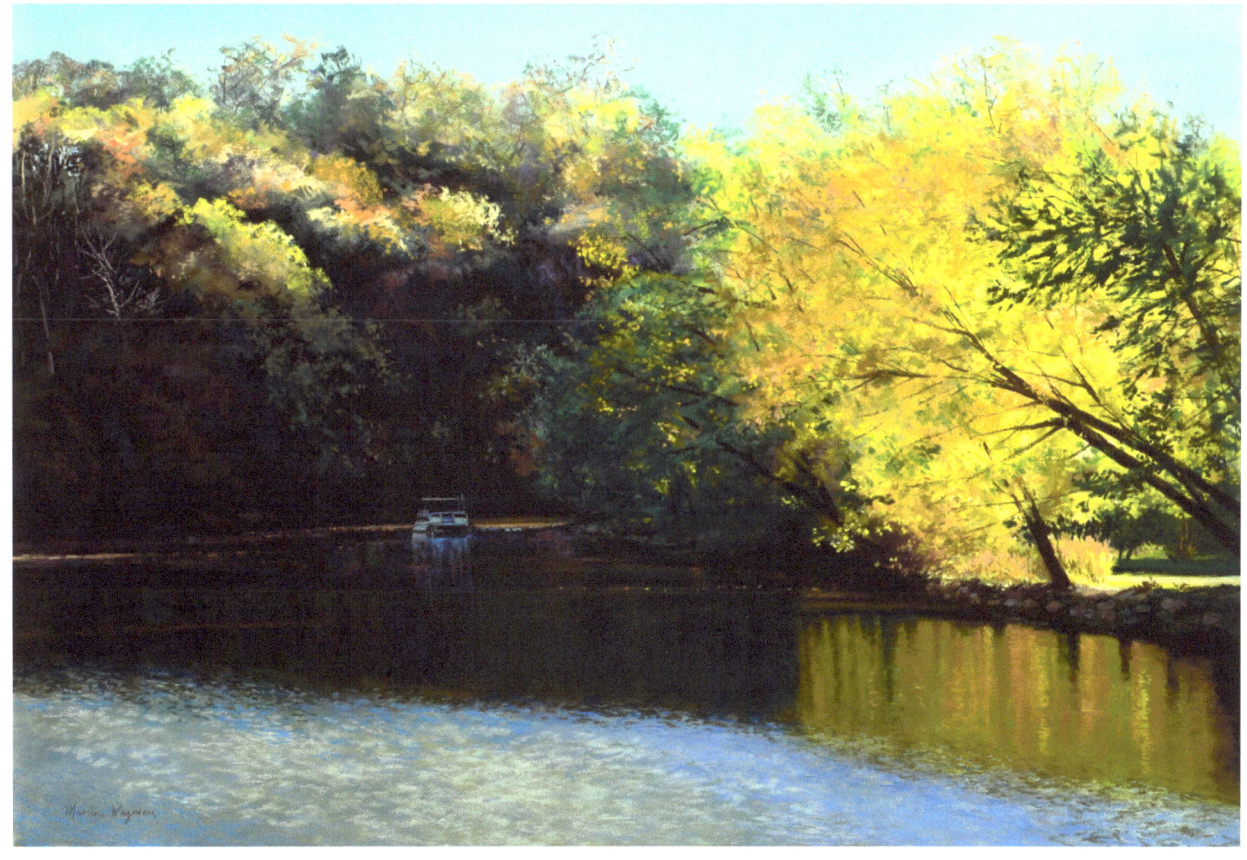
October River 24 x 36 in.

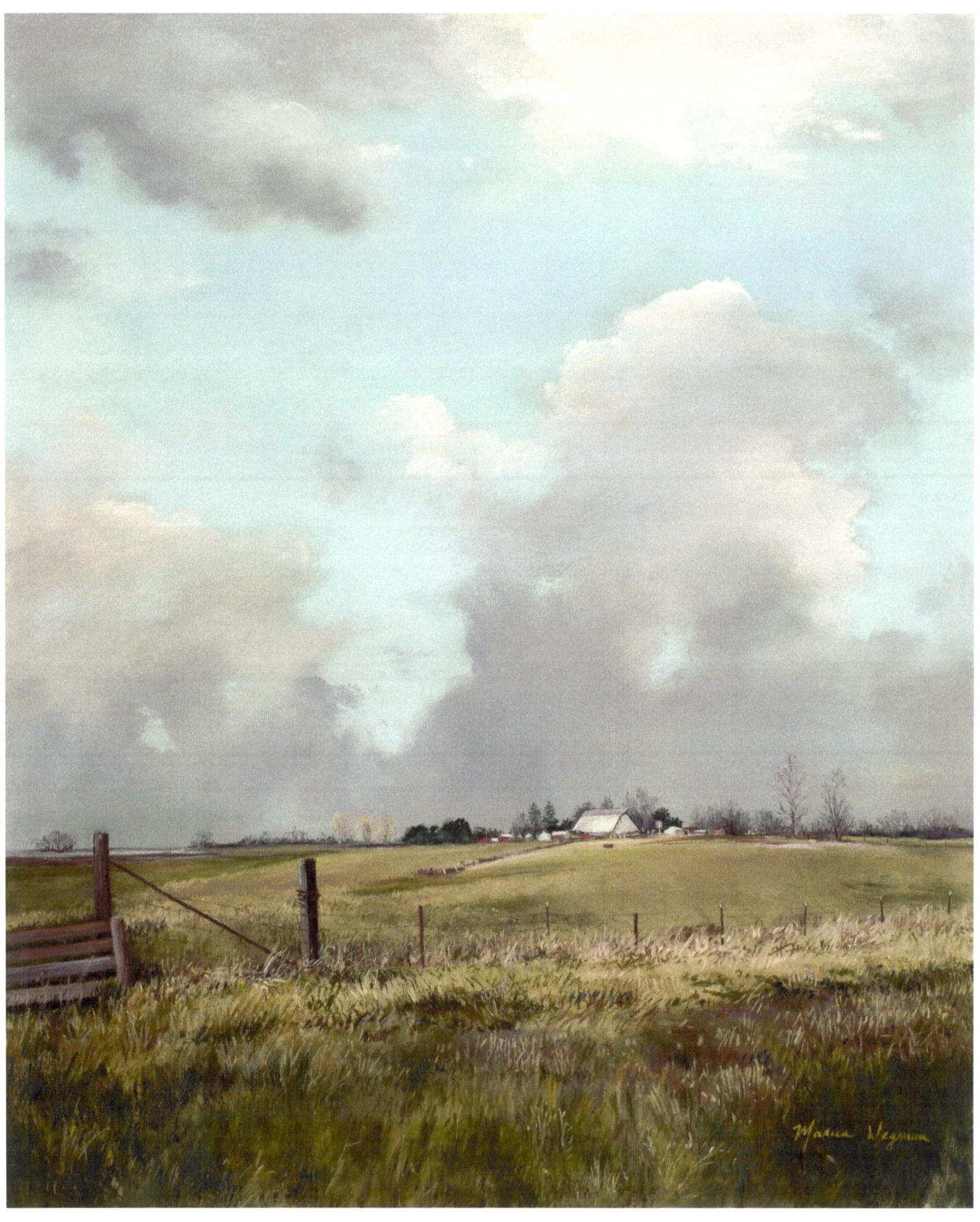

Early Spring 28 x 24 in.

Spring

Early April is perhaps my favorite week of the year, when the fields are a rich, dark brown, the grasses vivid green, and the trees glow with a halo of light, bright pink and green. It is all so promising, and so difficult to capture in pastel.

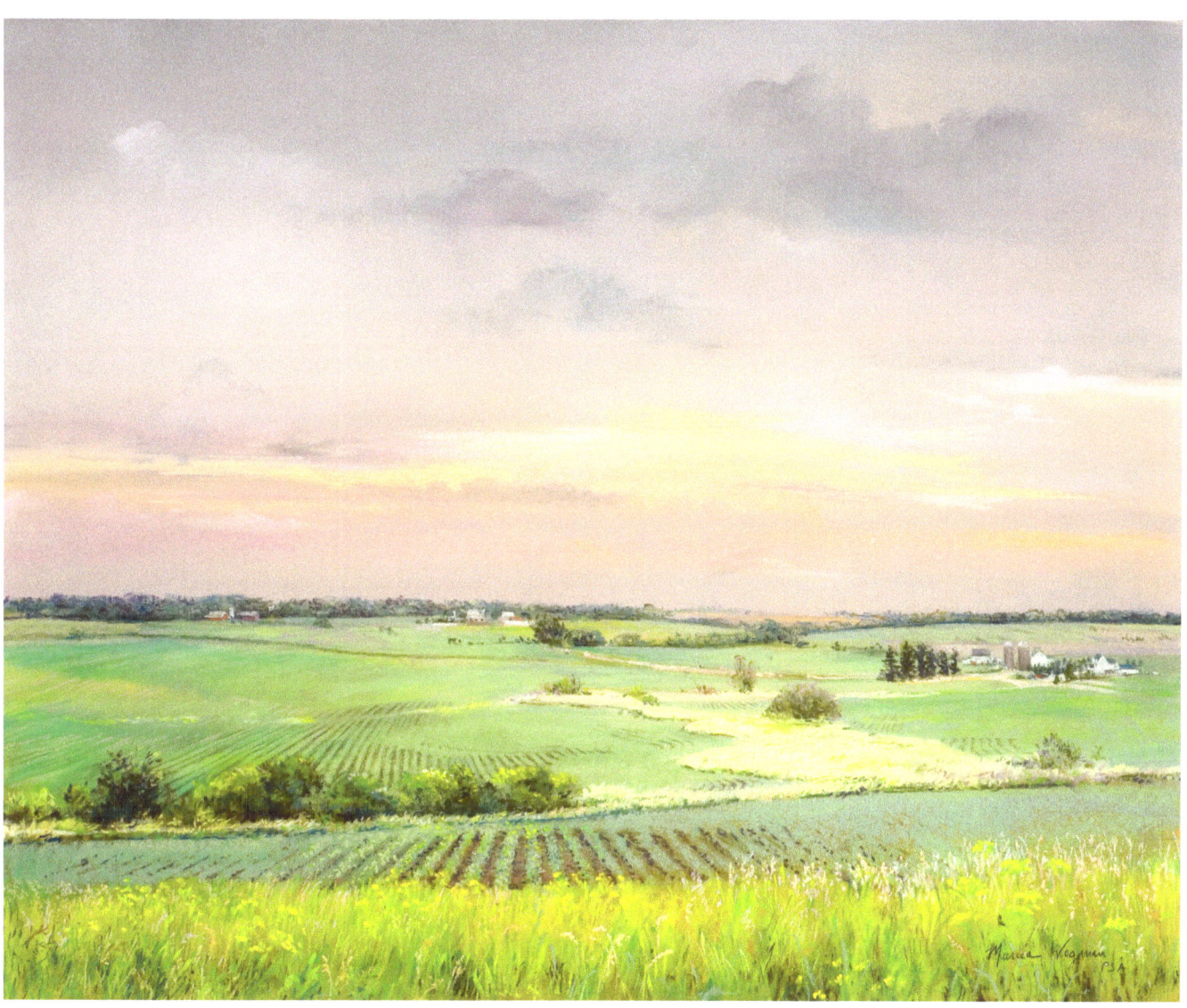

Spring Colors 18 x 24 in.

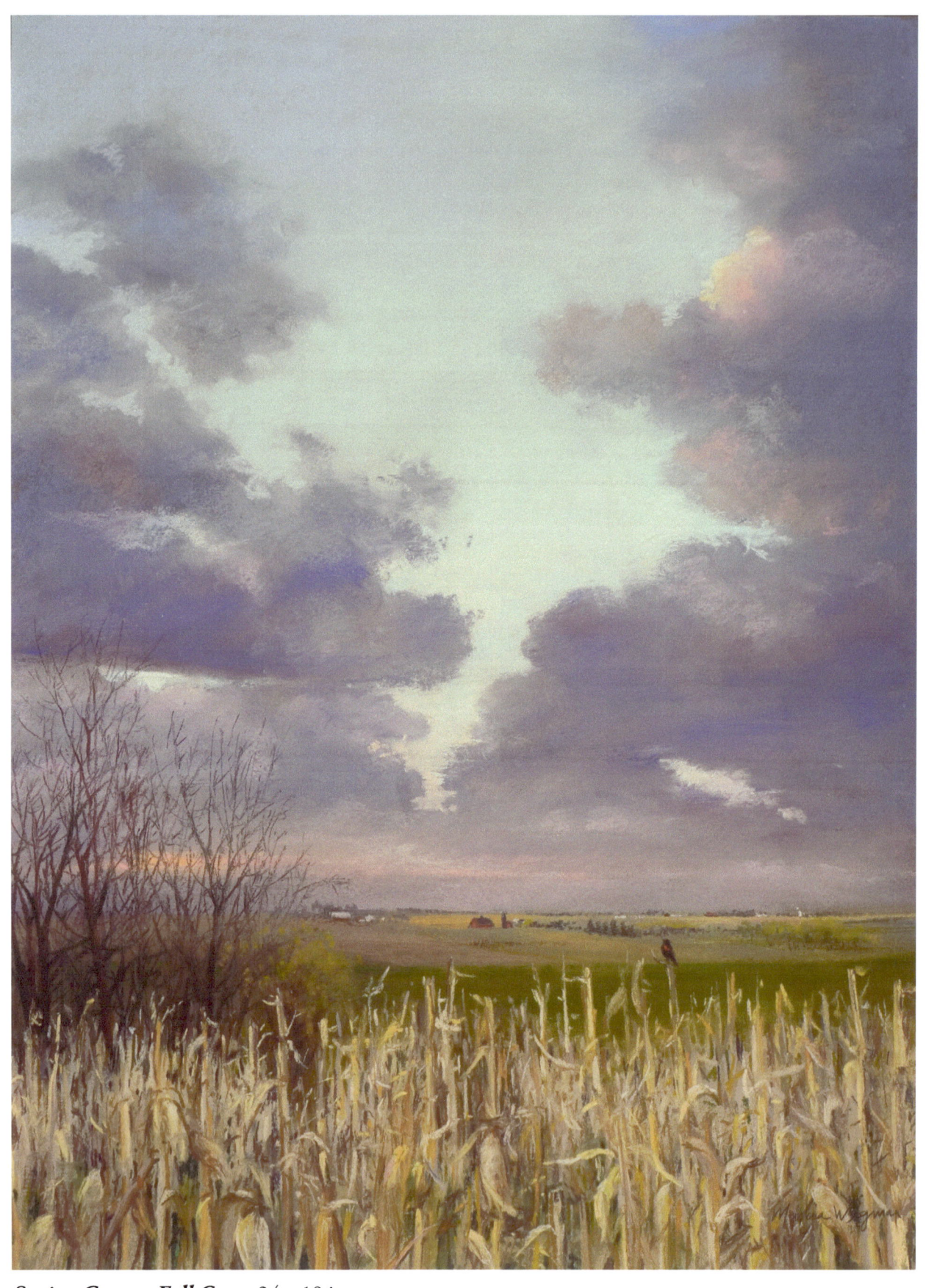

Spring Grass—Fall Corn 24 x 18 in.

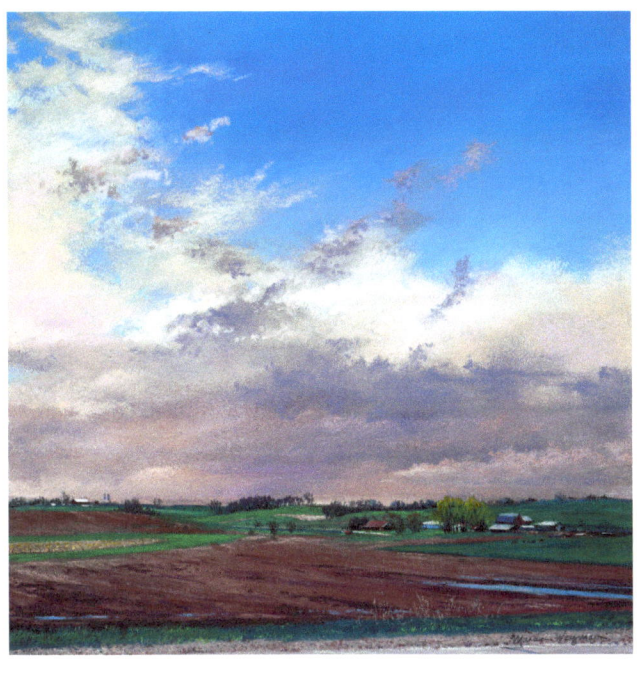
Spring Fields 18 x 18 in.

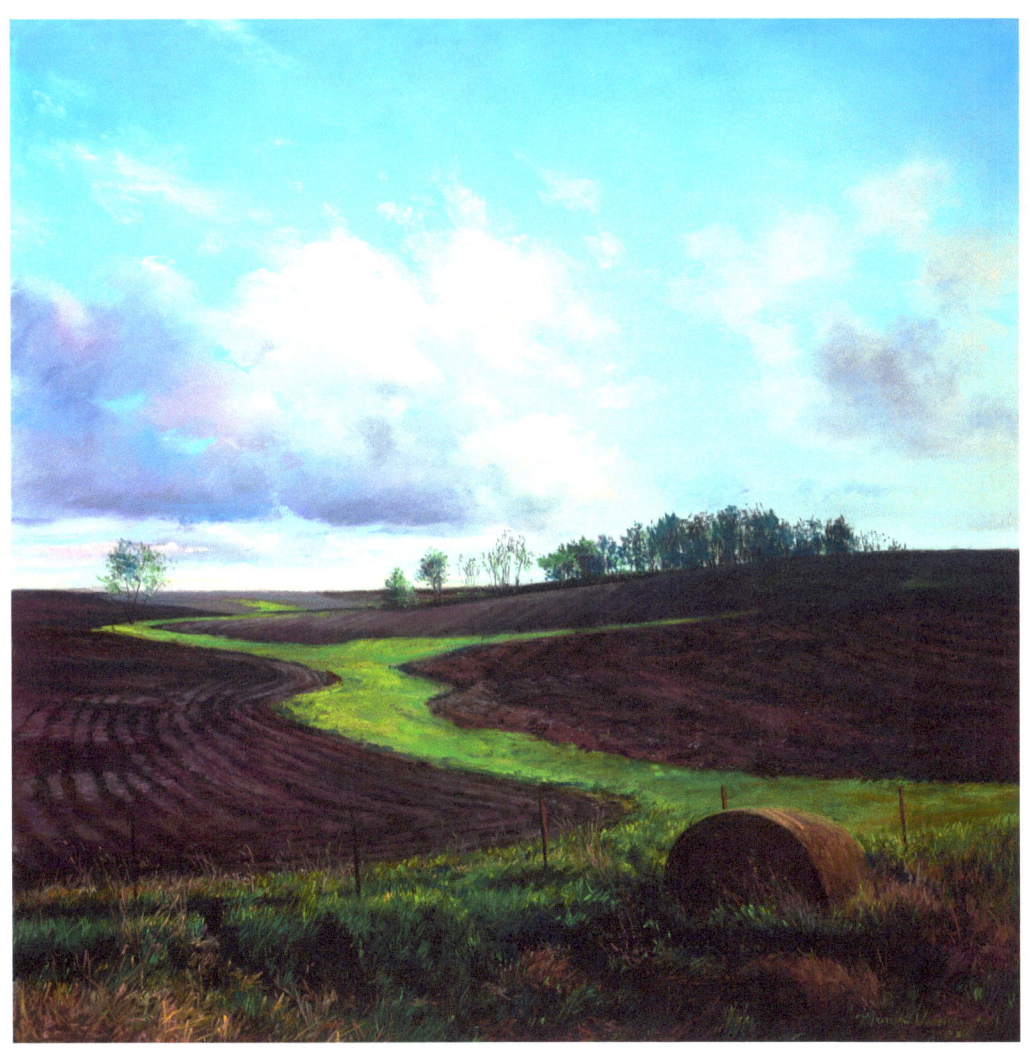
Spring Promise 27 x 27 in.

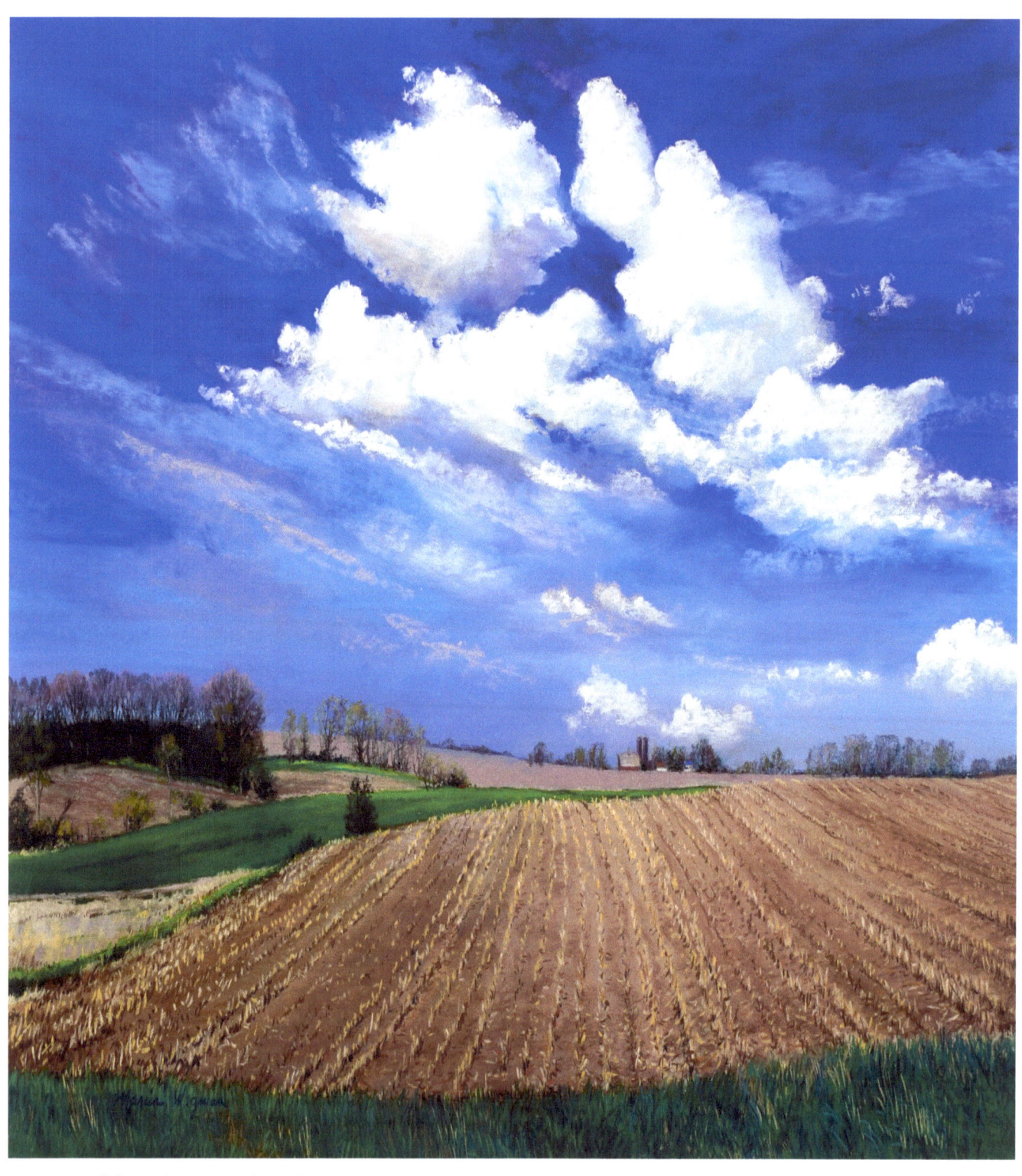

Farm Fields in Spring 24 x 36 in.

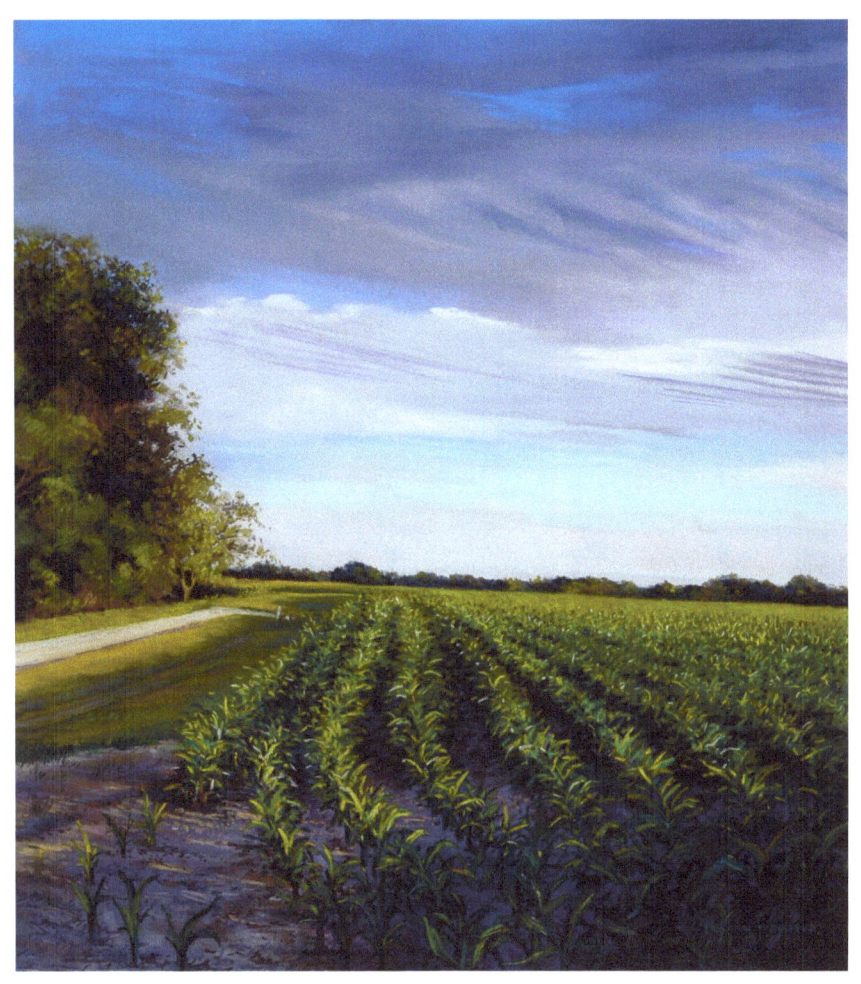

Young Corn 24 x 22 in.

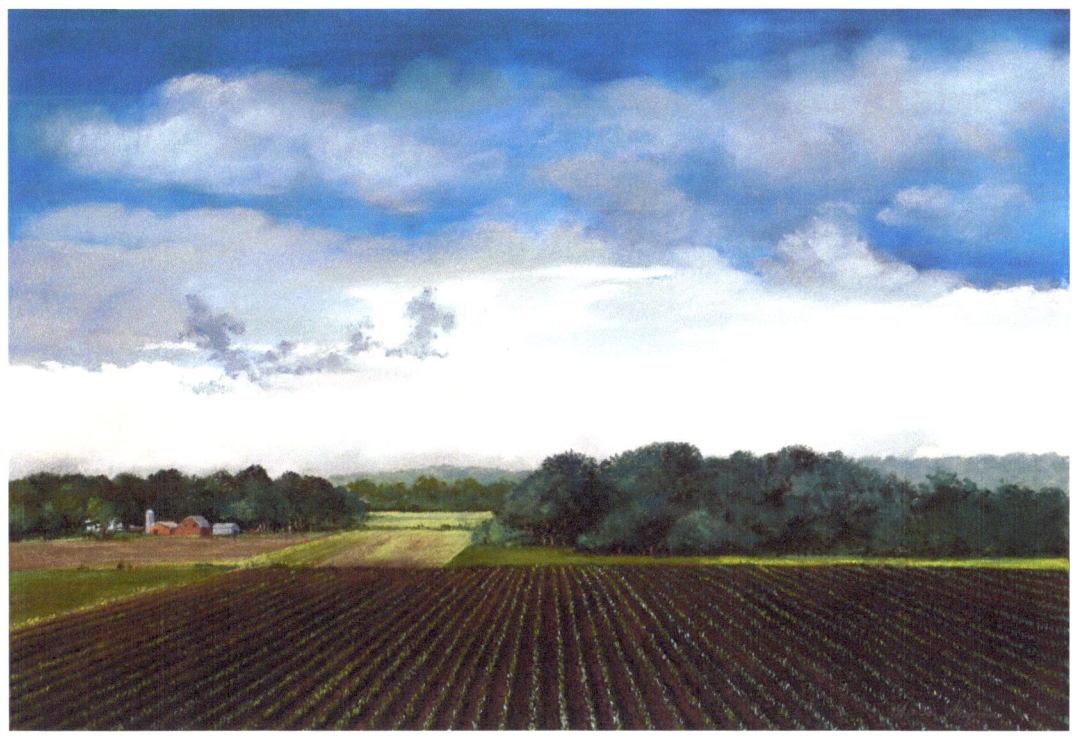

New Crop 21 x 31 in.

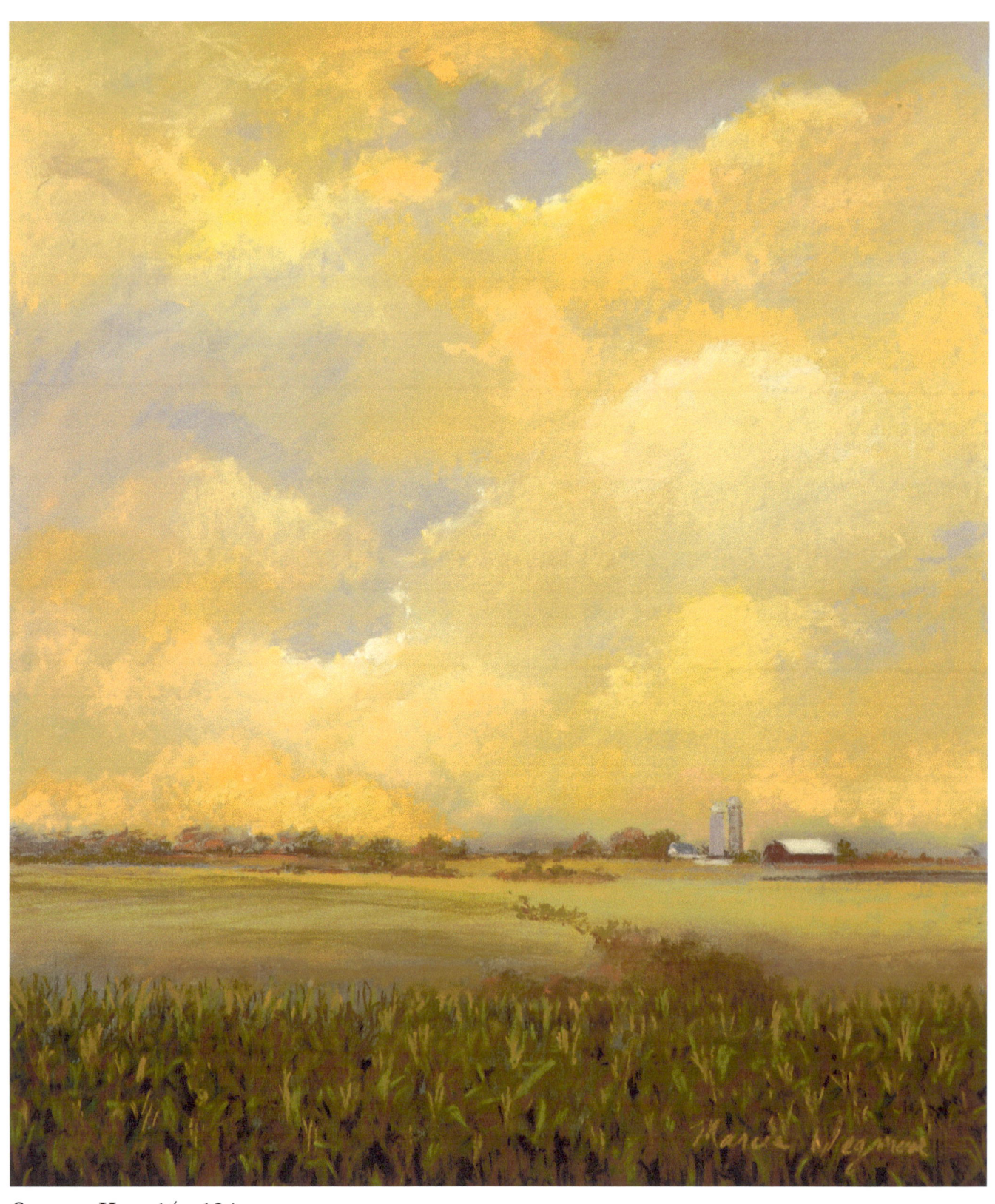

Summer Haze 14 x 12 in.

Summer

The challenge in painting the summer in Iowa is that it is so, so green. I must look for the varieties of green in the foliage of crops, grasses, wildflowers, trees, and shrubs. This time of year I try to go out early morning or early evening to take reference photographs. The sun is low then, which changes the light on the forms and creates a variety of color and shadows.

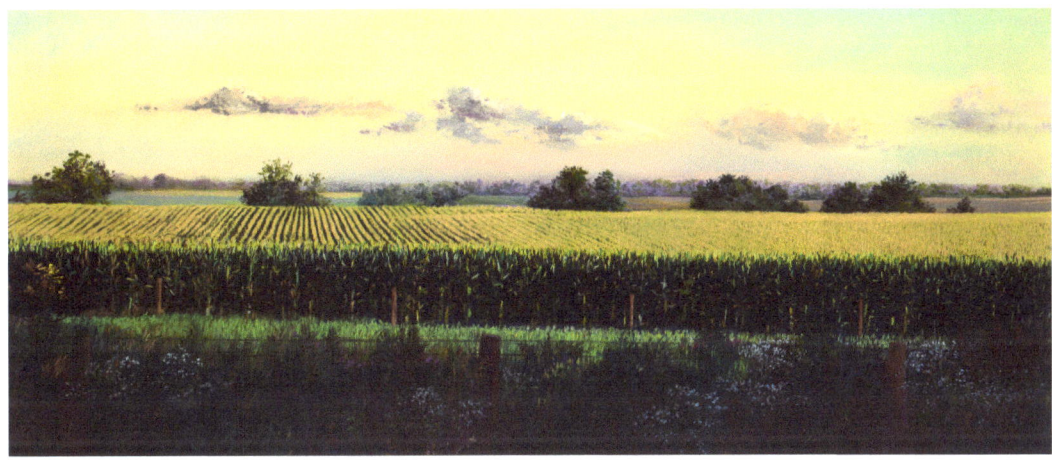

Late Summer Corn 10 x 24 in.

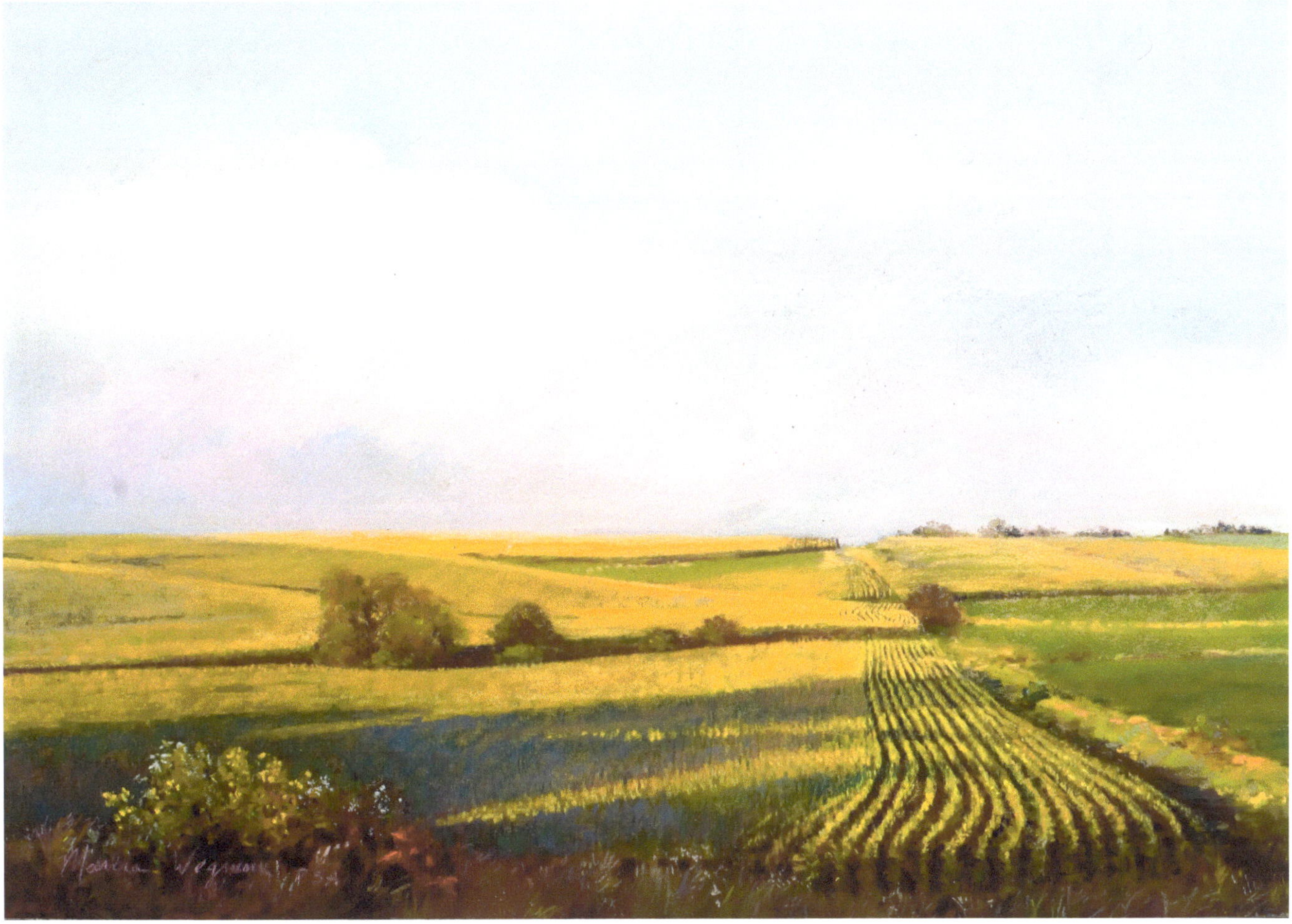

Late Day Sun 13 x 20 in.

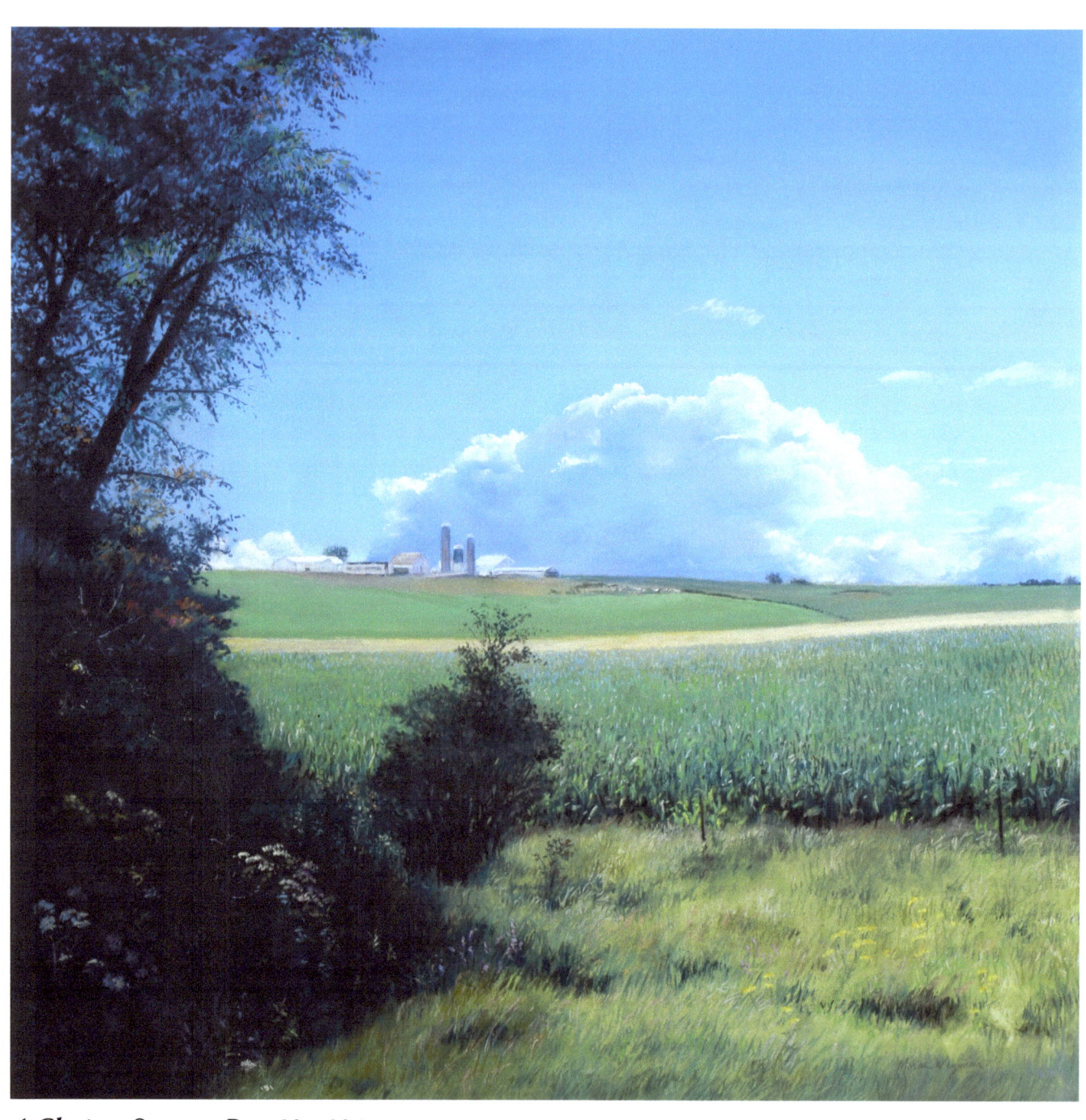

A Glorious Summer Day 30 x 30 in.

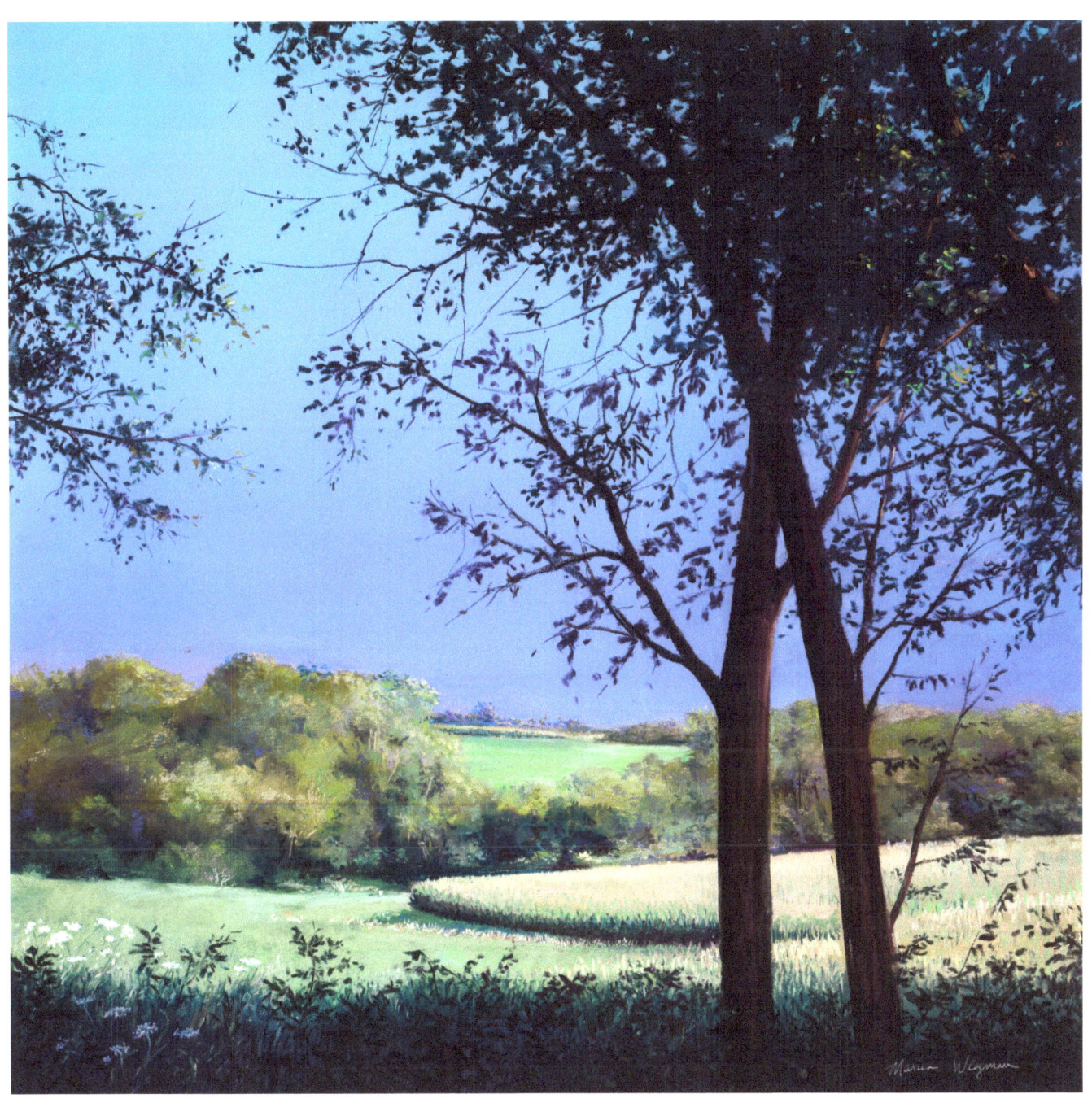

Approaching Summer Storm 21 x 21 in.

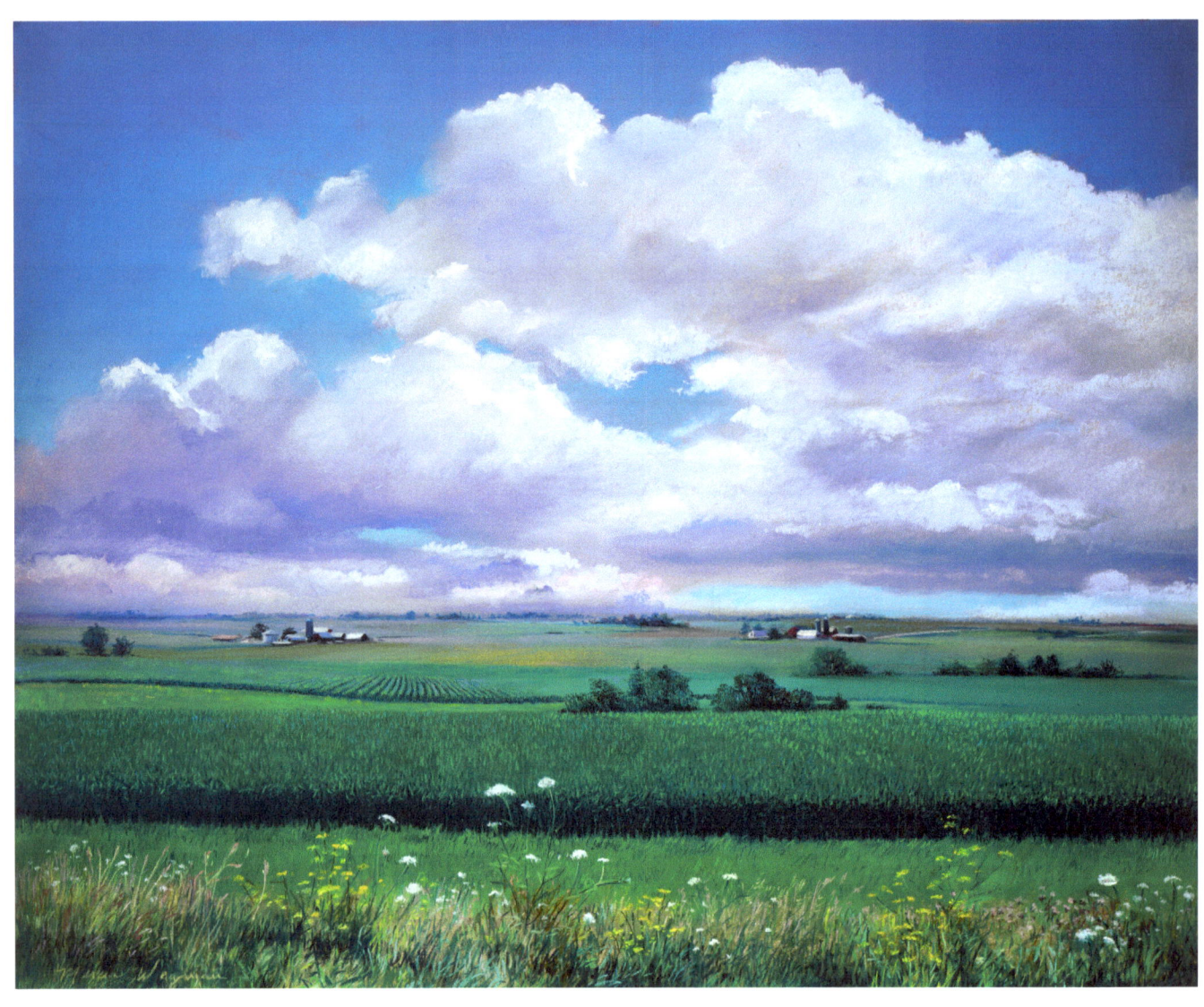

Iowa Summer 21 x 27 in.

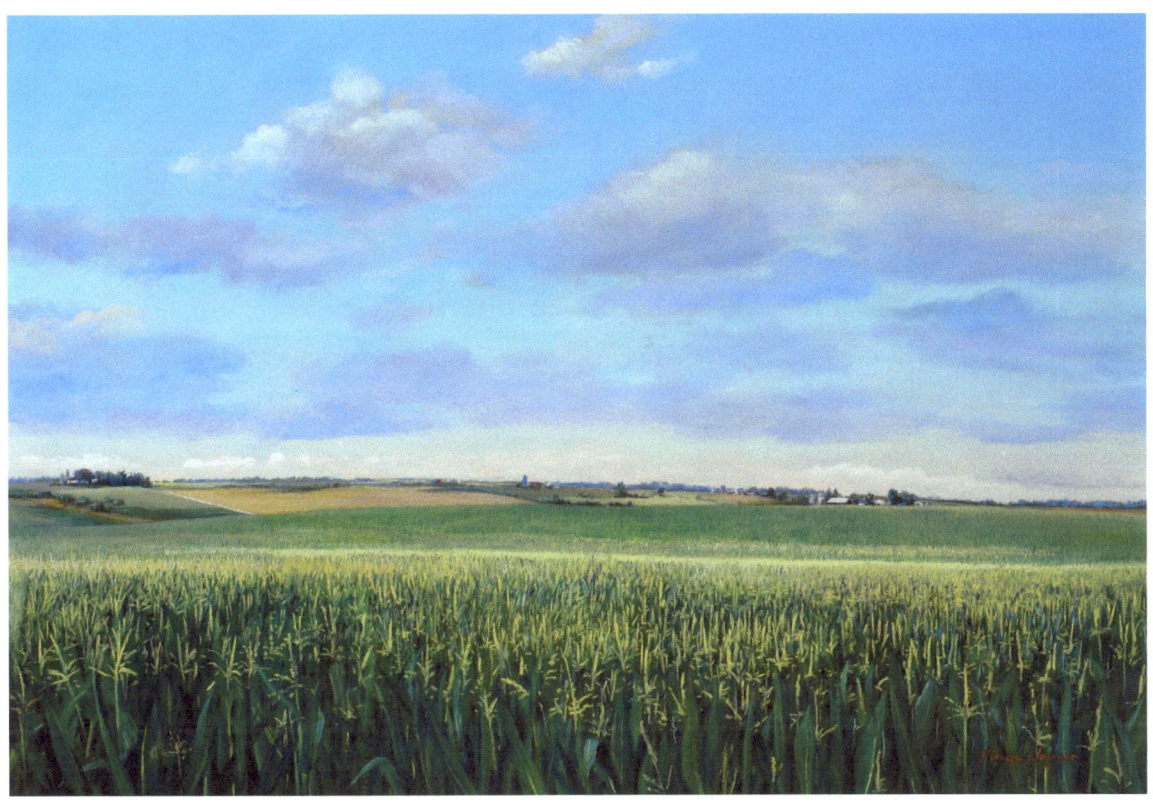

Iowa Summer Corn 24 x 36 in.

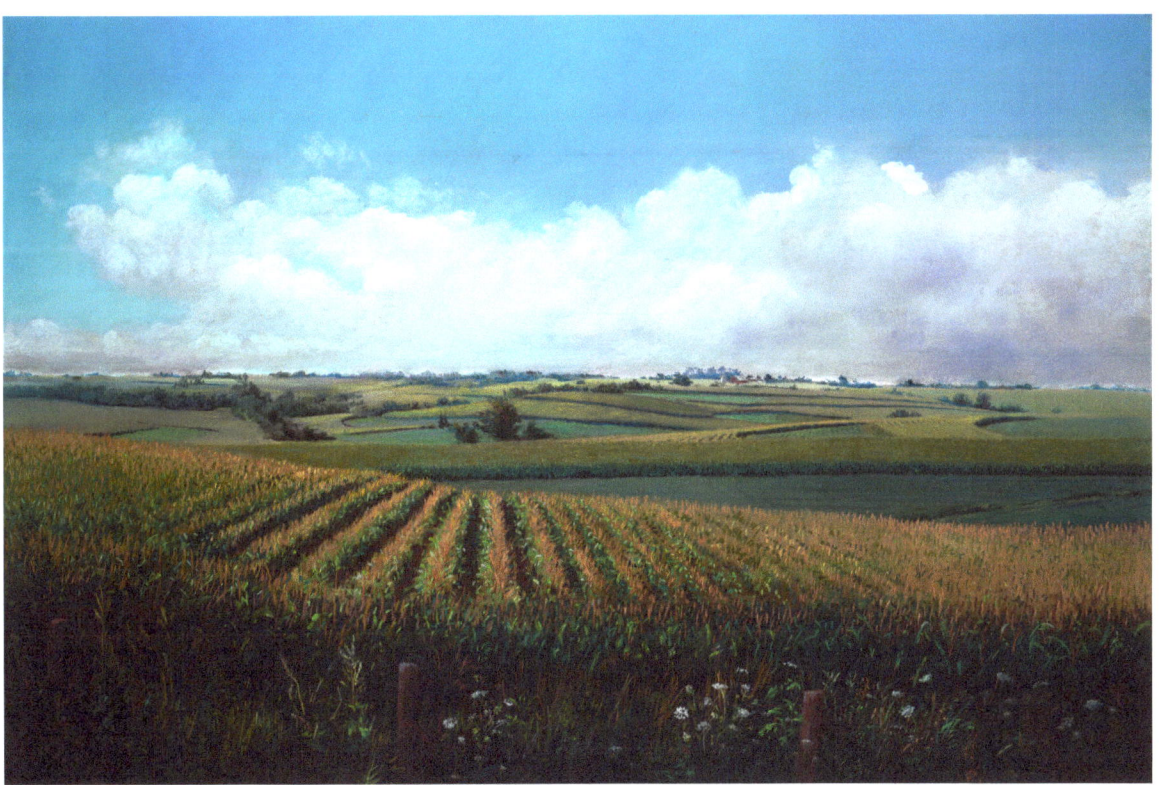

Iowa in August 22 x 34 in.

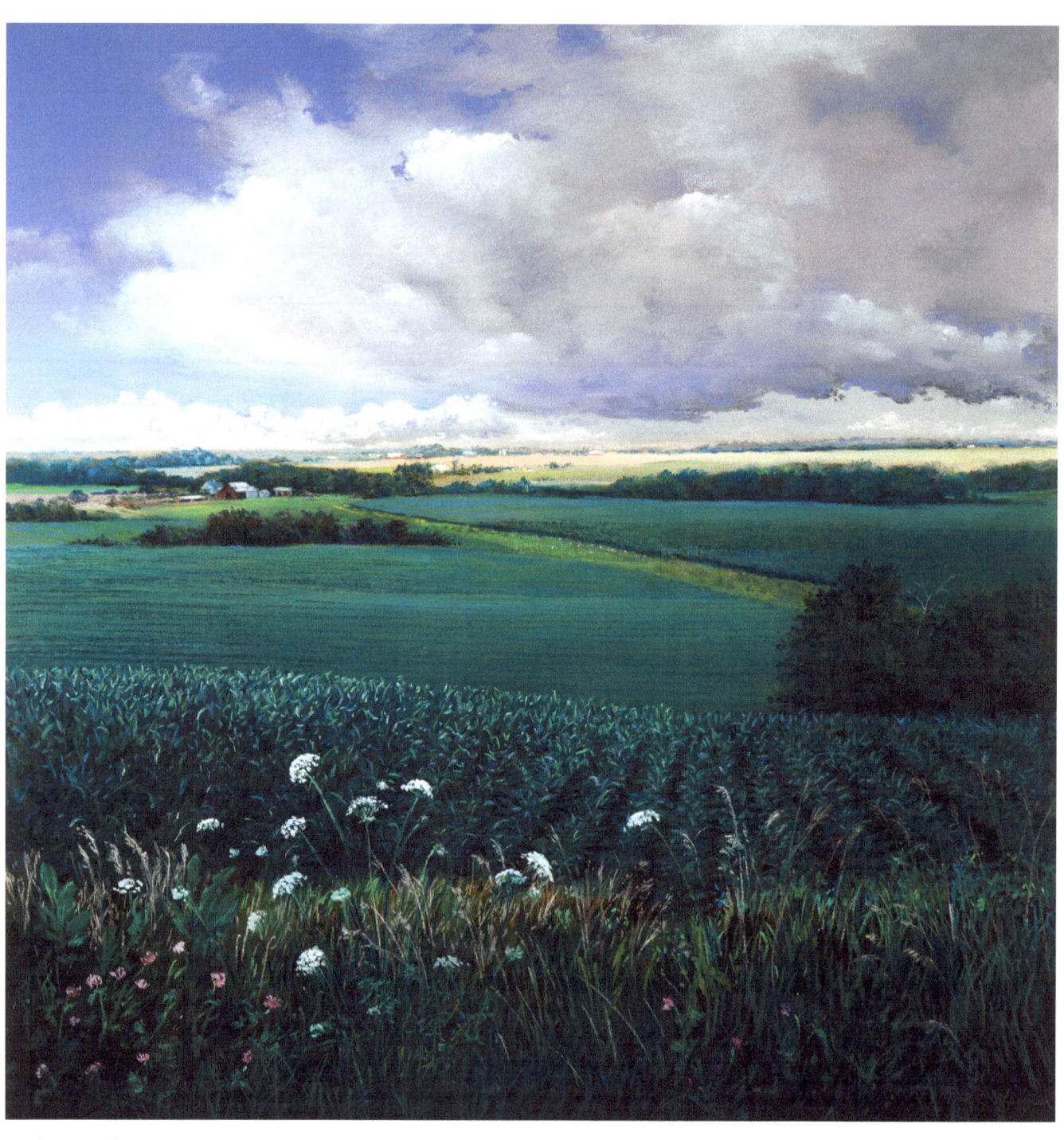

July Weather 24 x 24 in.

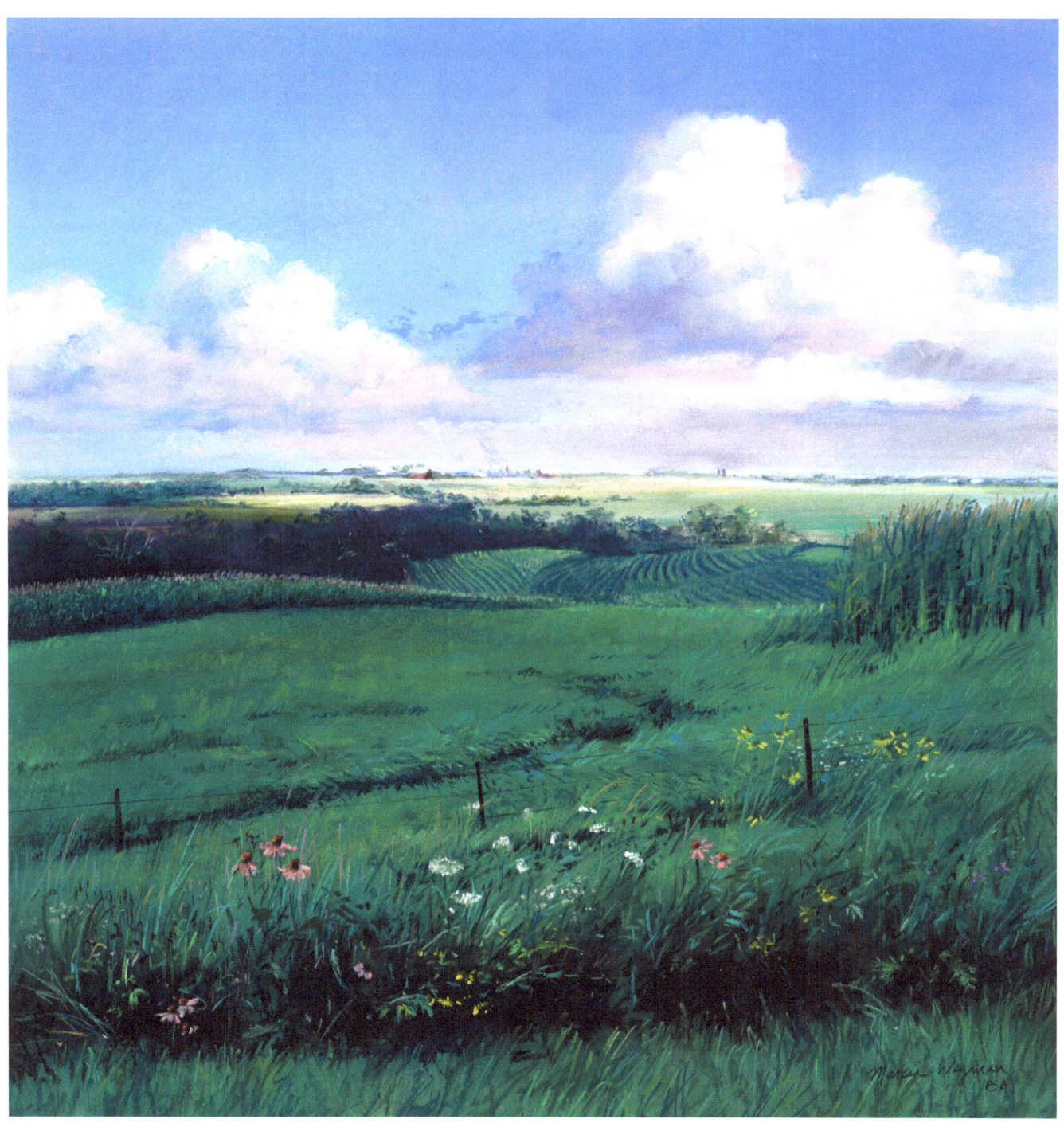

Rich Land, Rich Greens 21 x 21 in.

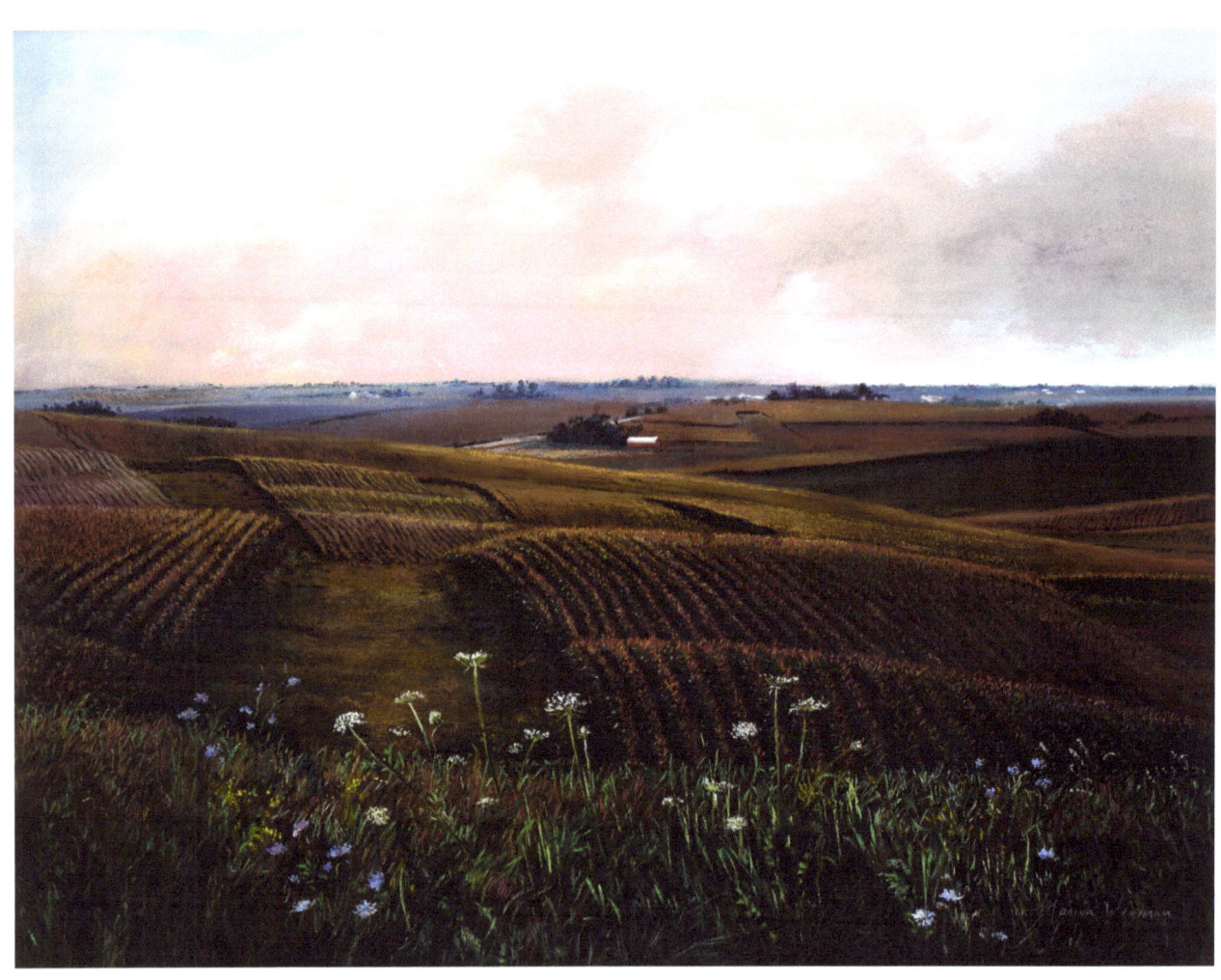

Hills of Corn 18 x 24 in.

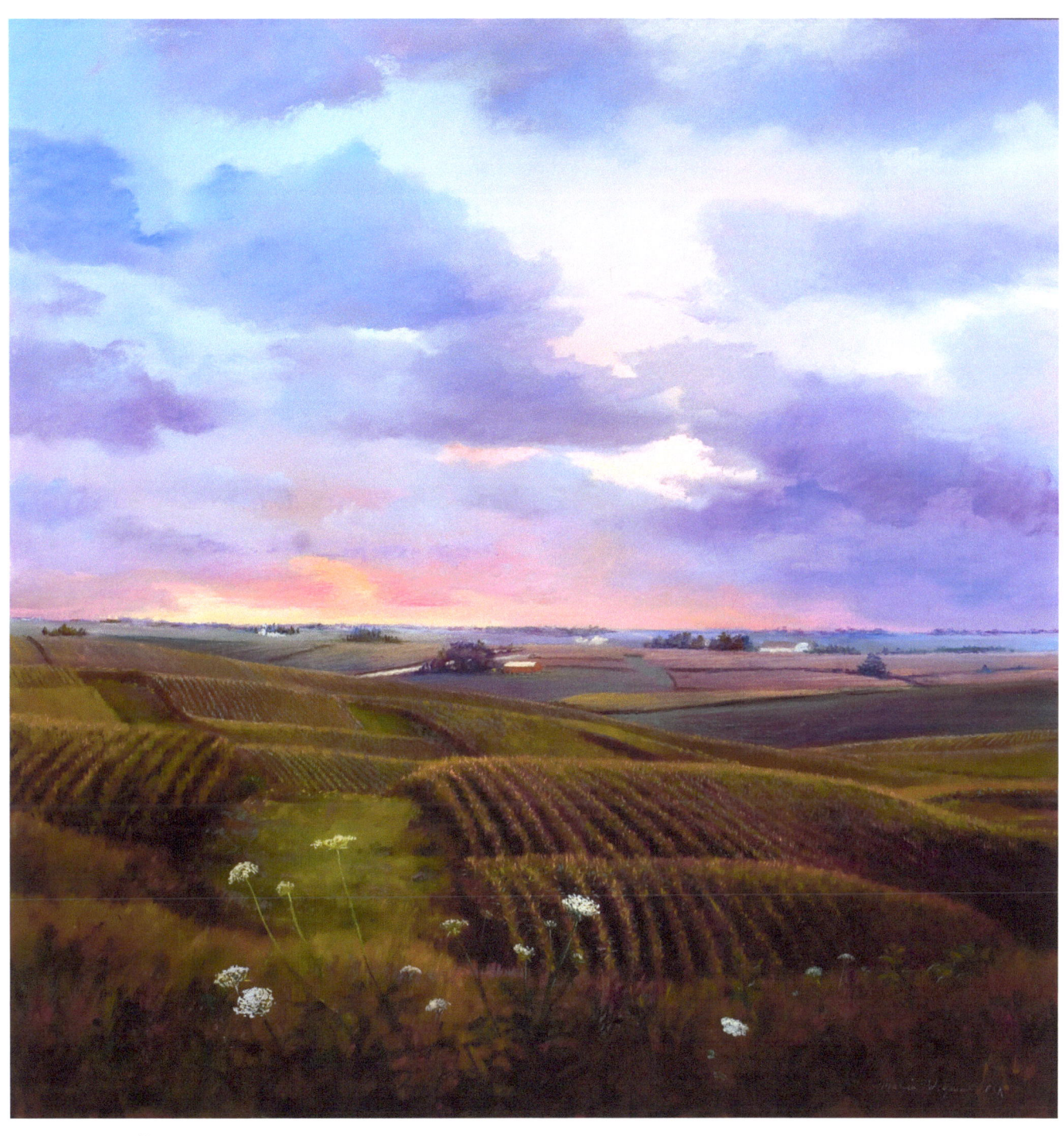

Anamosa Hills 30 x 30 in.

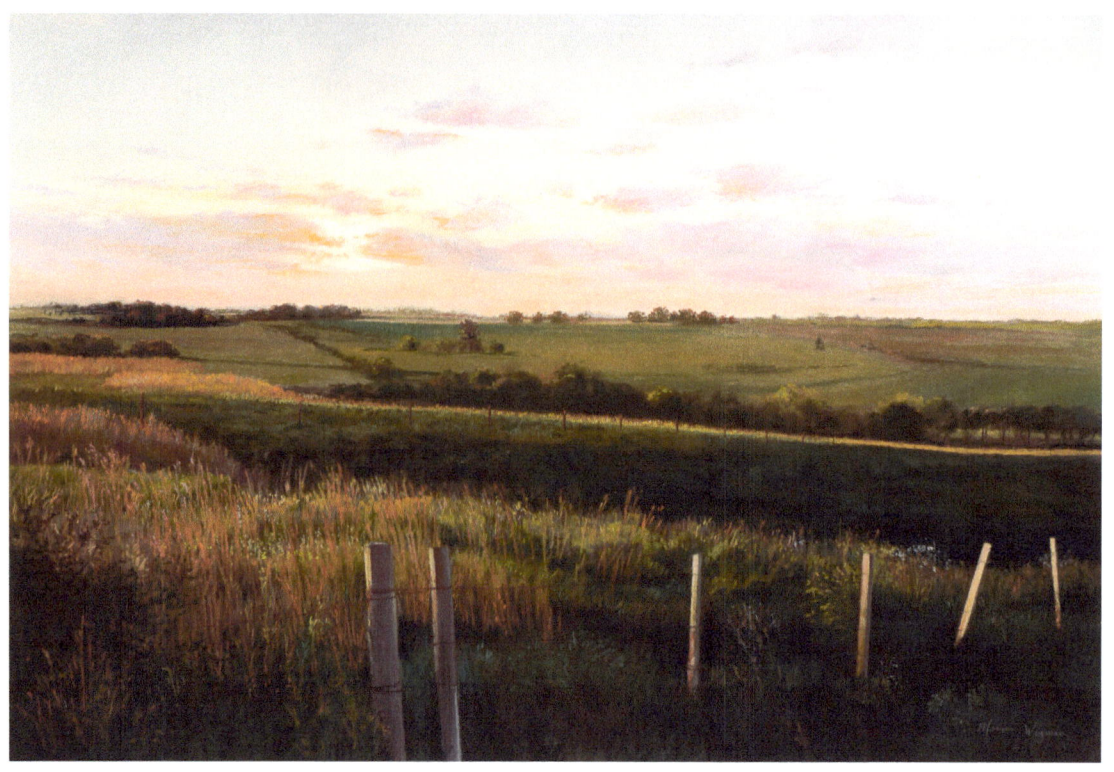

Iowa Sunrise 24 x 36 in.

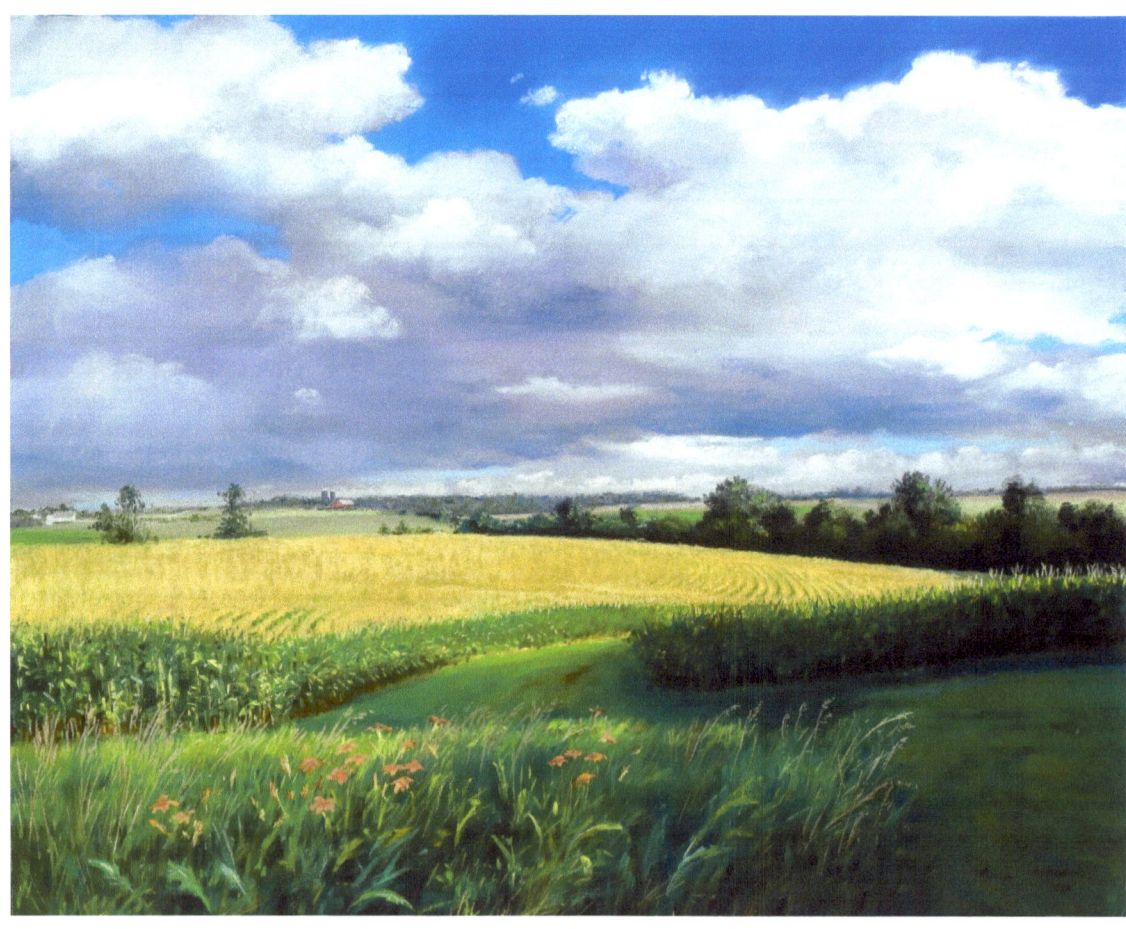

Layered Clouds, Layered Land 21 x 27 in.

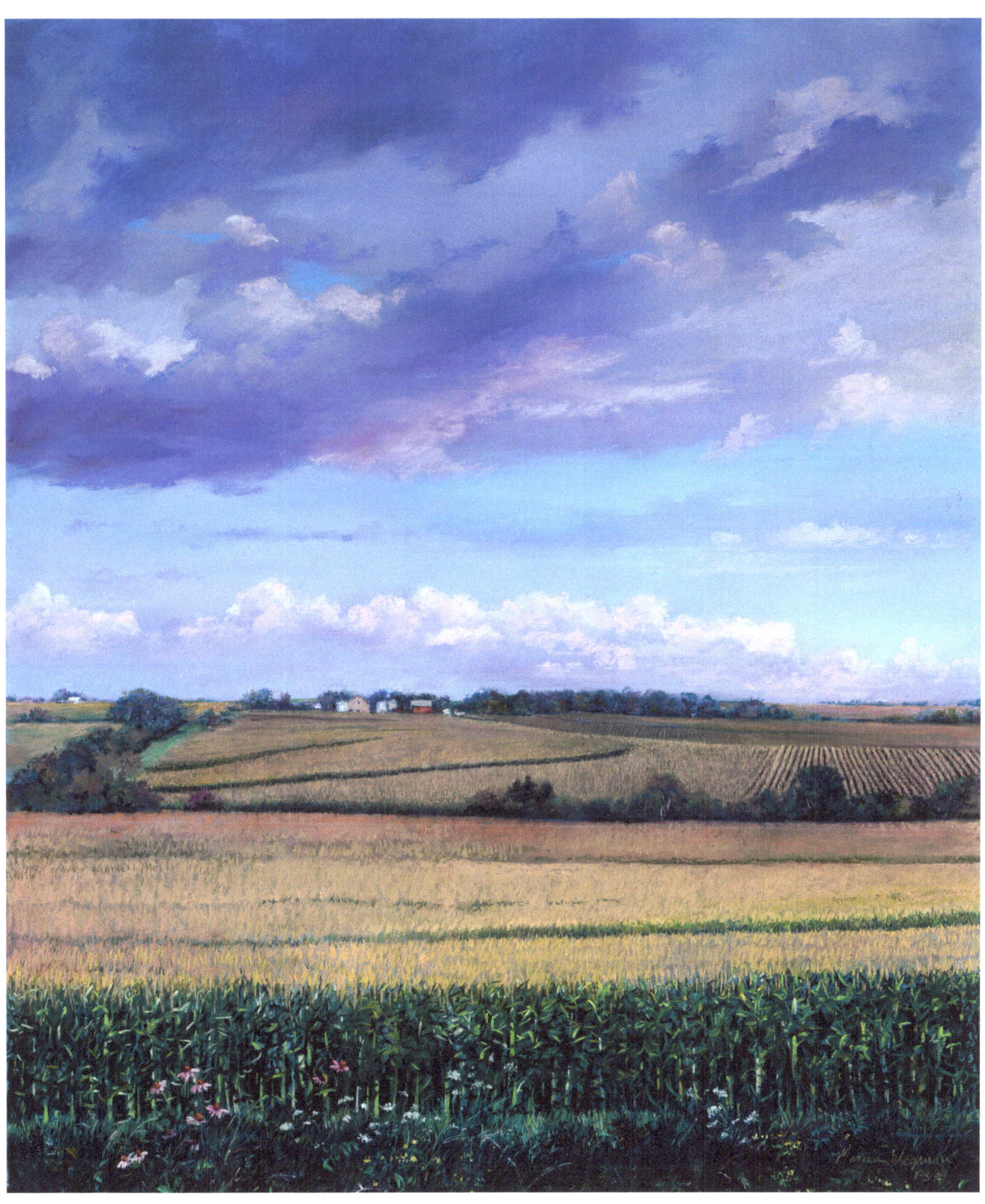

Tasseling Cornfields 28 x 24 in.

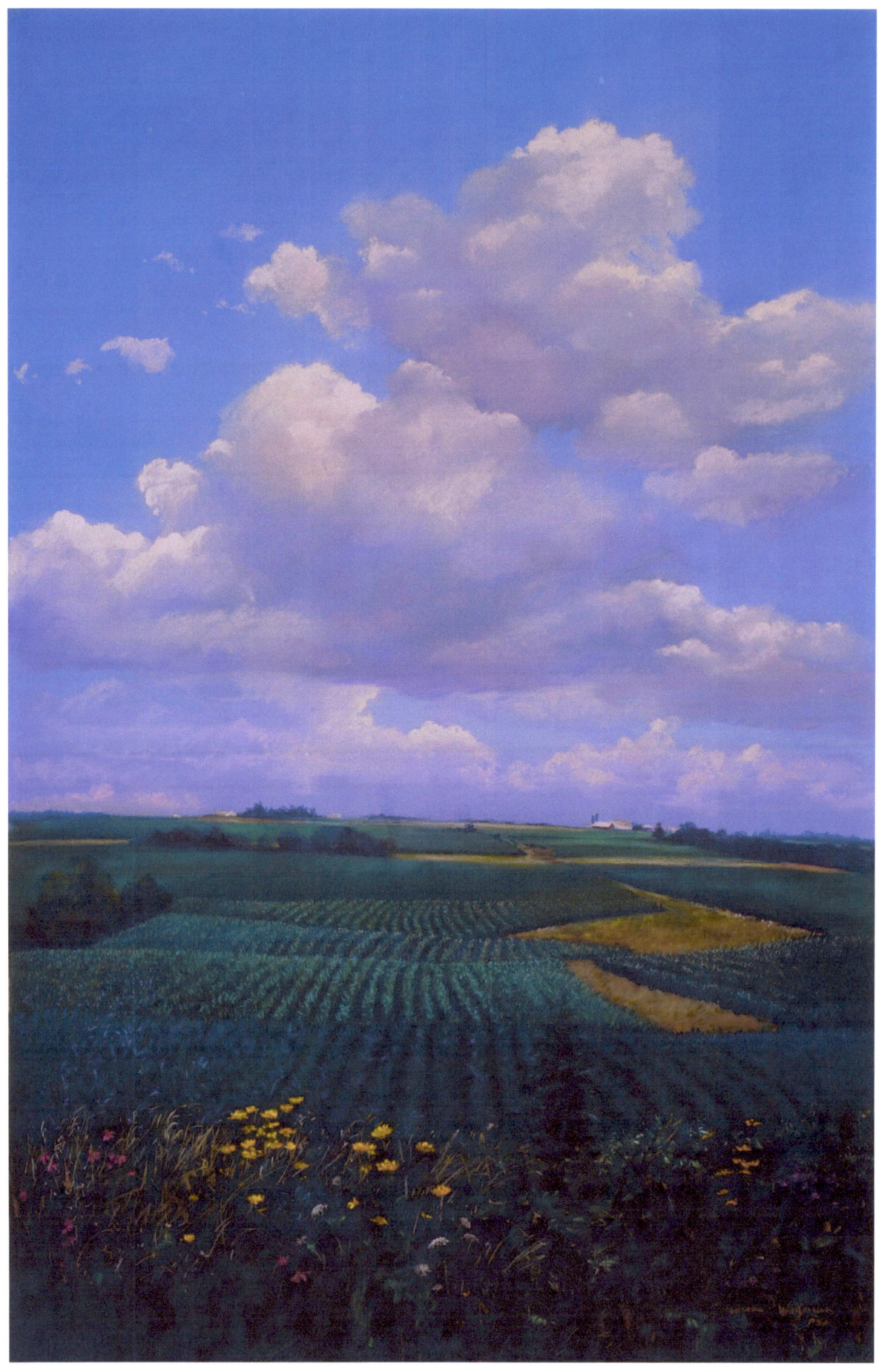

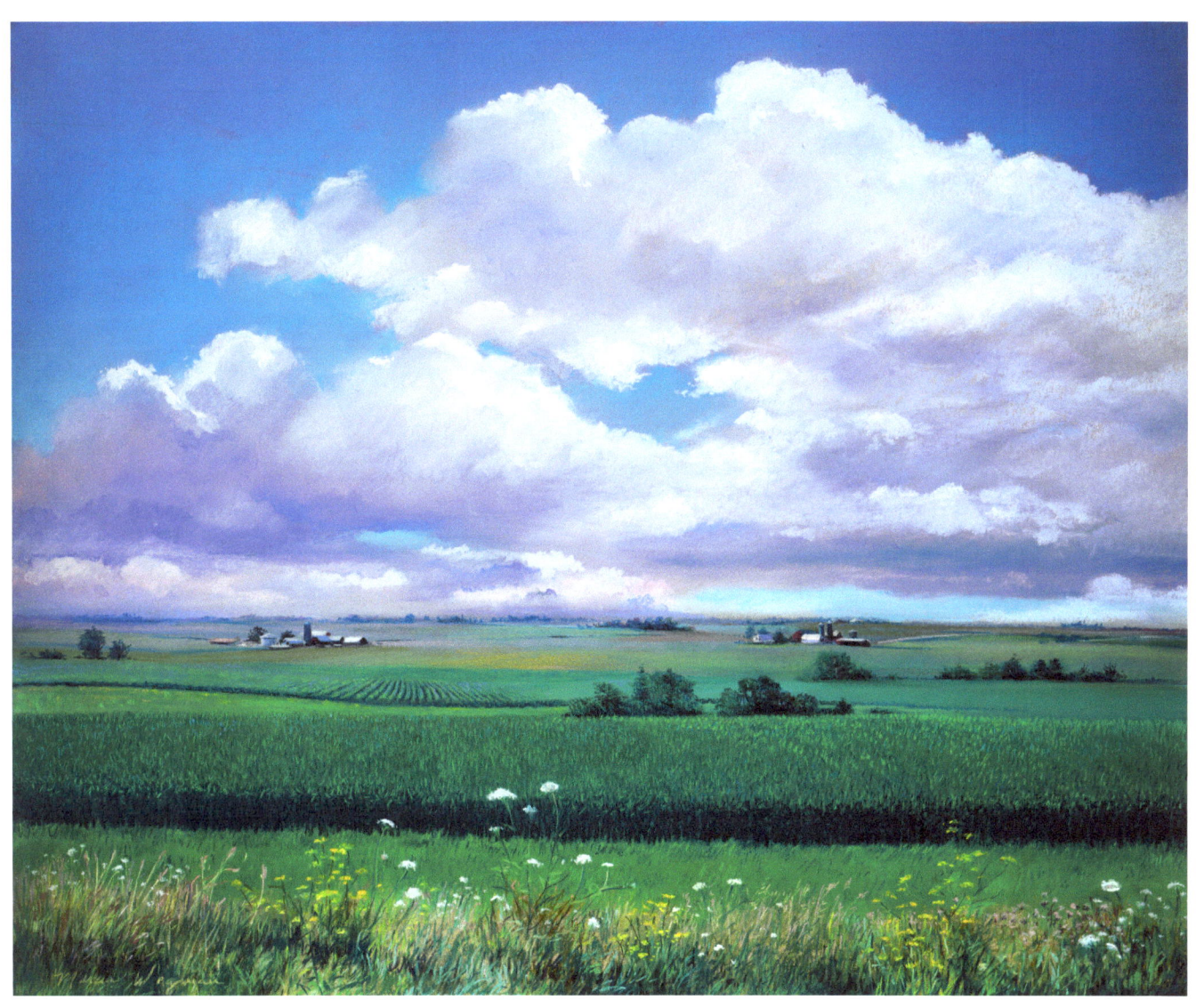

Iowa Summer 21 x 27 in.

Left: *Summer Sky and Fields* 21 x 27 in.

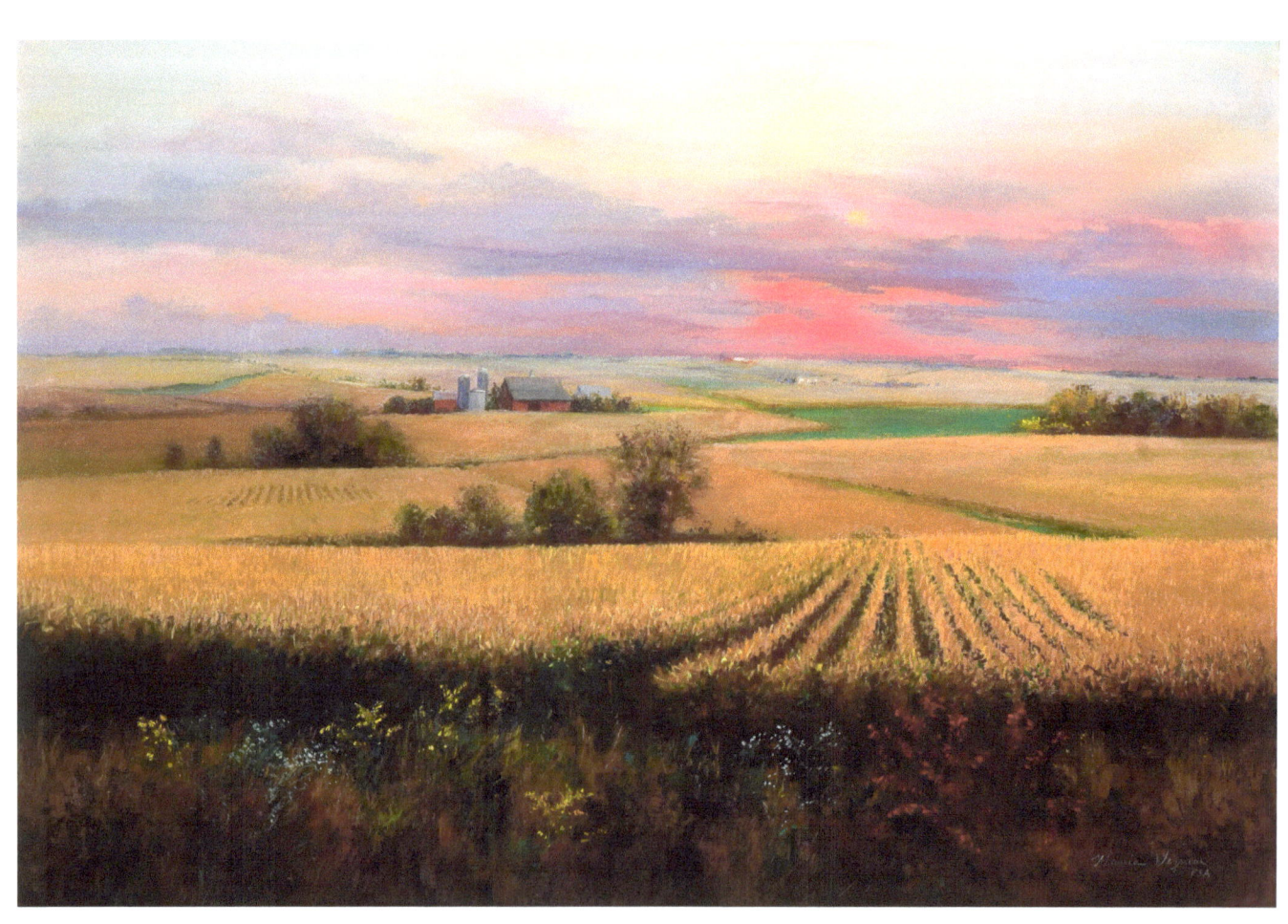

Autumn Light 24 x 36 in.

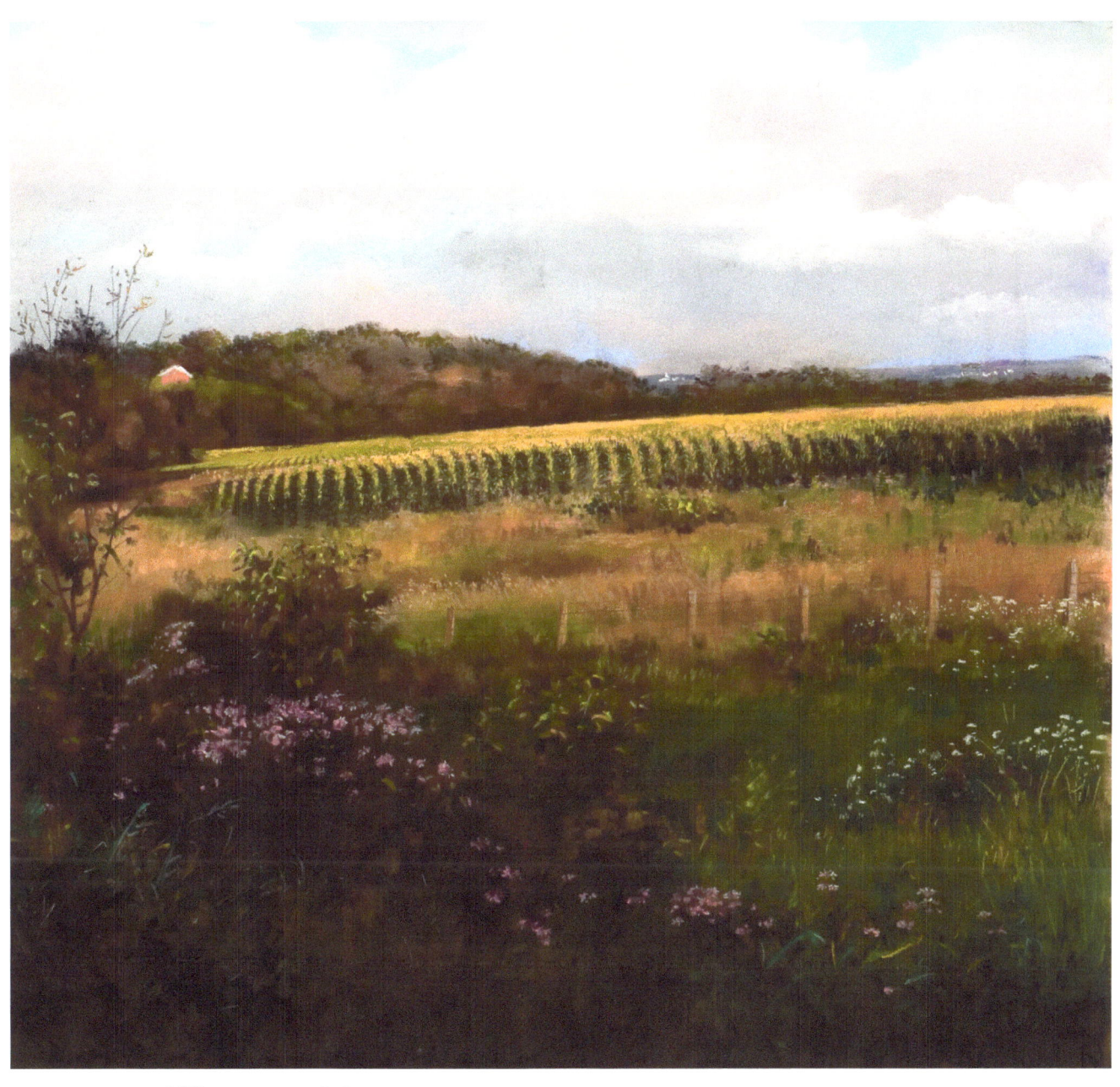

Summer Wildflowers and Corn 19 x 21 in.

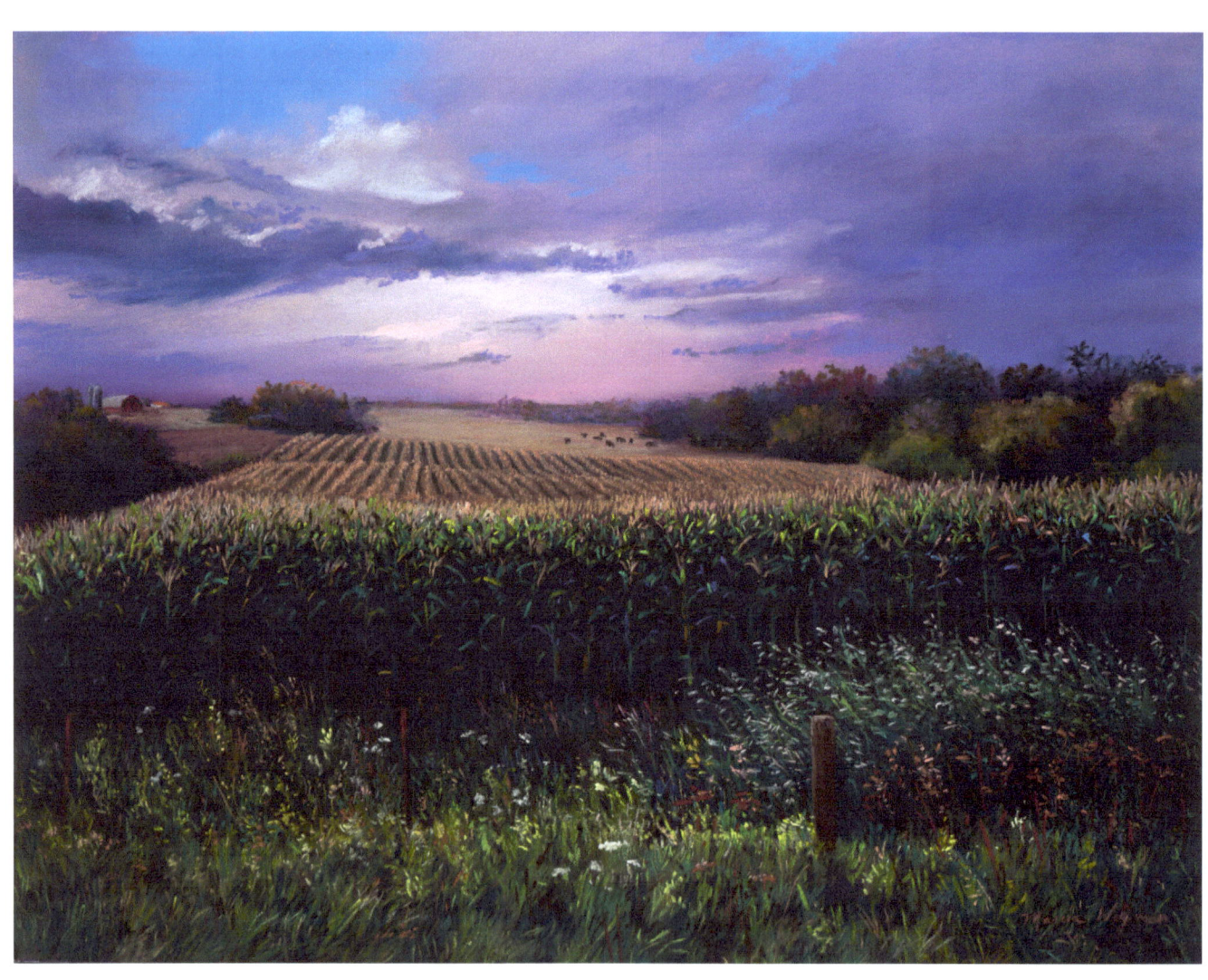
Prairie Corn and Cattle 18 x 24 in.

Fall

September and early October are the most colorful months to paint the Iowa landscape. There is a nice balance of the warm colors of tasseled and drying cornstalks with the still vibrant green grasses and darkening tree colors. The addition of blue skies makes for a dynamic composition. Wildflowers add bright color accents. Changing leaf colors are a challenge because of their great variety, bold and subtle hues. When doing commissioned paintings, this is the season most frequently preferred.

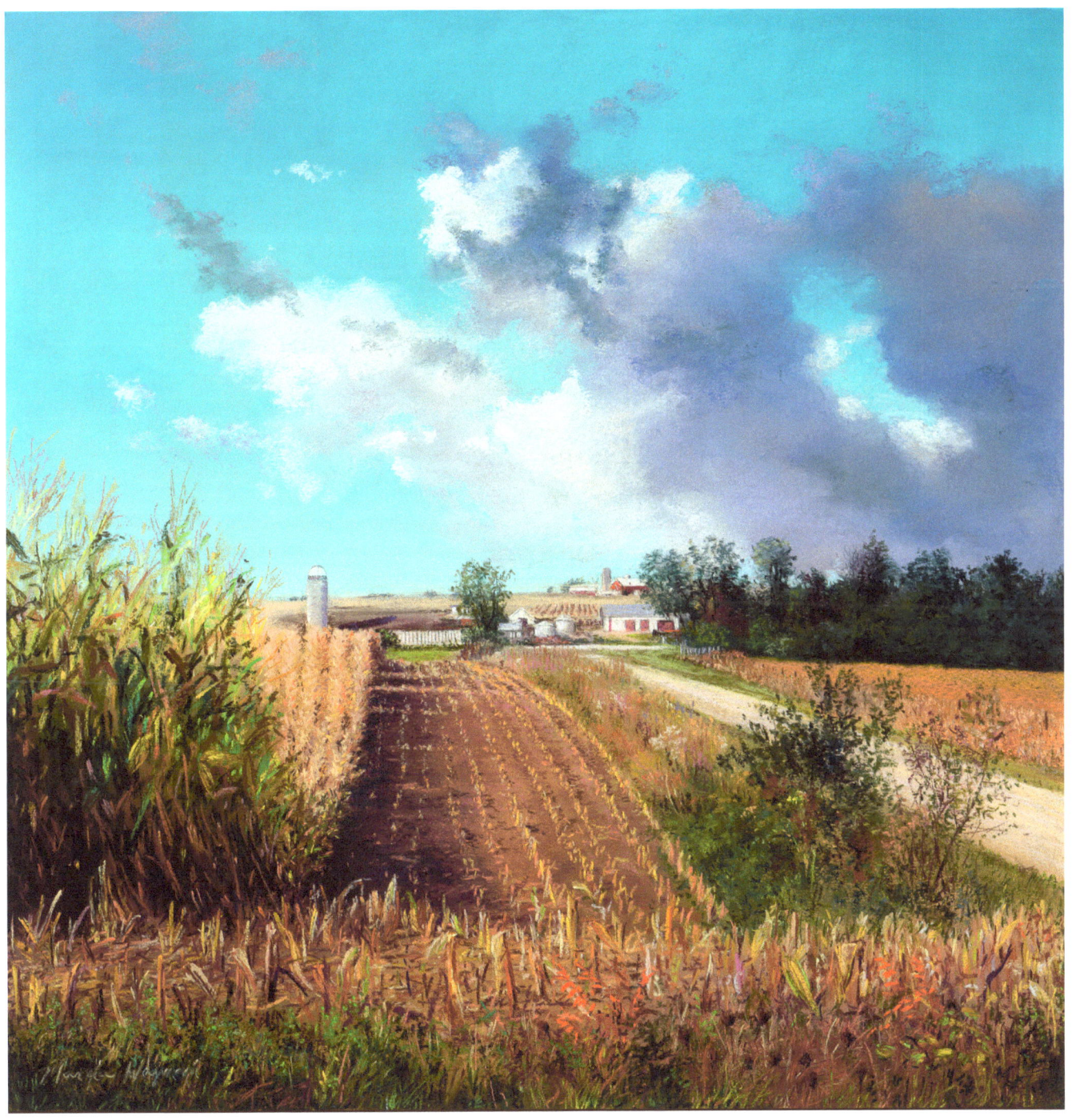

Corn Harvesting Weather 24 x 24 in.

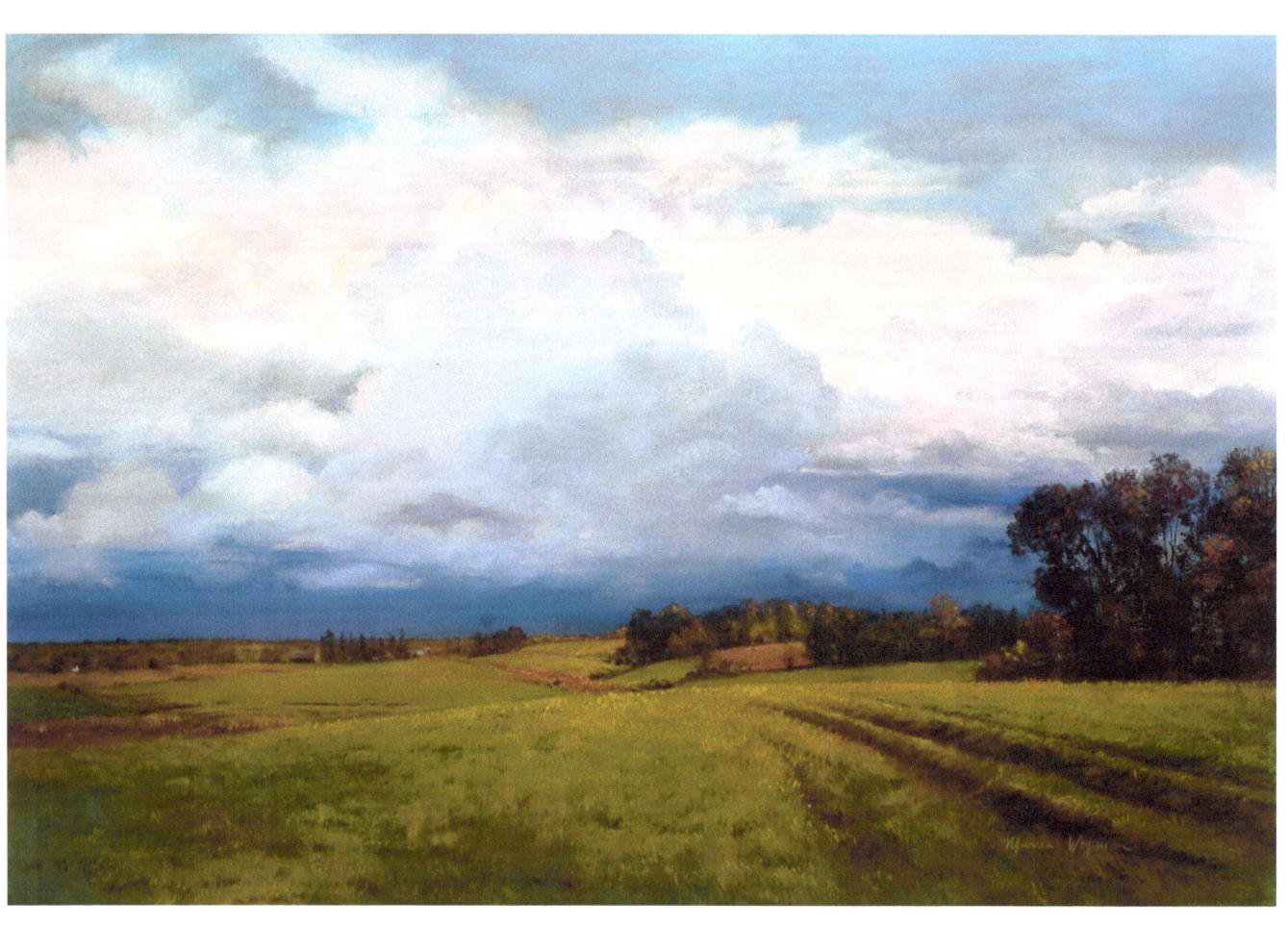

Early Fall Weather 24 x 36 in.

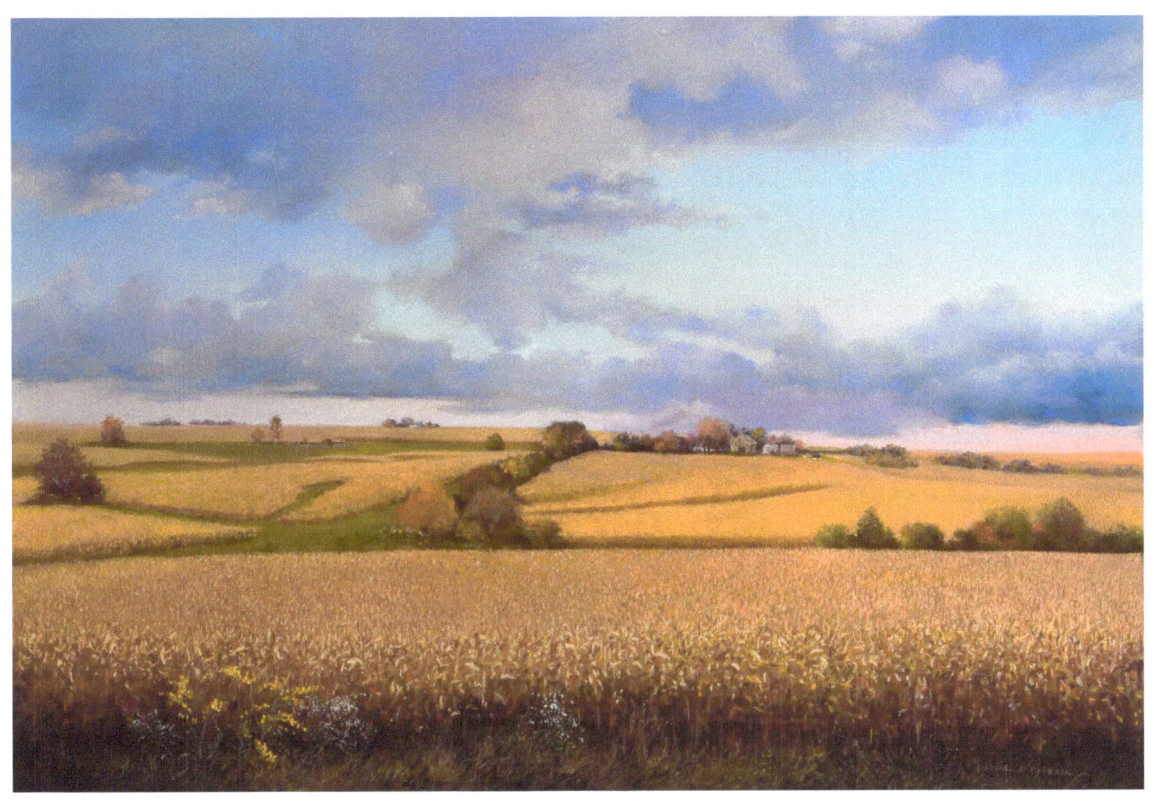

Fall Land and Sky in Iowa 24 x 36 in.

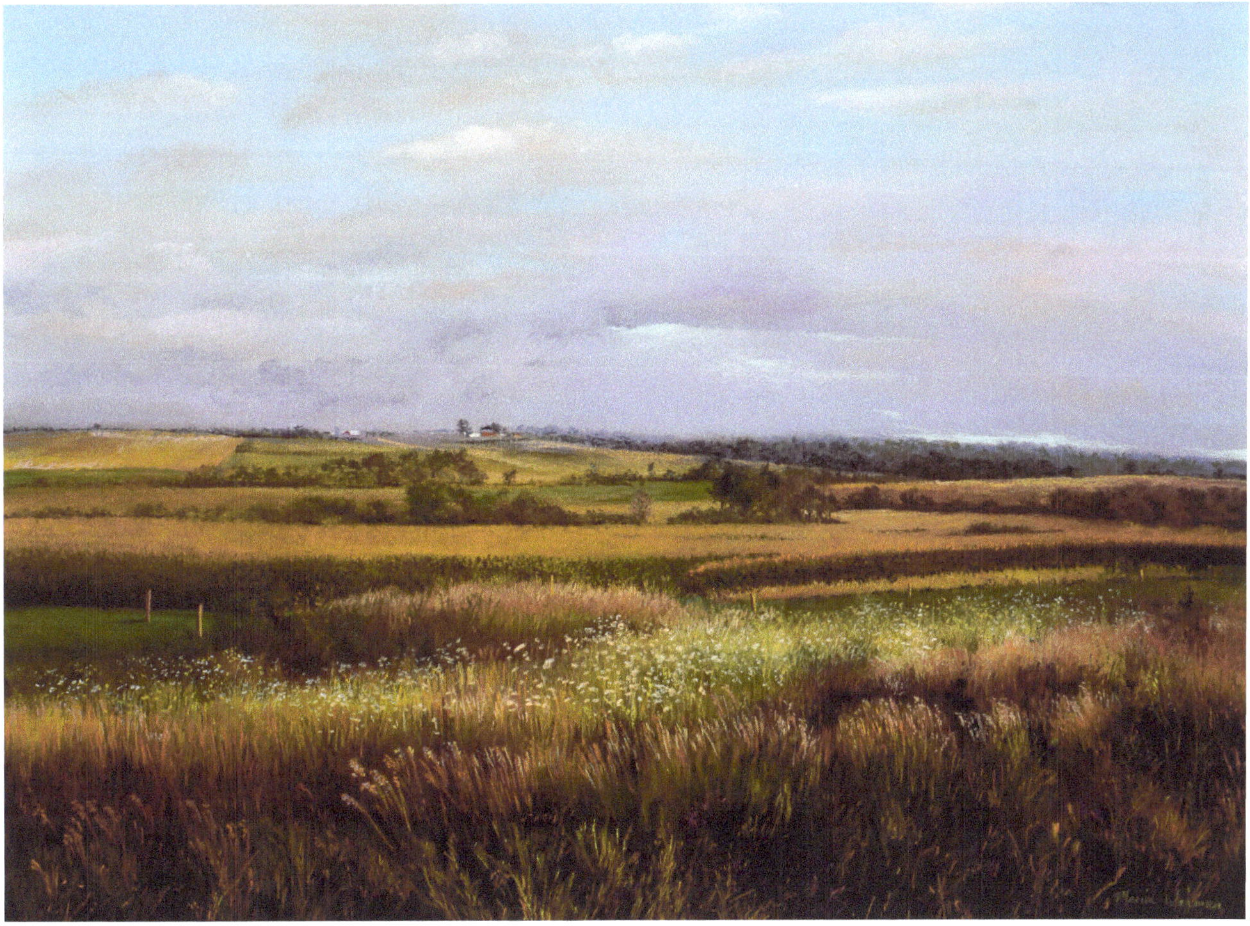

Fall Poetry 24 x 36 in.

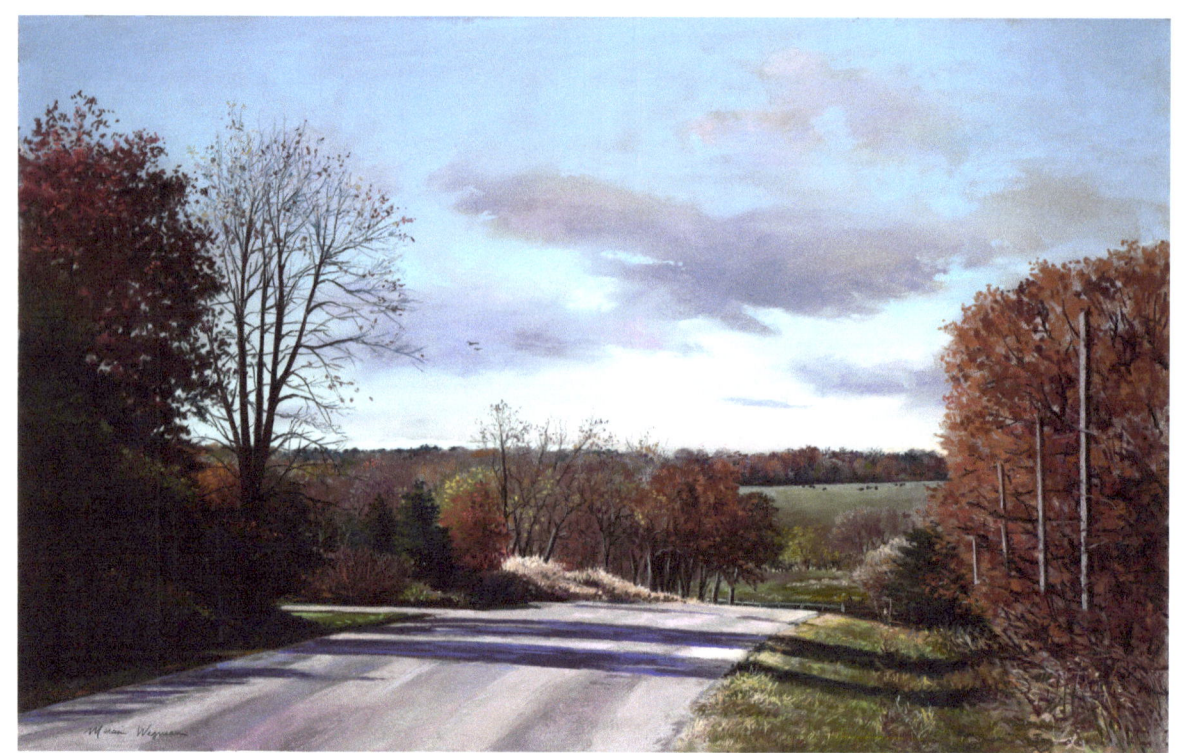

Hill Road 17 x 28 in.

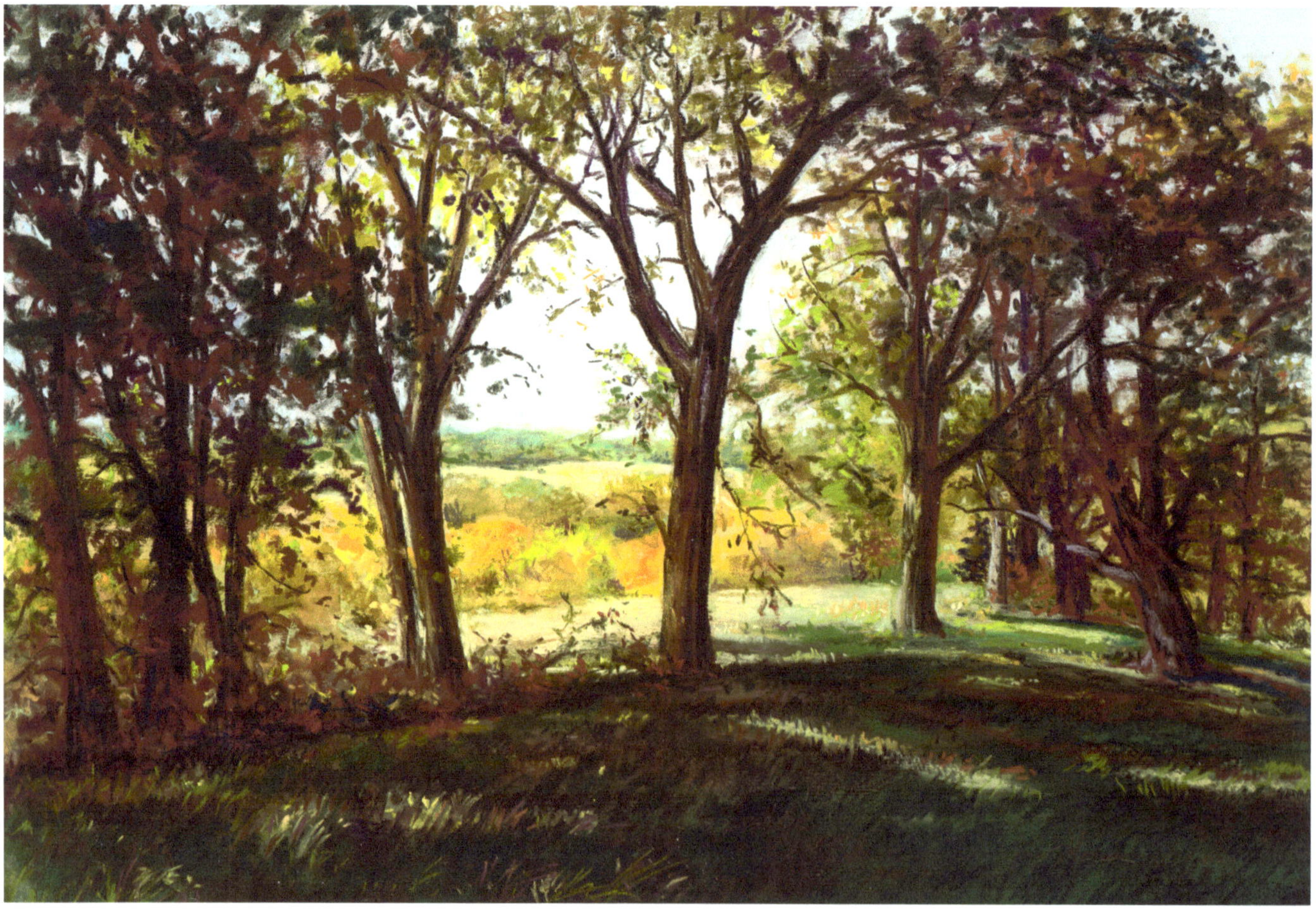

High in the Loess Hills 12 x 18 in.

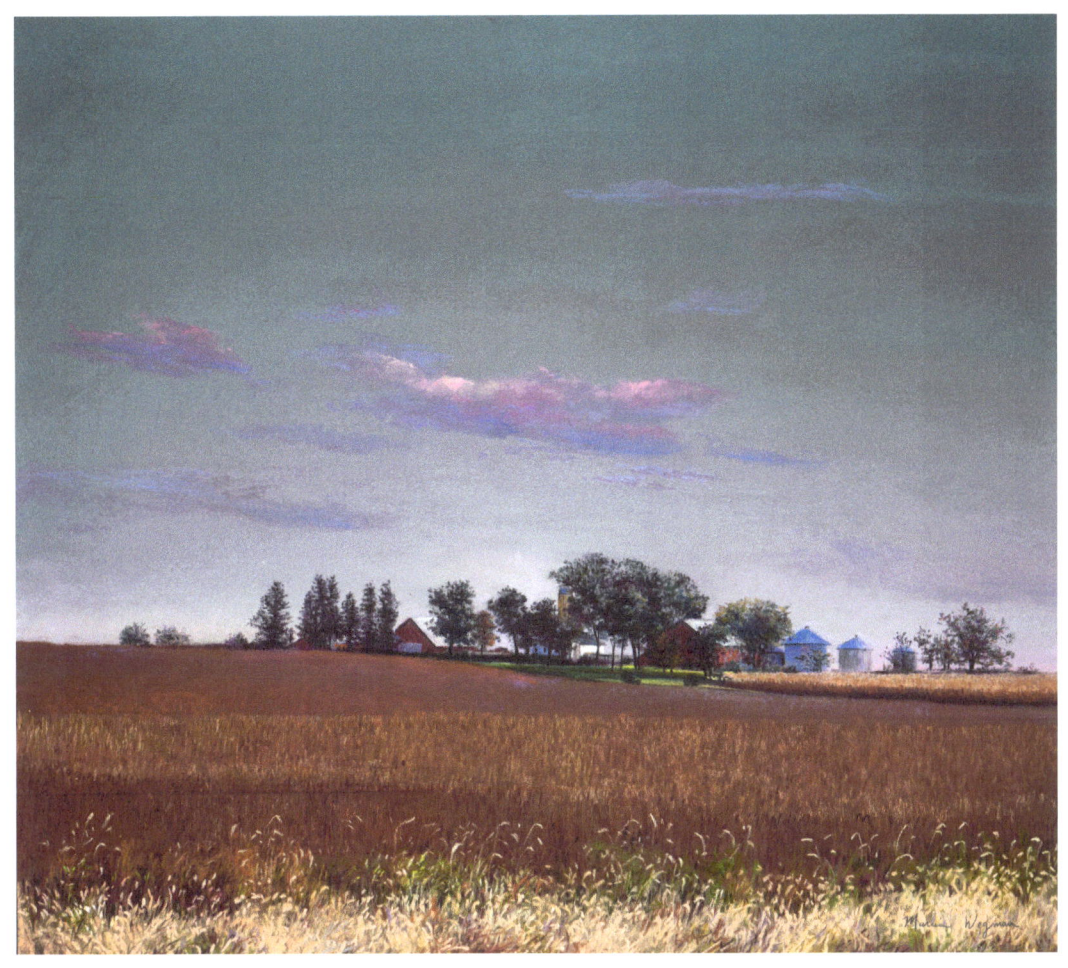

Fall Soybean Fields 21 x 24 in.

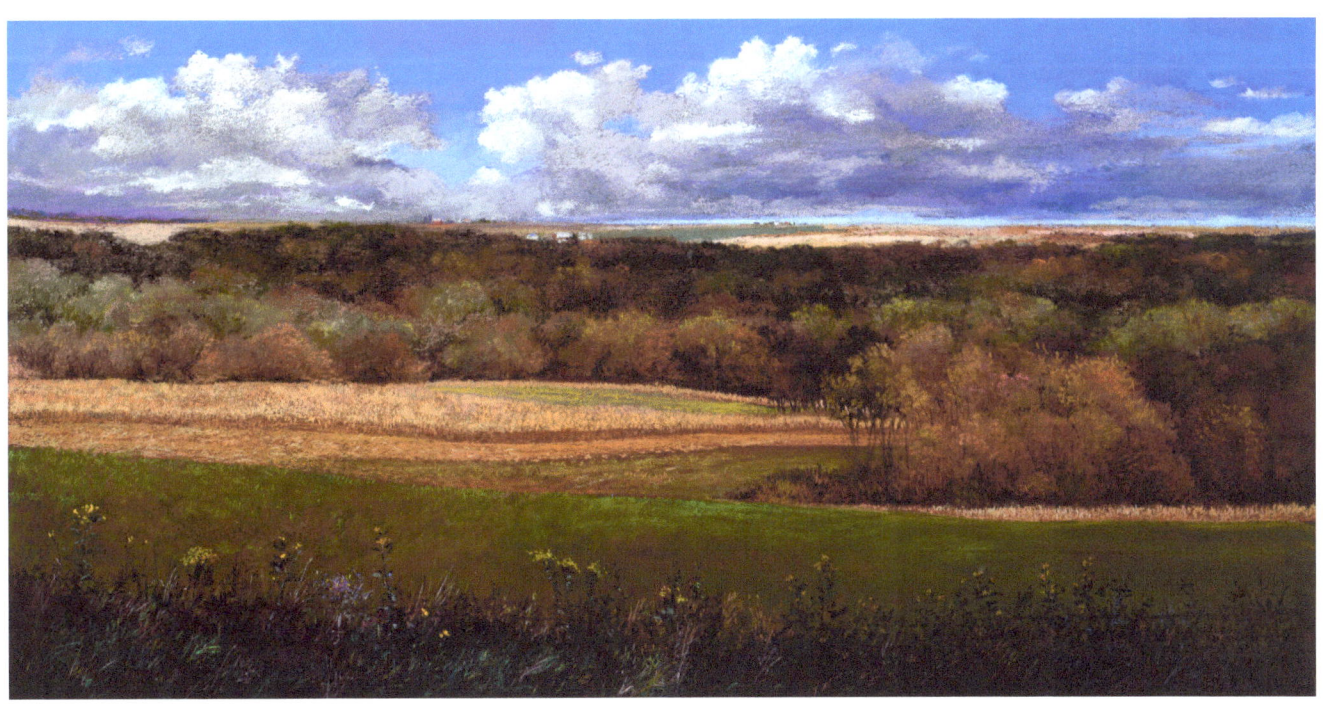

Harvest Time 18 x 36 in.

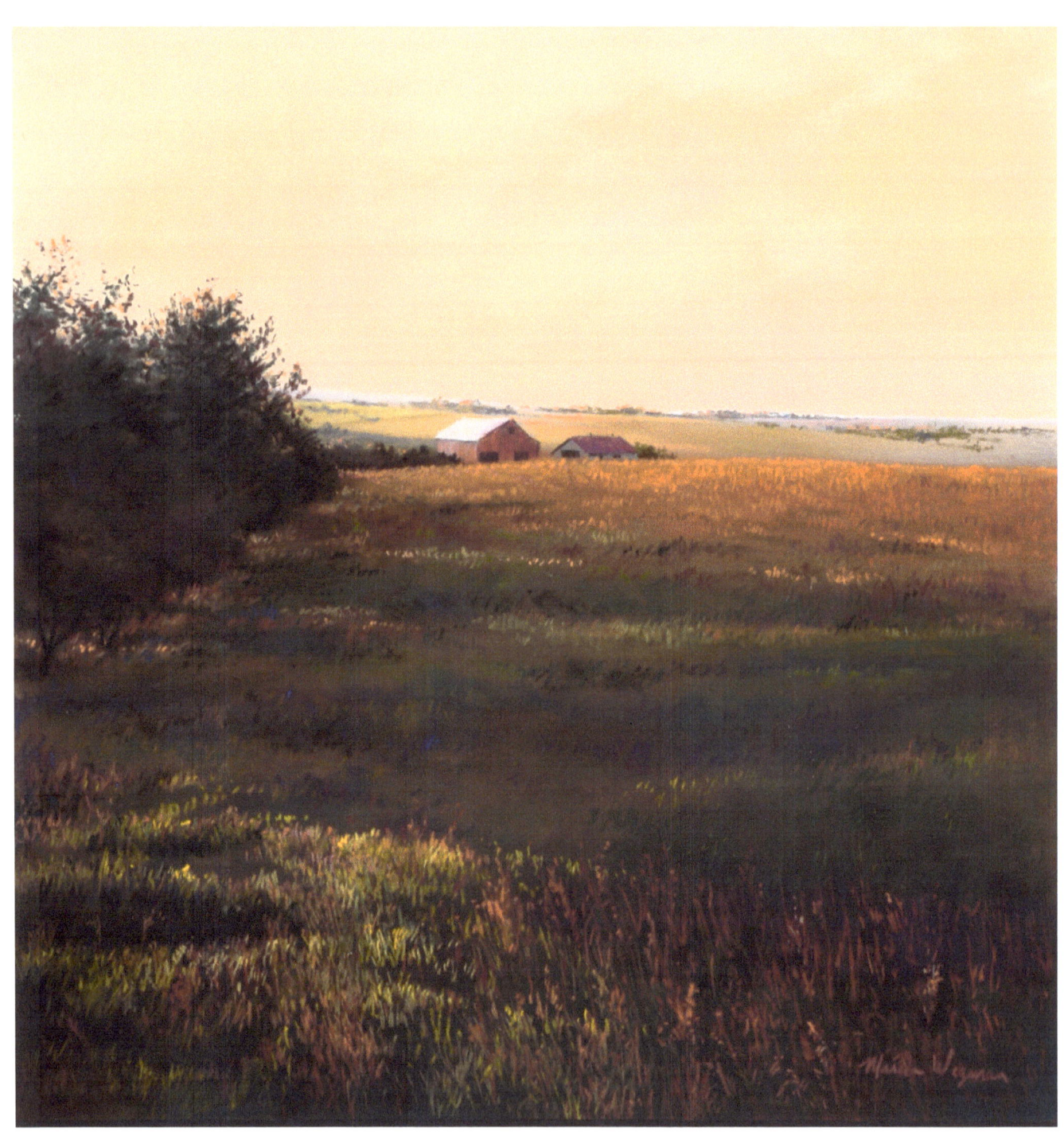

September Country 18 x 18 in.

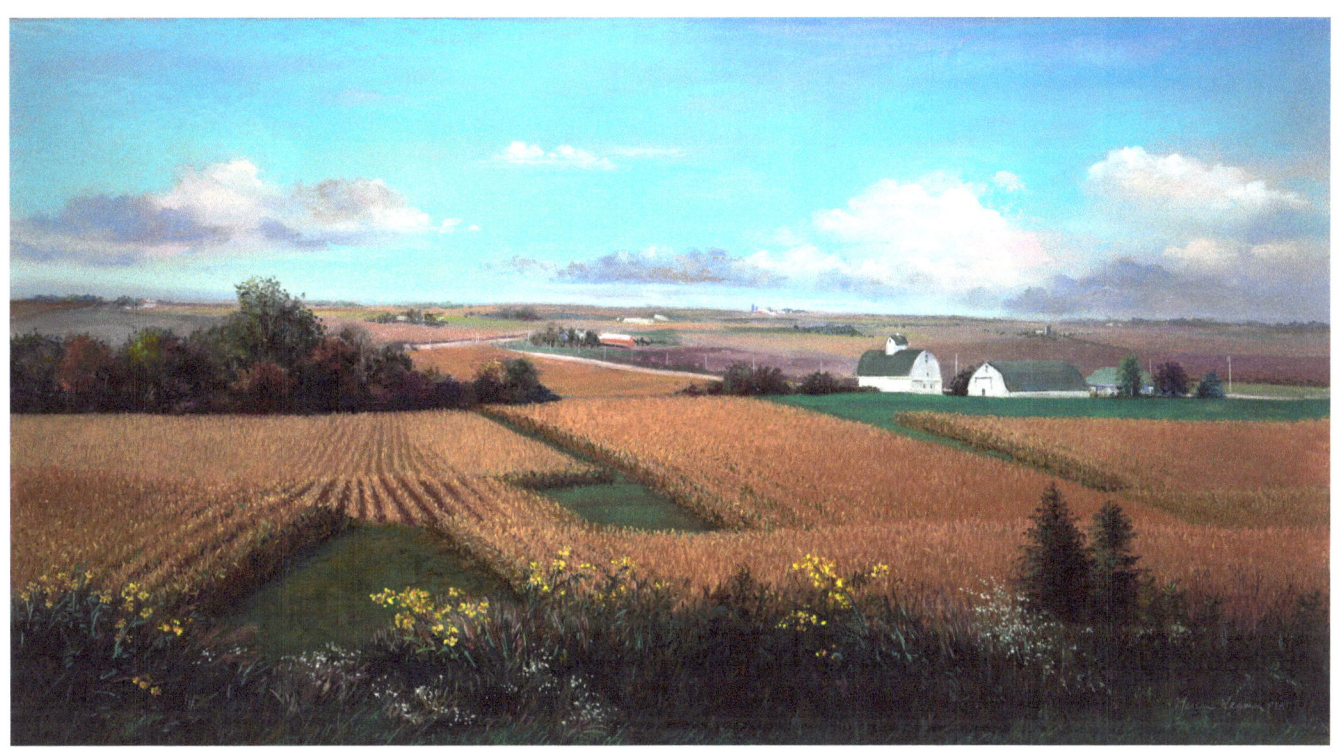

White Farm 19 x 36 in.

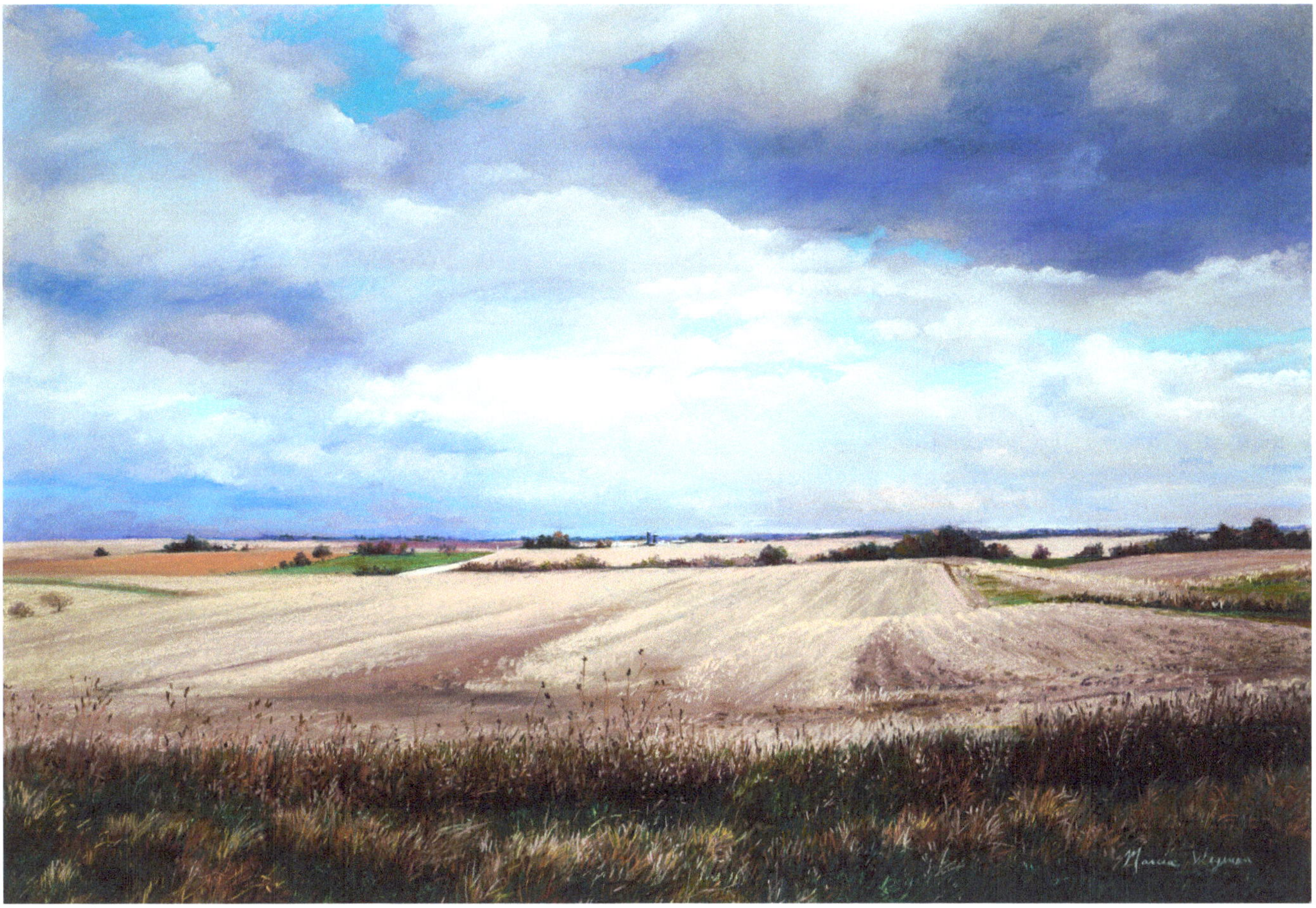

Ready for Winter 24 x 36 in.

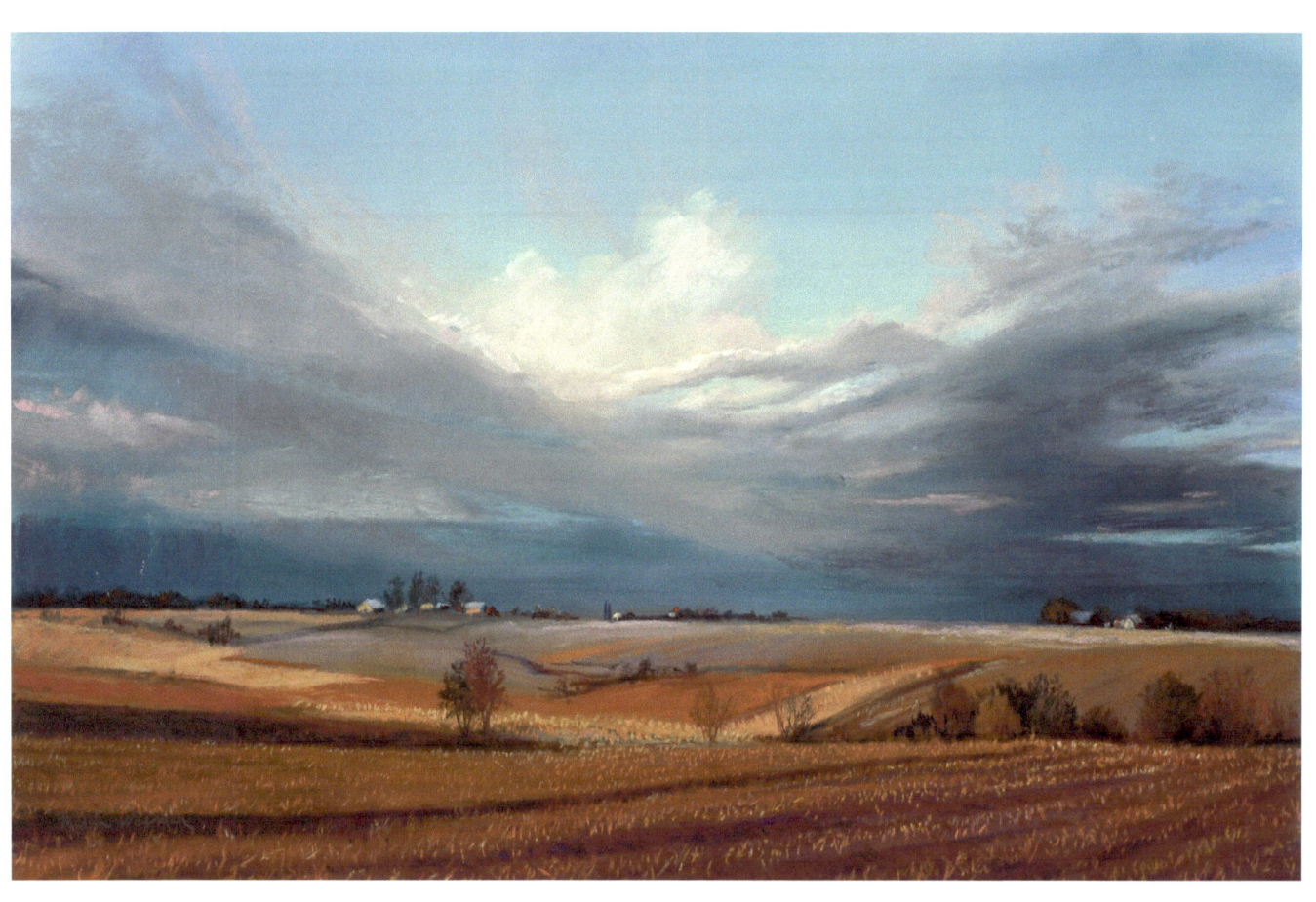

Winter in the Air 12 x 24 in.

Winter

Winter reveals the bones of the land. The rolling hills are made more evident by the barren fields and skeletal trees. When blanketed lightly or thickly by snow, a new color scheme is created. Shadows take on more color.

The dark accents of farm buildings and trees add a different kind of accent that is fun to work with. A red barn makes a bold statement. The skies, either overcast or exceptionally bright, can make for a change in composition.

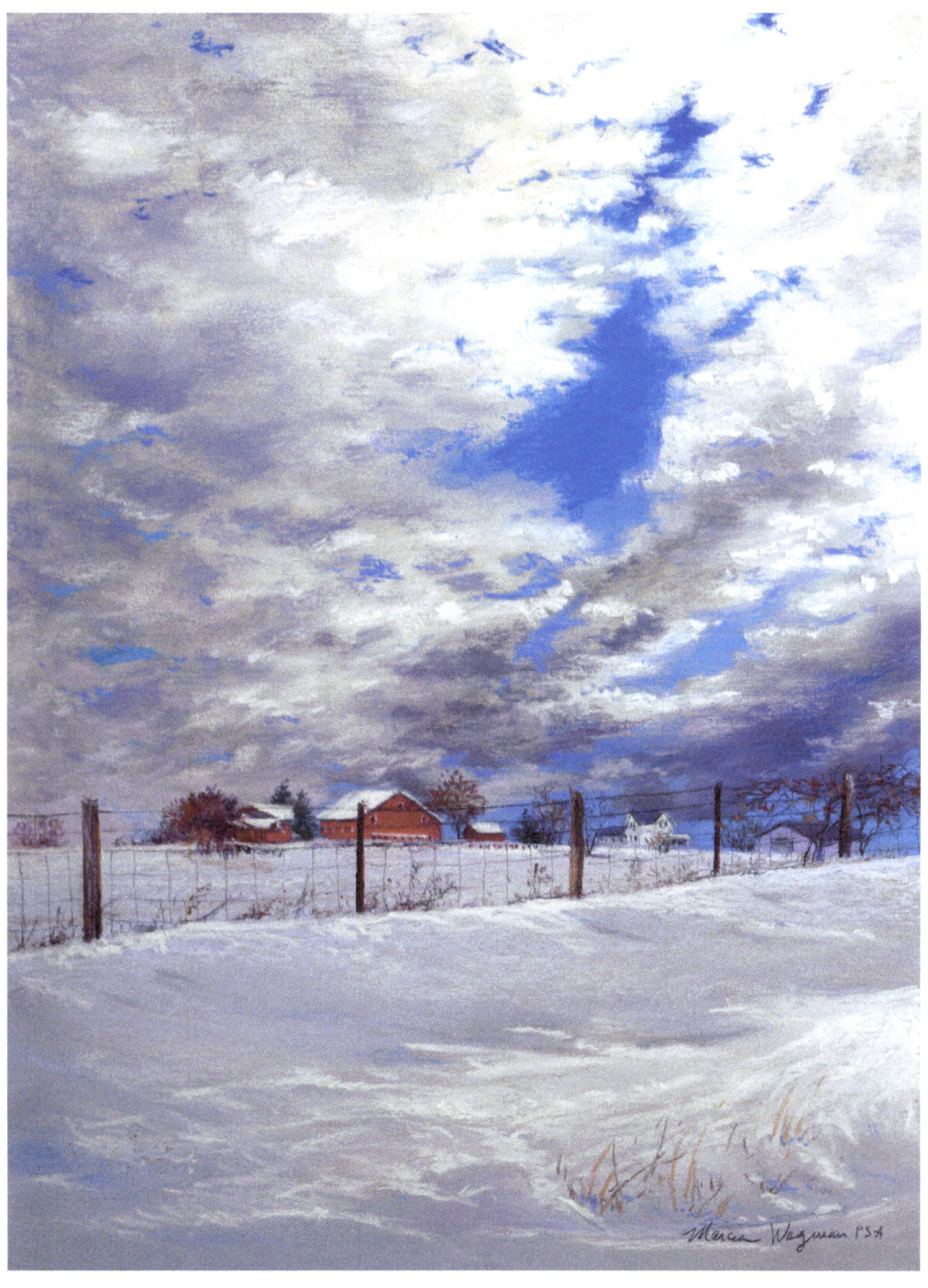

Iowa Seasons: Winter 12 x 9 in.

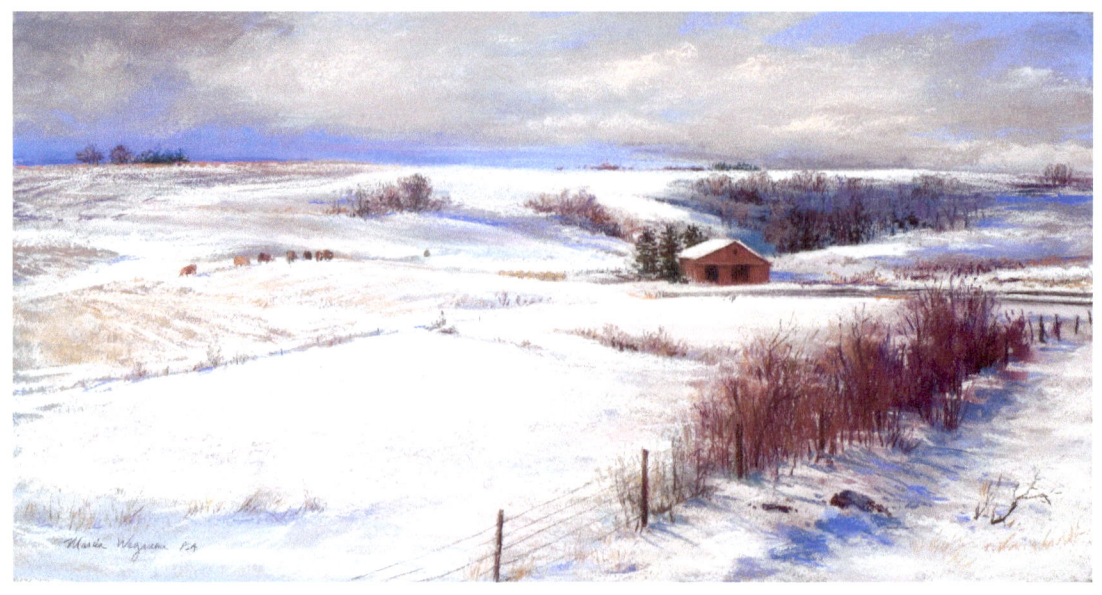

Winter Winds 12 x 24 in.

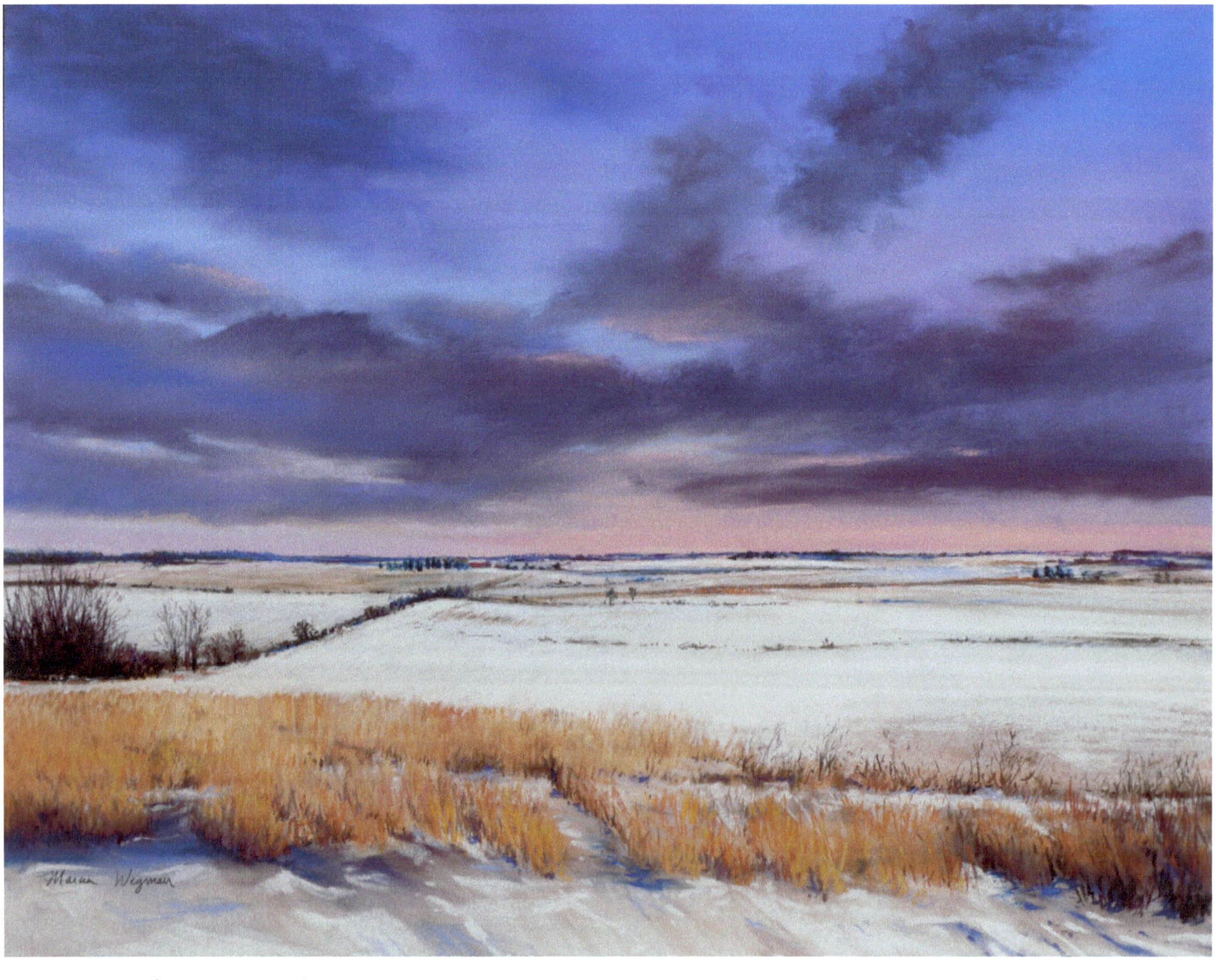

Winter Colors 19 x 24 in.

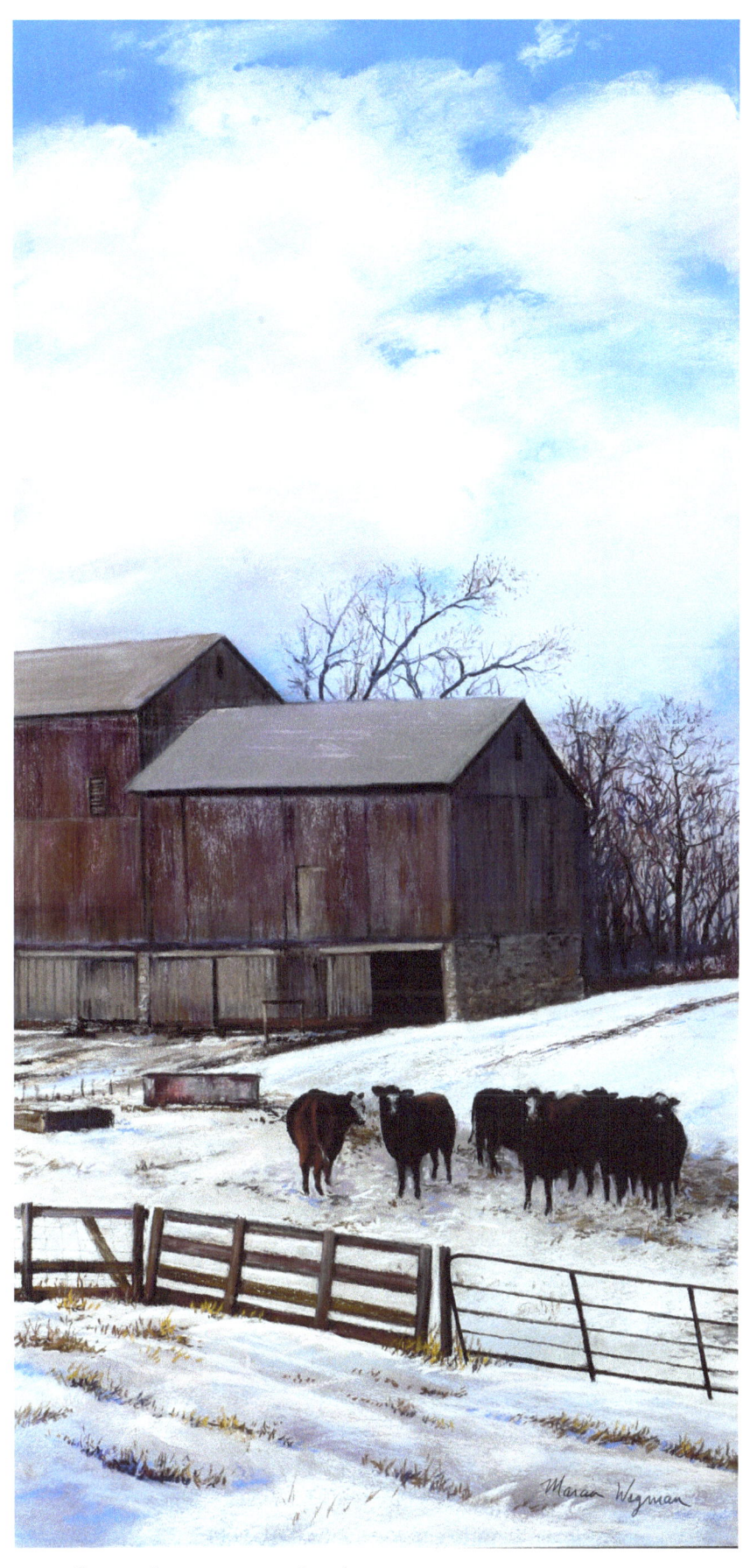

Cattle in the Barnyard 24 x 12 in.

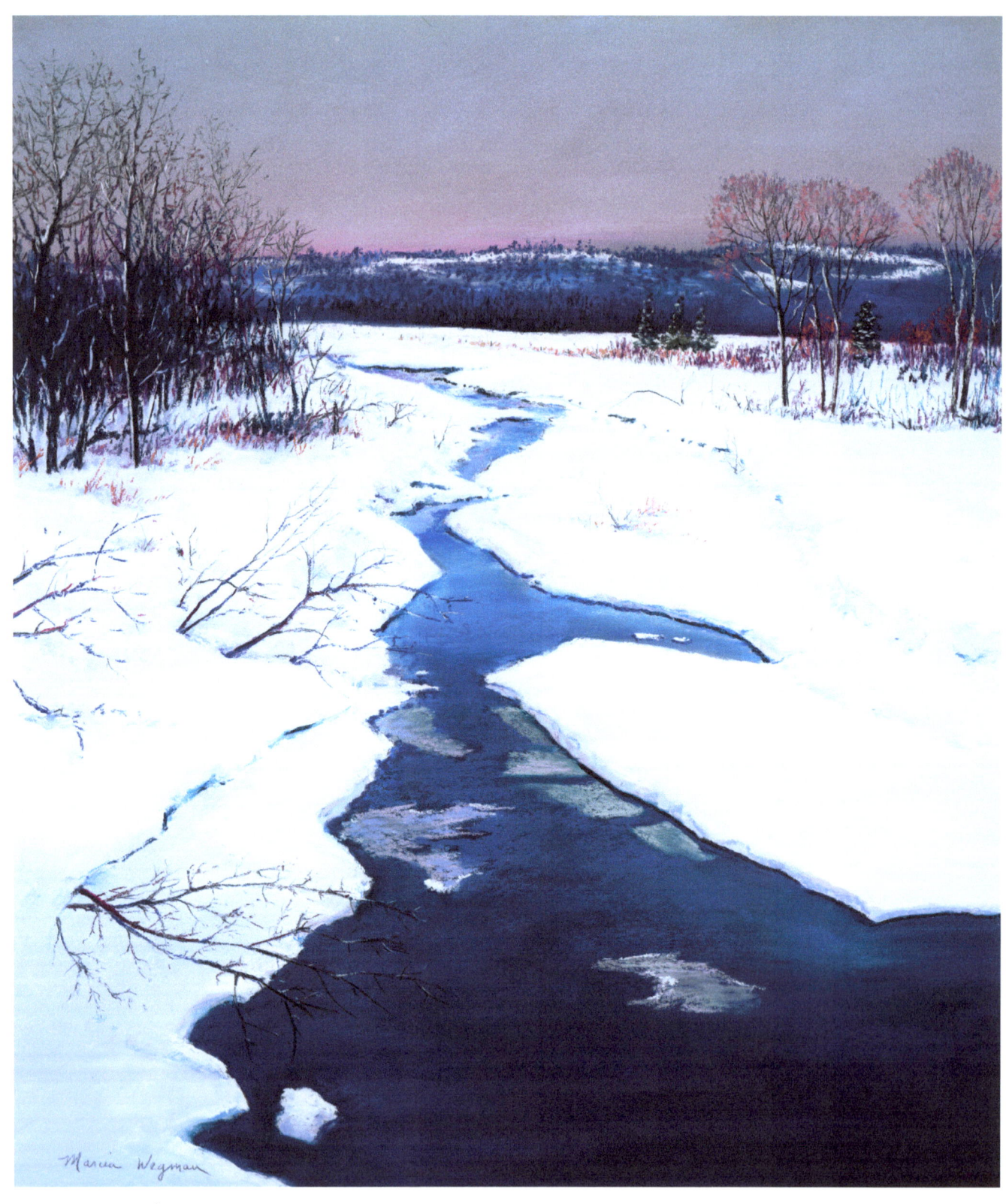

Winter Creek 21 x 18 in.

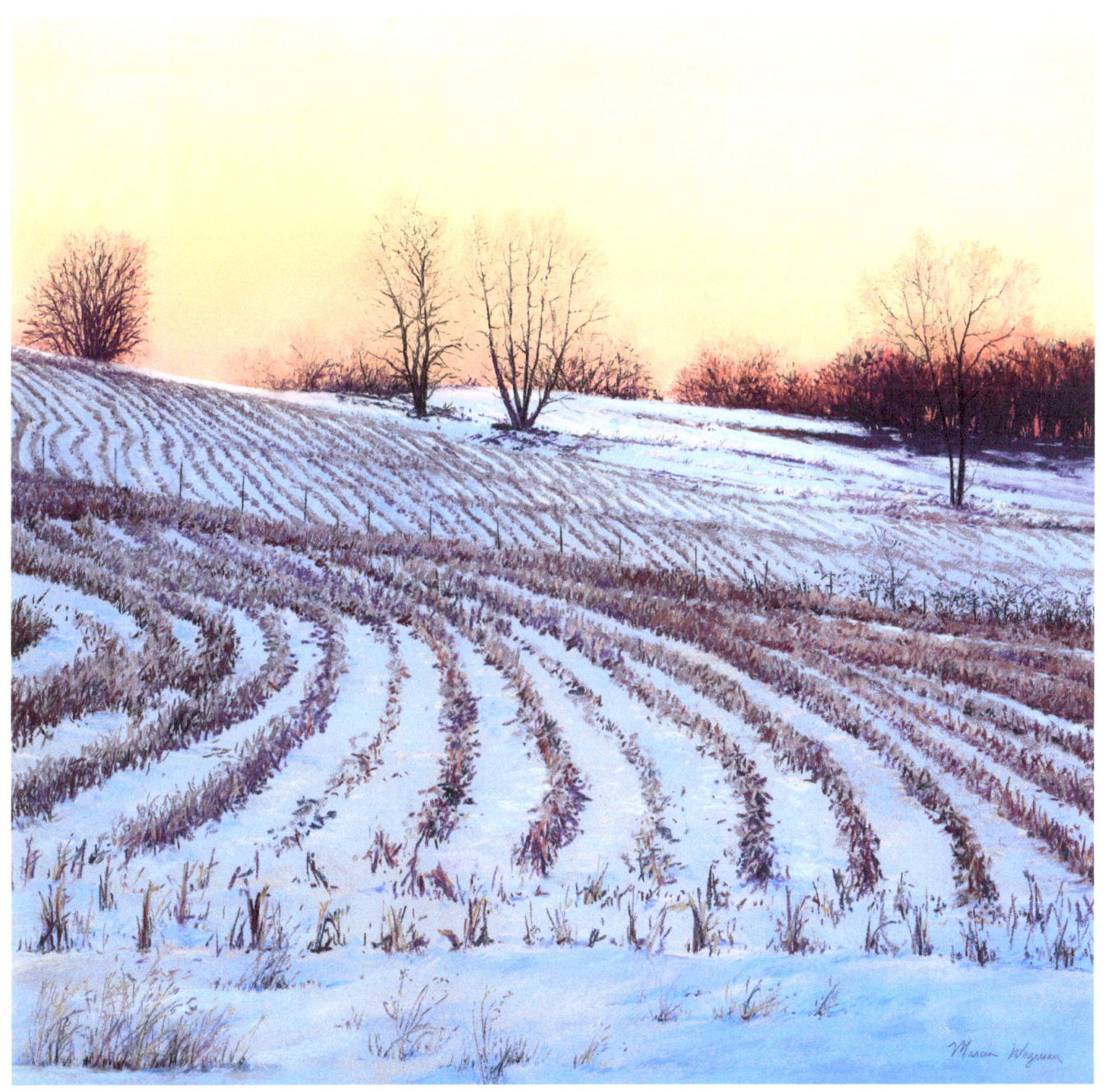

Winter Cornfields at Sunset 24 x 30 in.

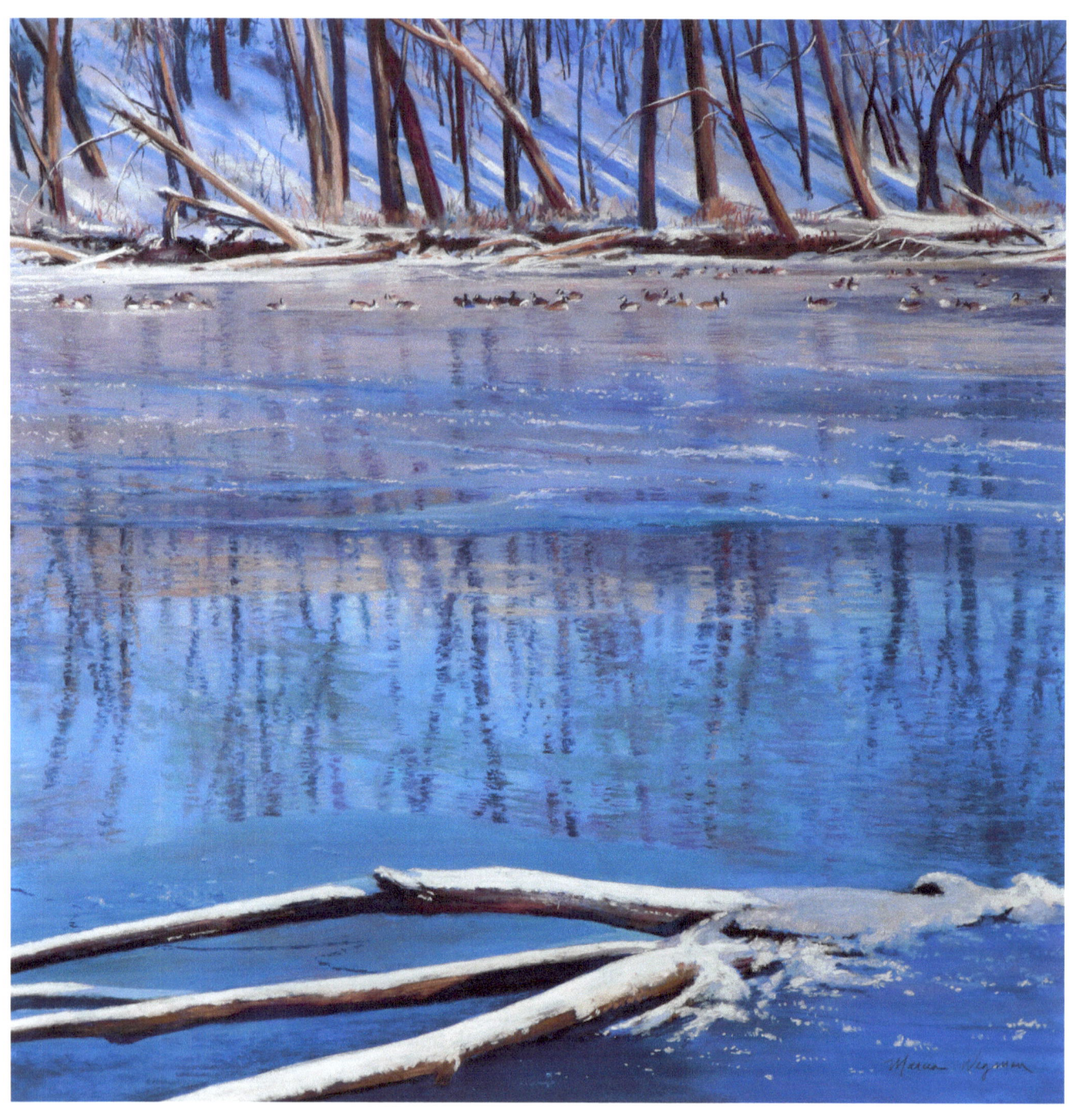

Winter River Geese 24 x 24 in.

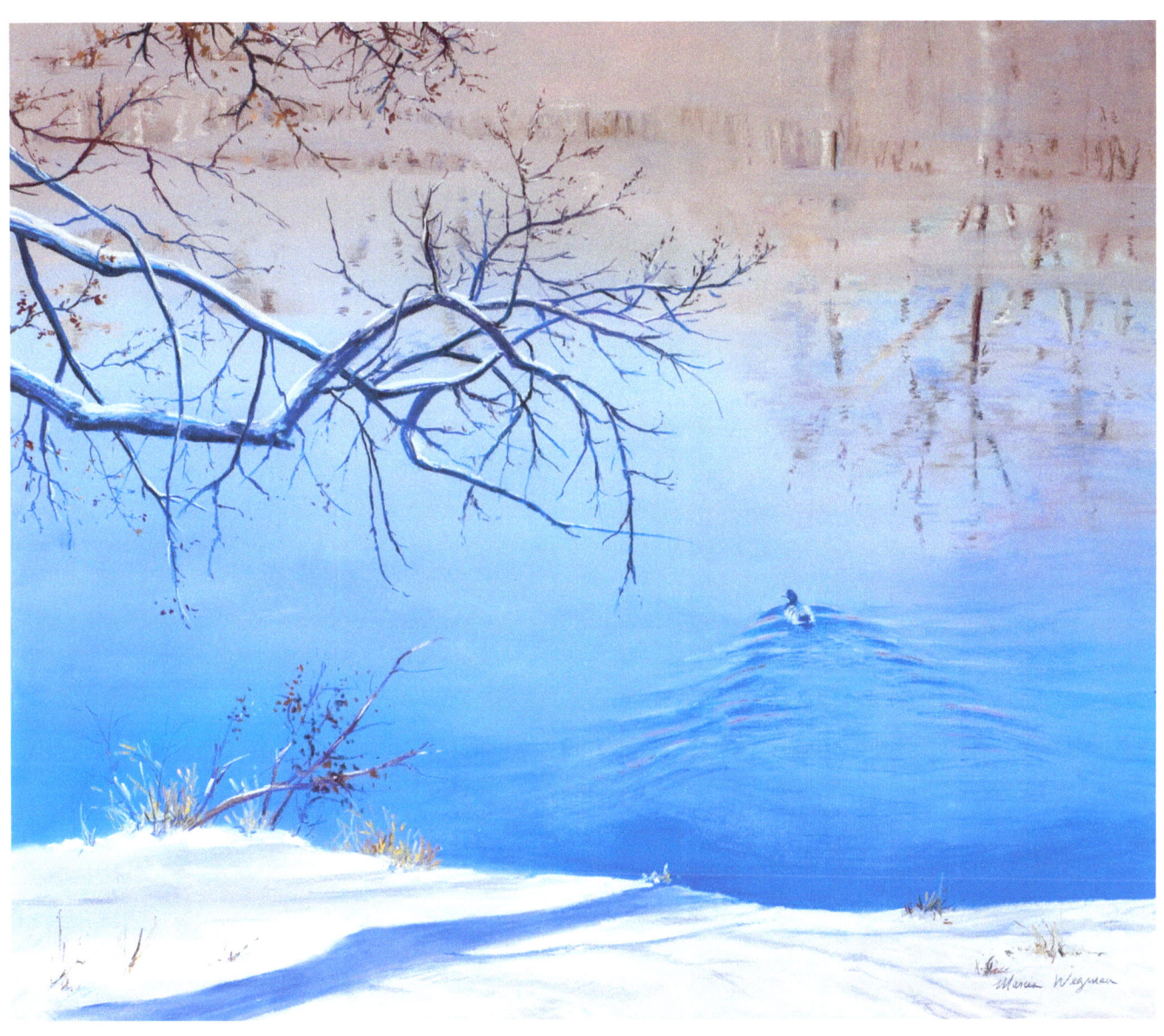

Winter Ice and Snow 18 x 22 in.

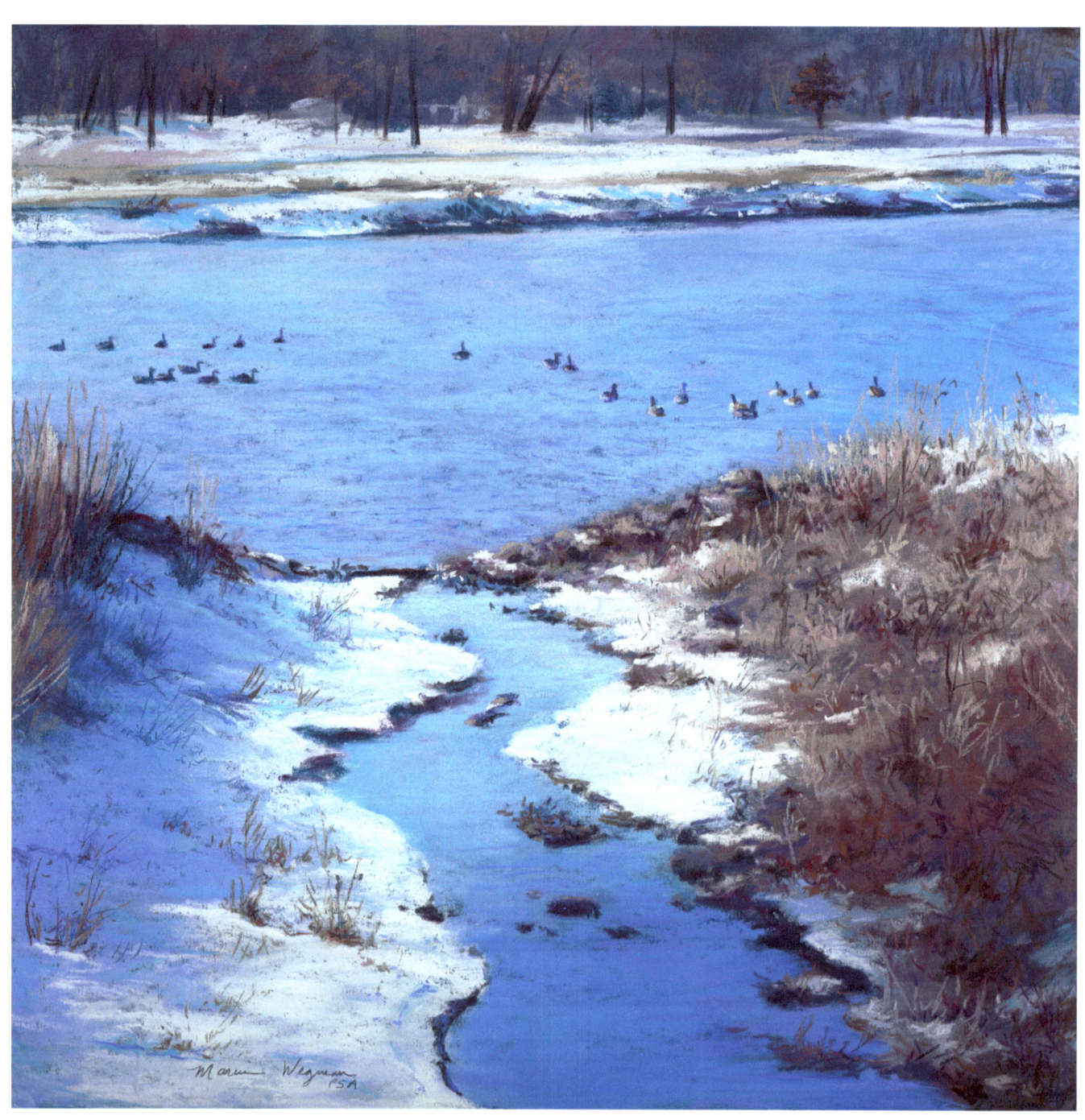

Winter Geese 16 x 16 in.

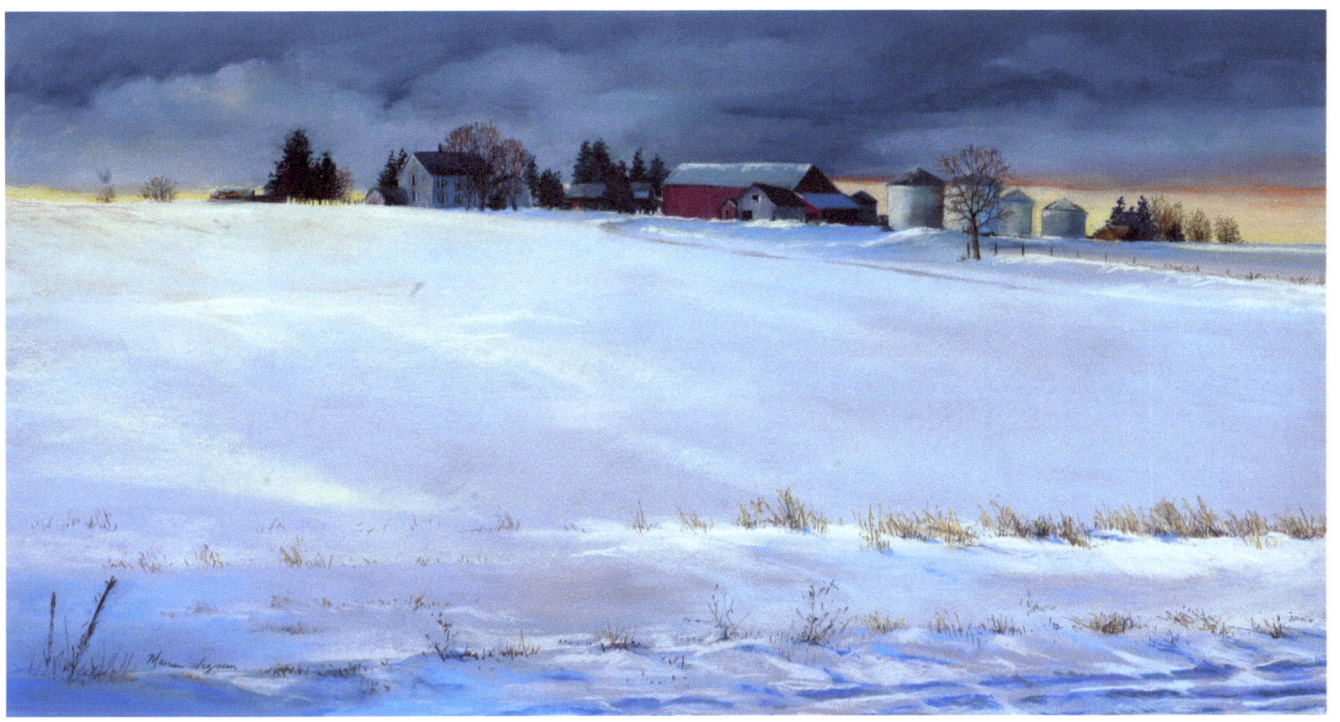

Winter Farm 19 x 36 in.

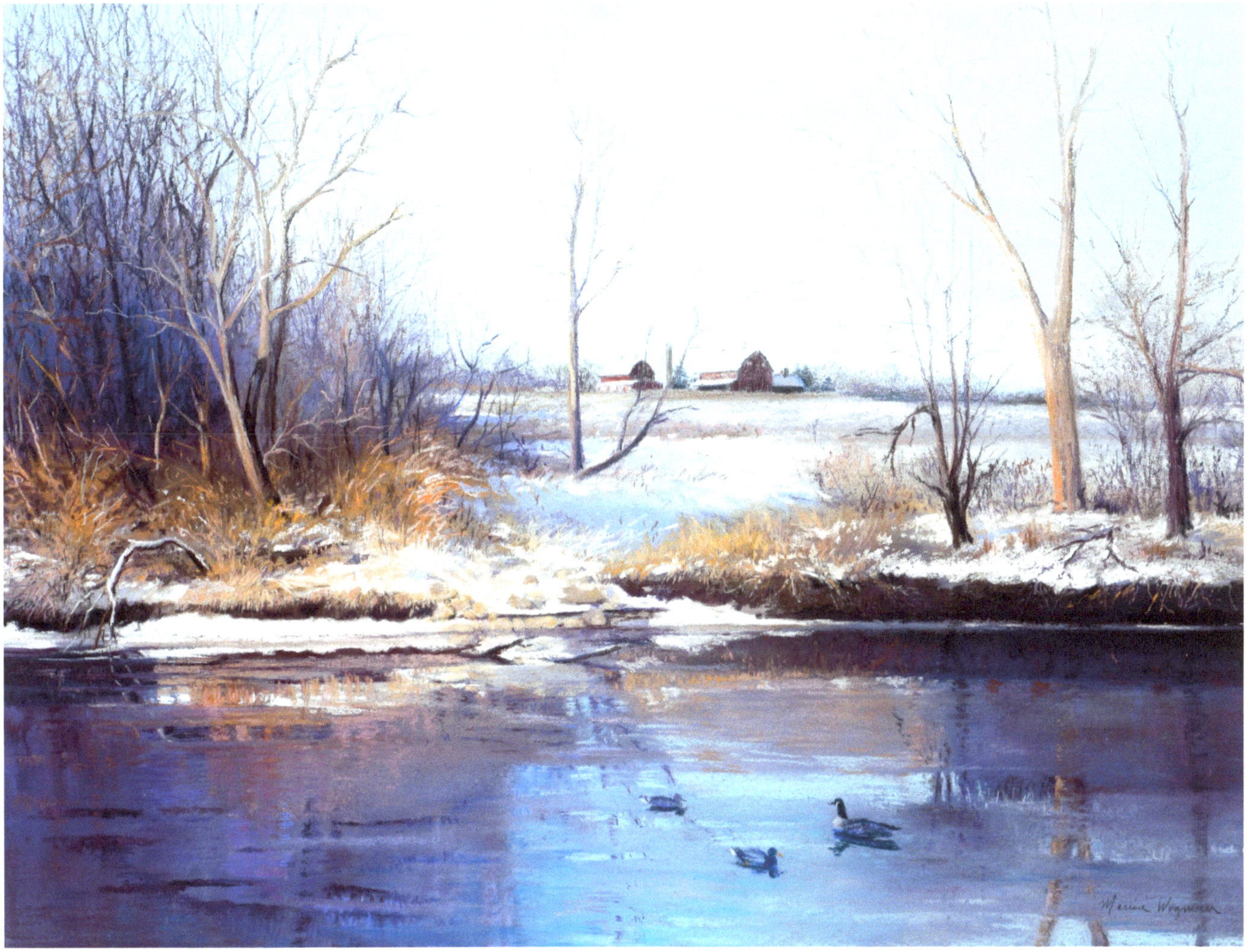

Winter River Reflections 18 x 24 in.

—105

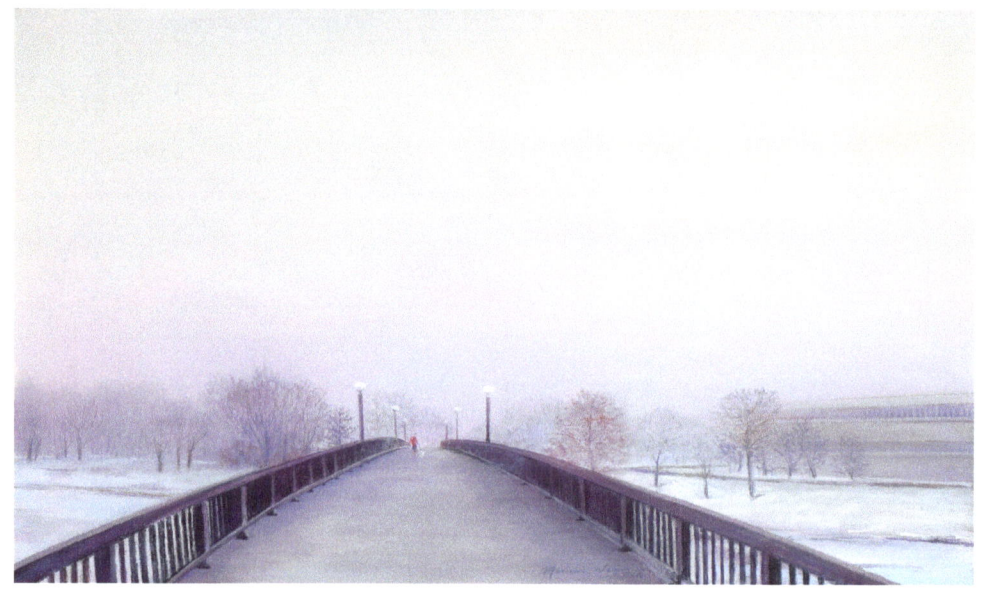

Footbridge 14 x 18 in.

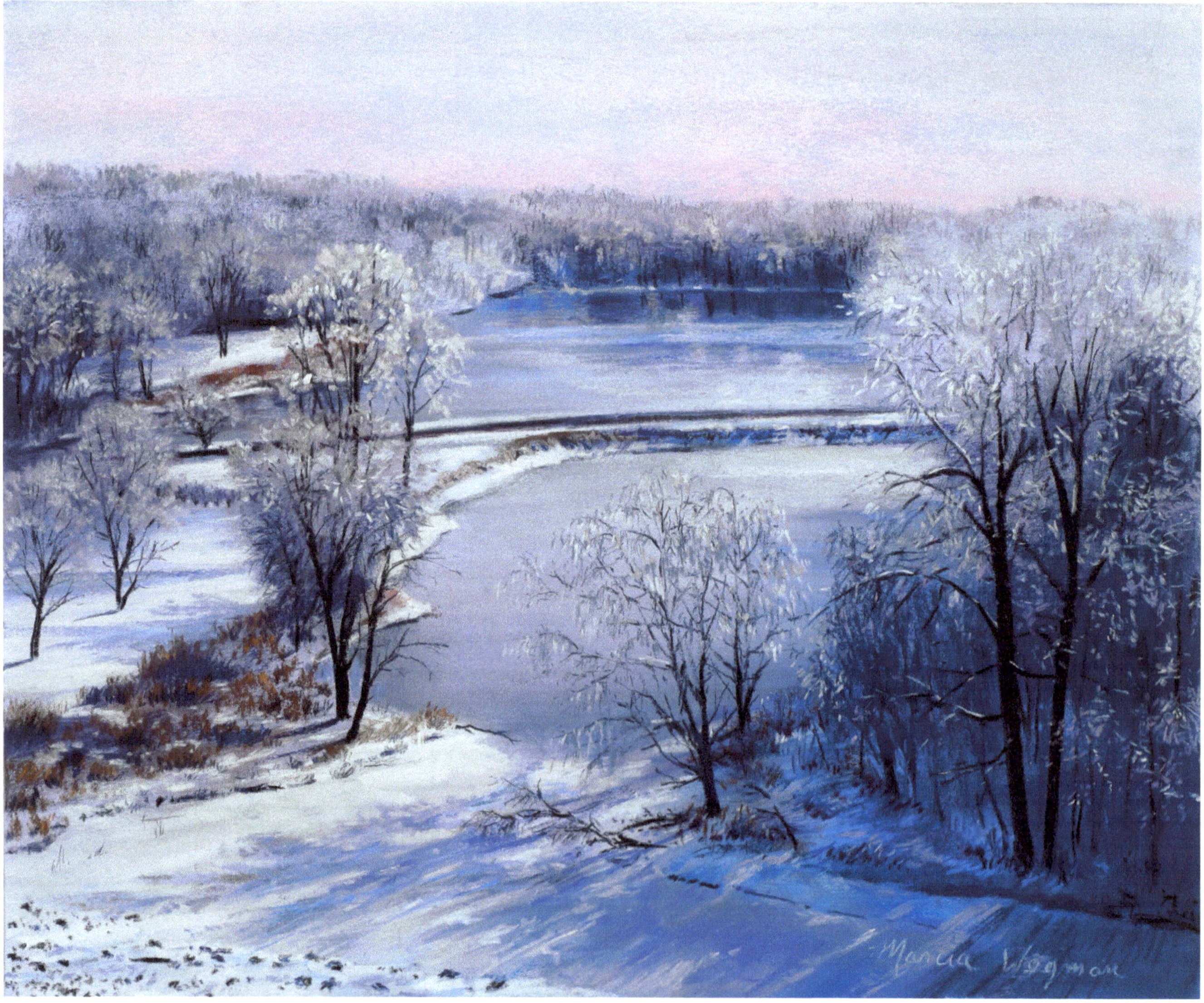

After the Storm: From the Dam 12 x 15 in.

Roads and Trails

When on a photographic expedition, primarily in Johnson County, but also in other parts of the state, I take the small, gravel roads so I can make quick stops when I see a promising scene. Including the road expands the compositional possibilities. I love to hike.

Once a week, I join a local hiking group. In good weather, we go to nearby parks to walk. I take my camera along. A trail disappearing into the woods or following around a lake makes for an appealing subject.

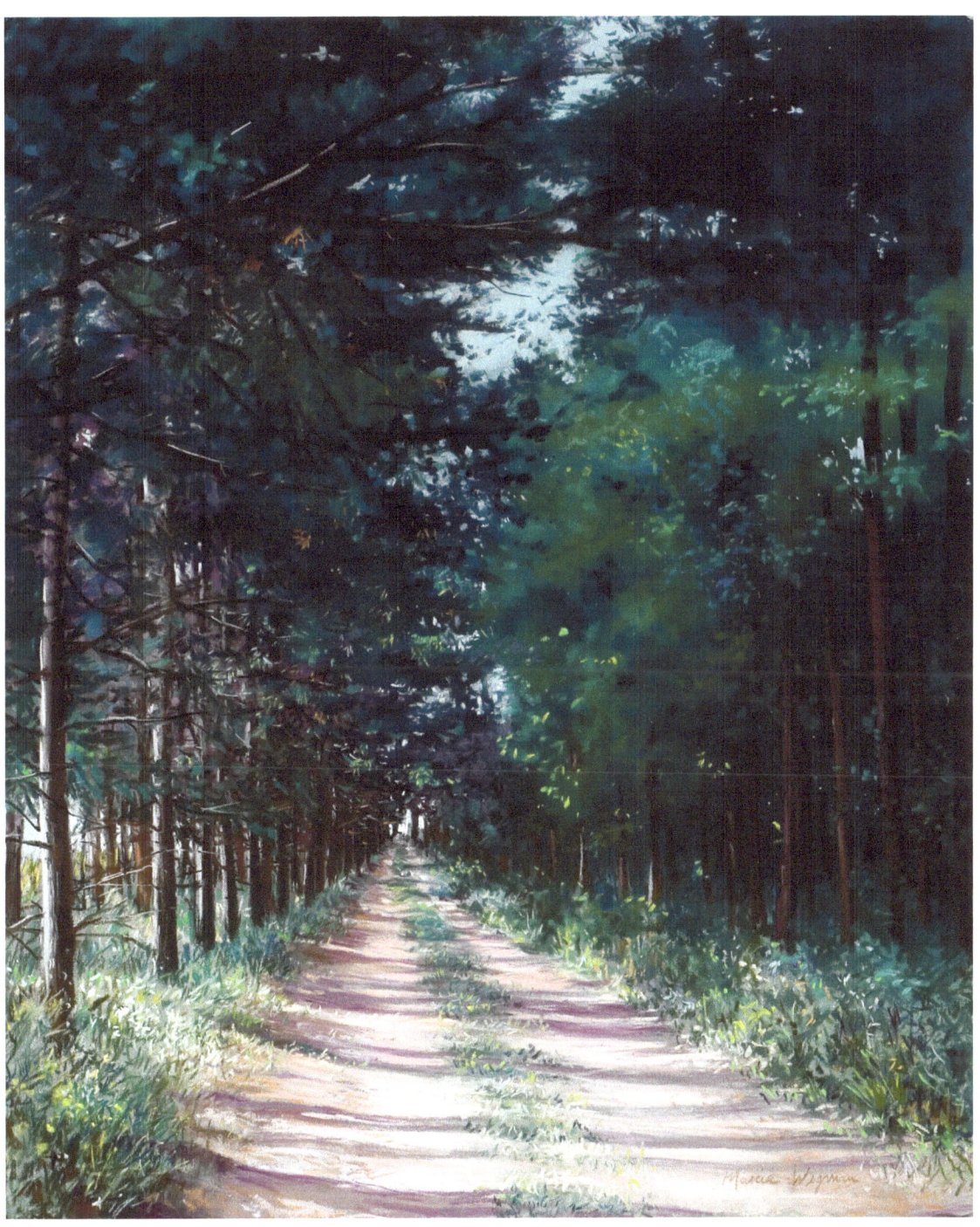

Trail at Kent Park 21 x 18 in.

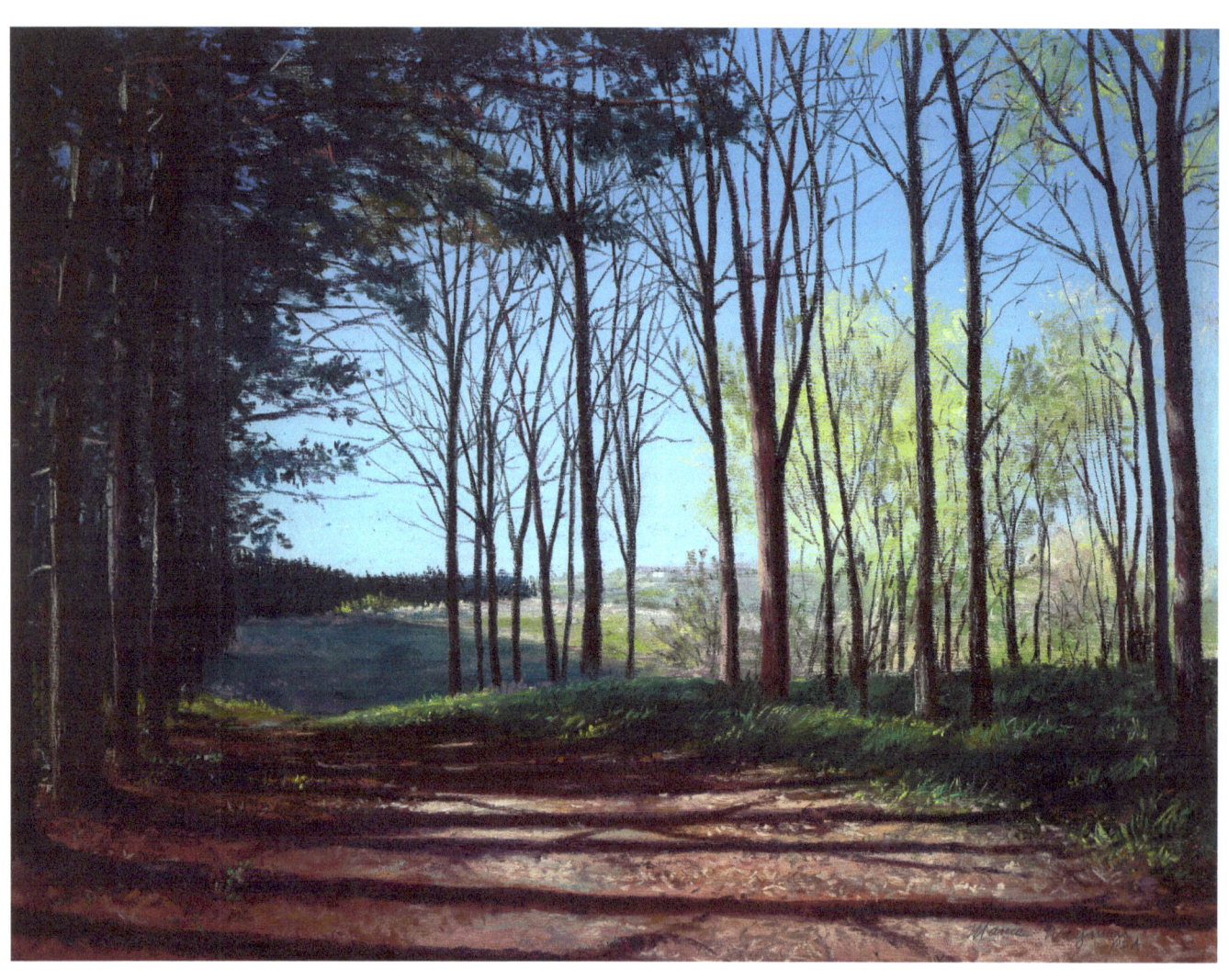

A Walk in Kent Park II 15 x 20 in.

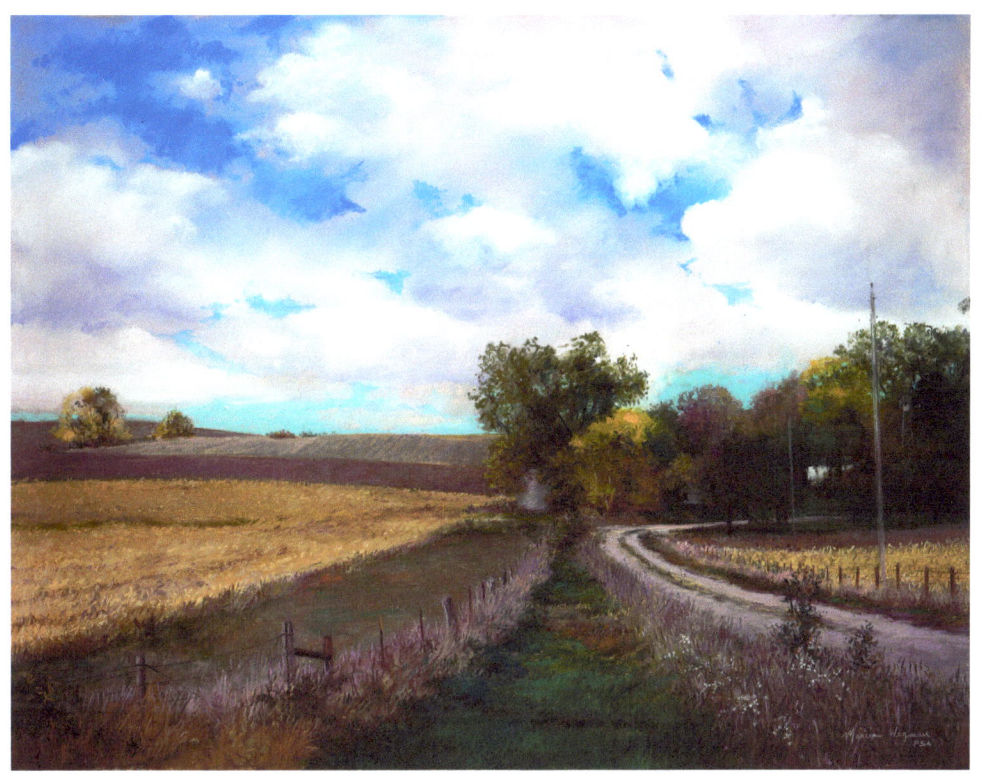

End of the Road 24 x 32 in.

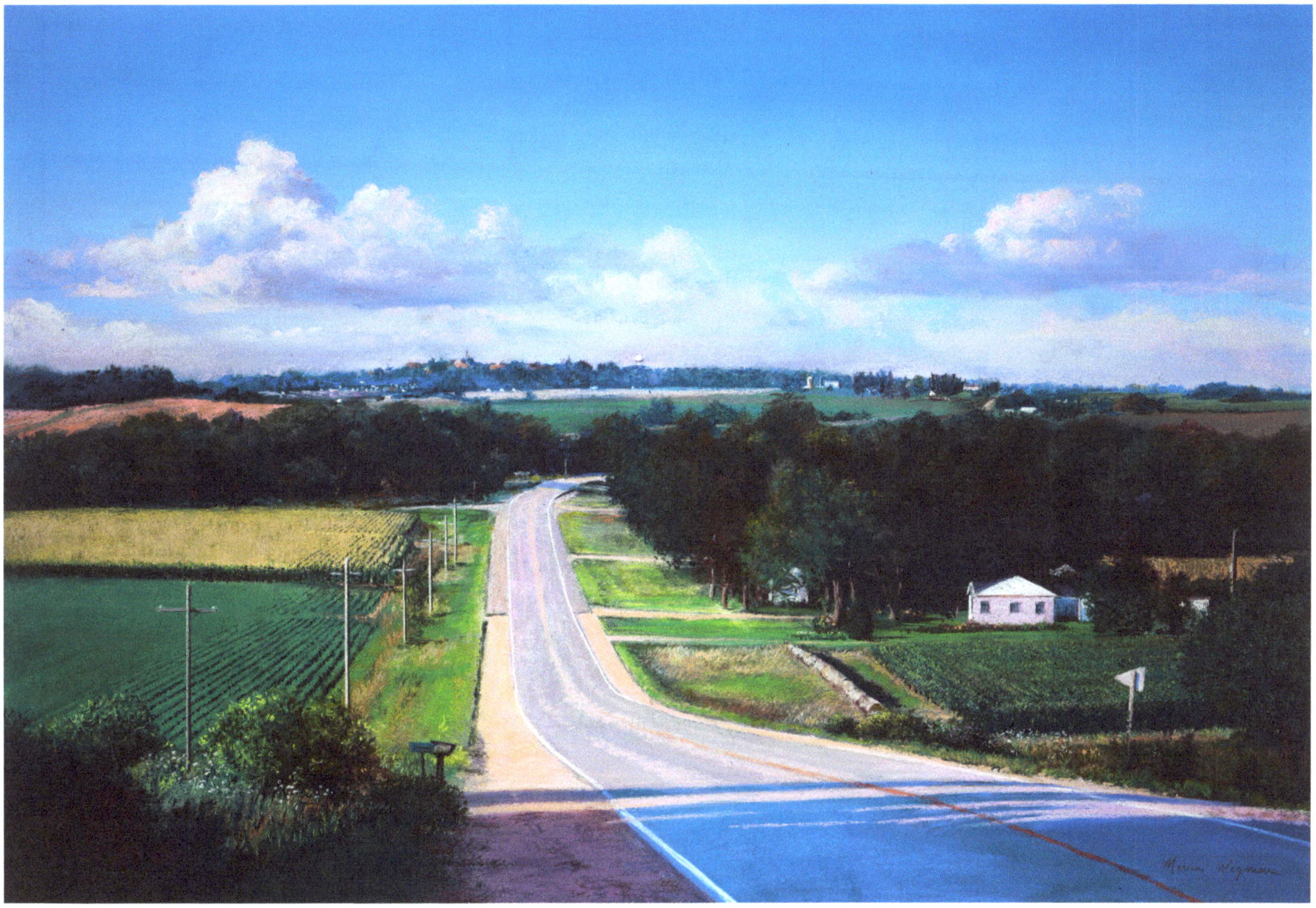

Cedar River Valley at Mount Vernon 24 x 36 in.

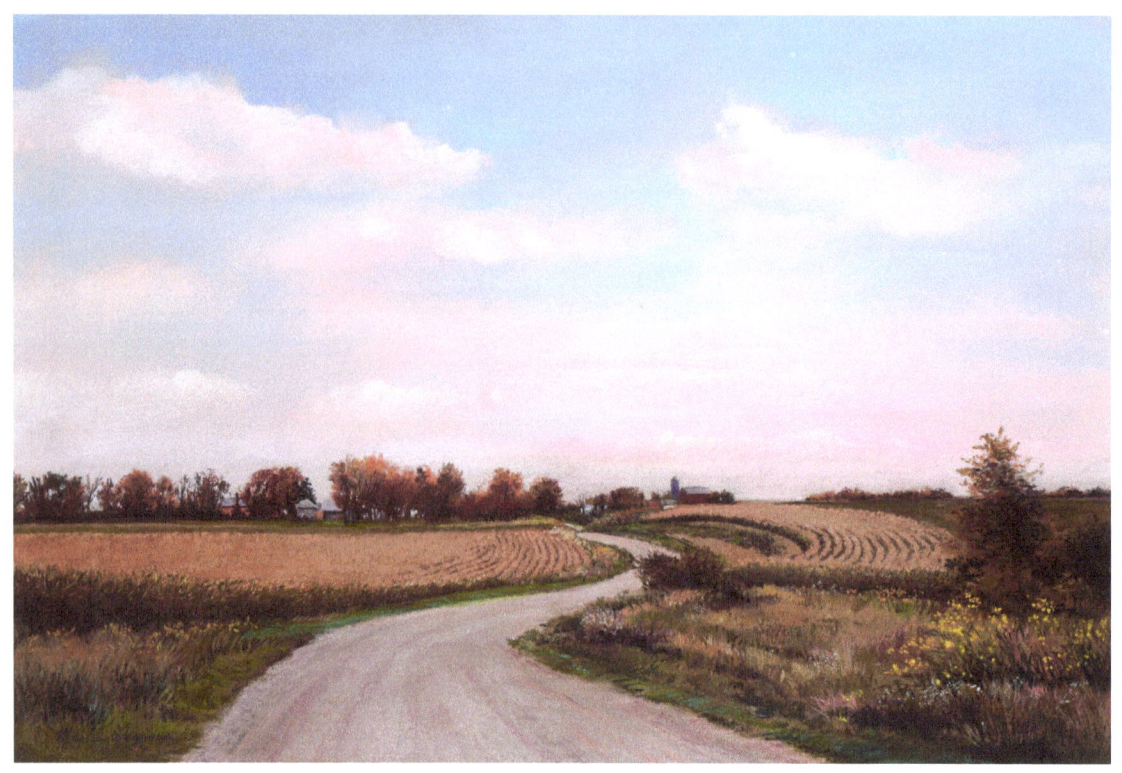

Through the Fields 15 x 24 in.

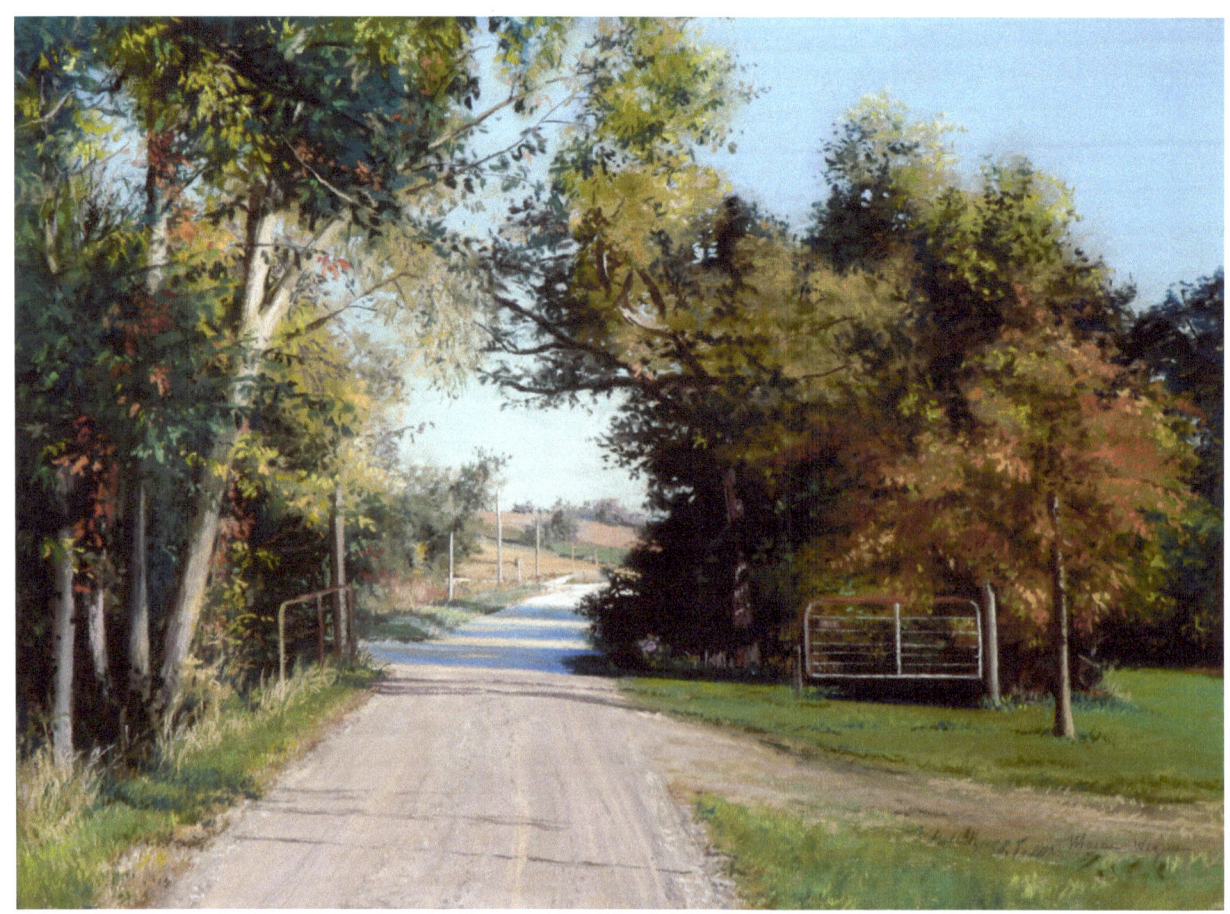

Gateway 15 x 21 in.

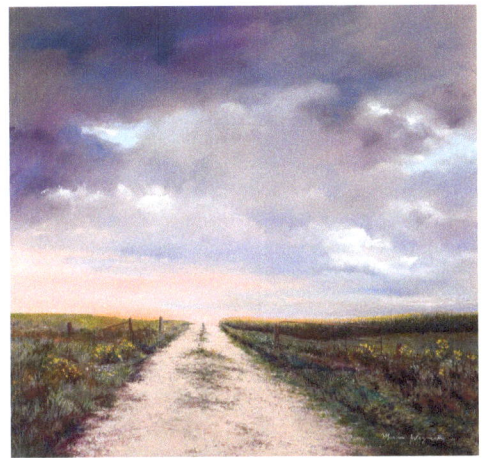
Into the Fields 24 x 26 in.

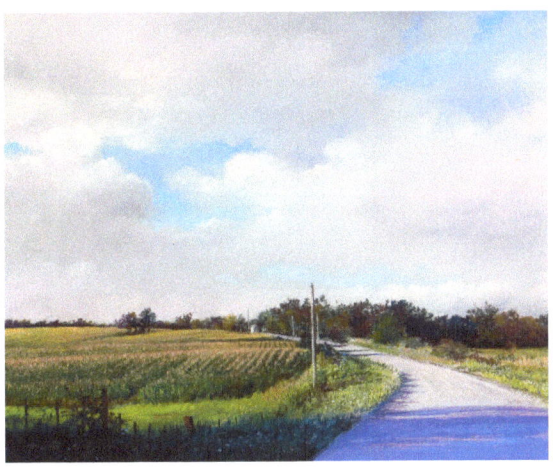
Evening Clouds and Shadows 12 x 15 in.

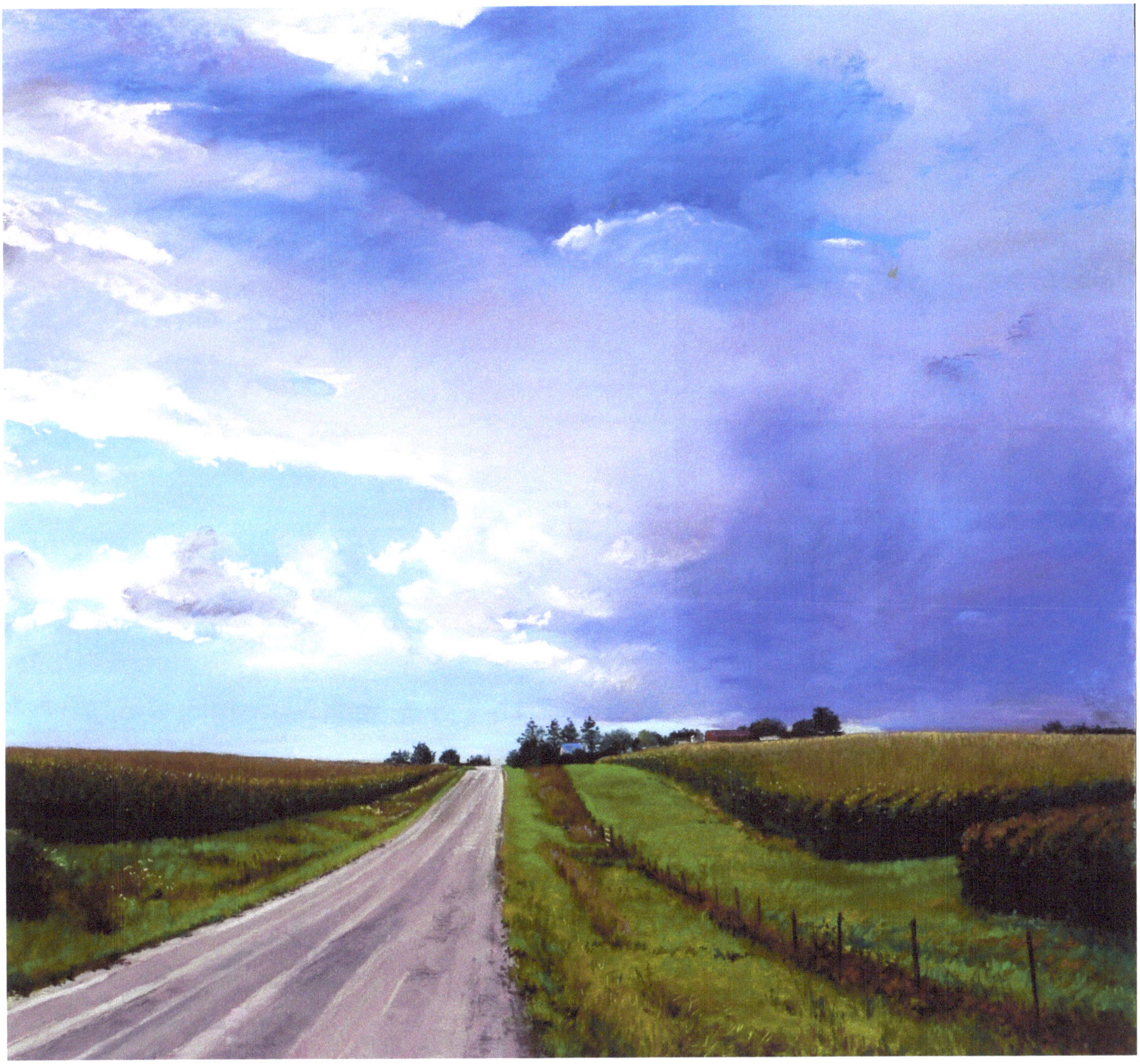

Kalona Road 24 x 25 in.

—111

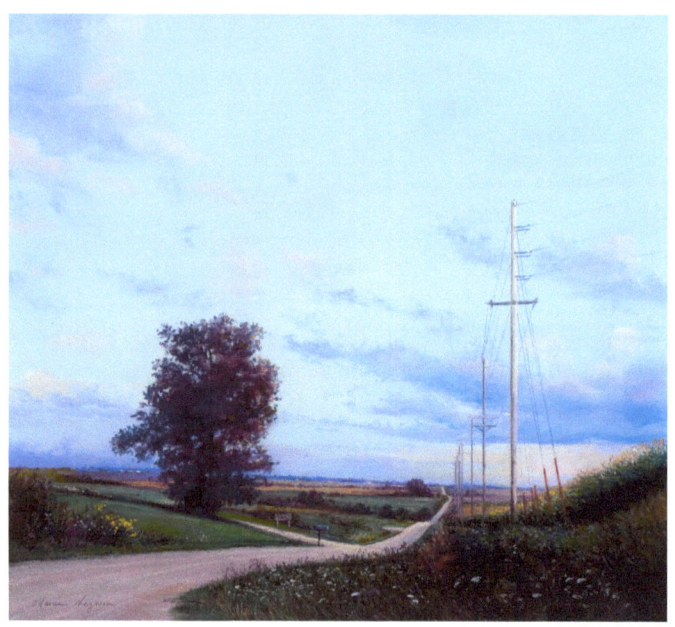

Evening Road 18 x 20 in.

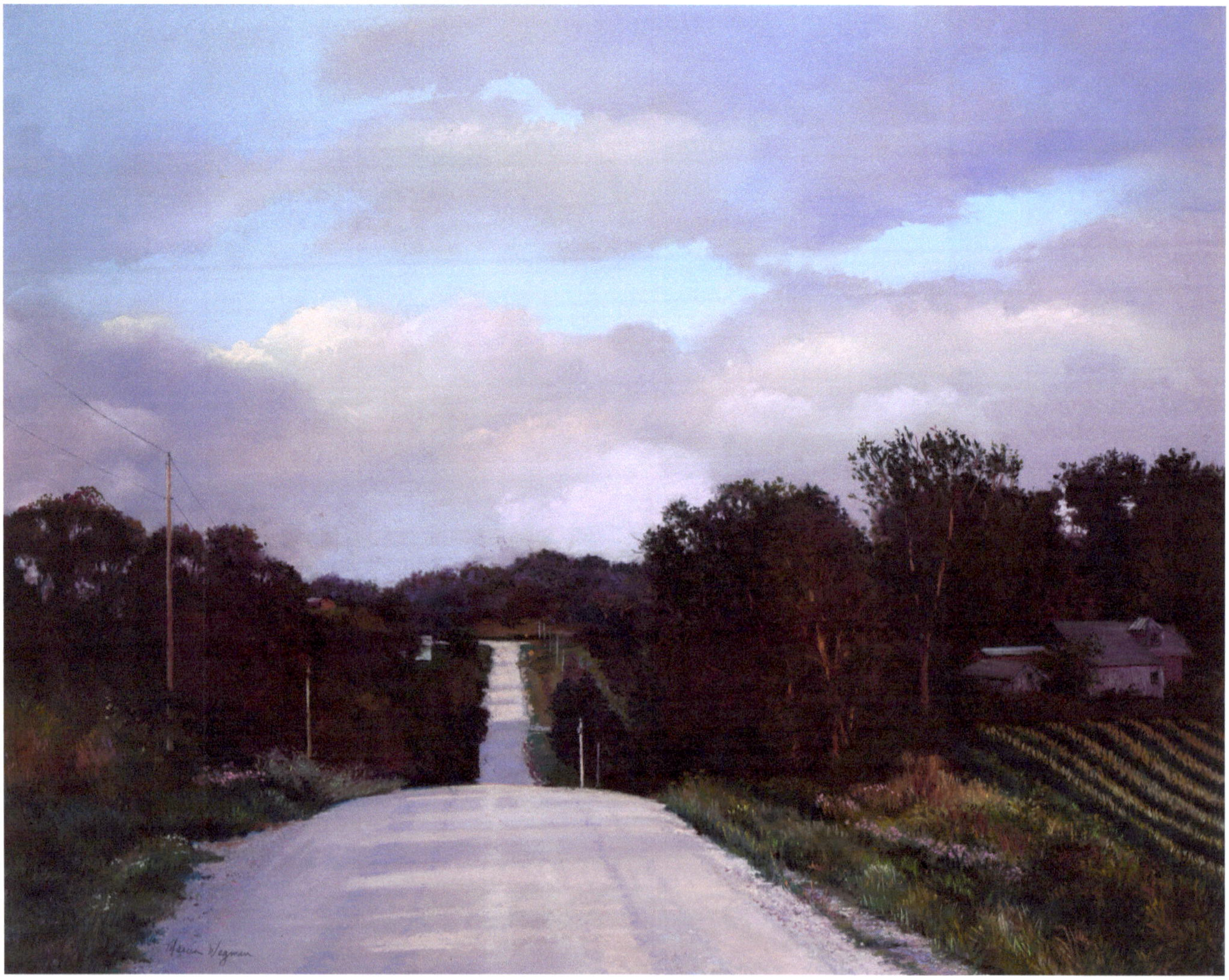

Late Afternoon in the Country 21 x 27 in.

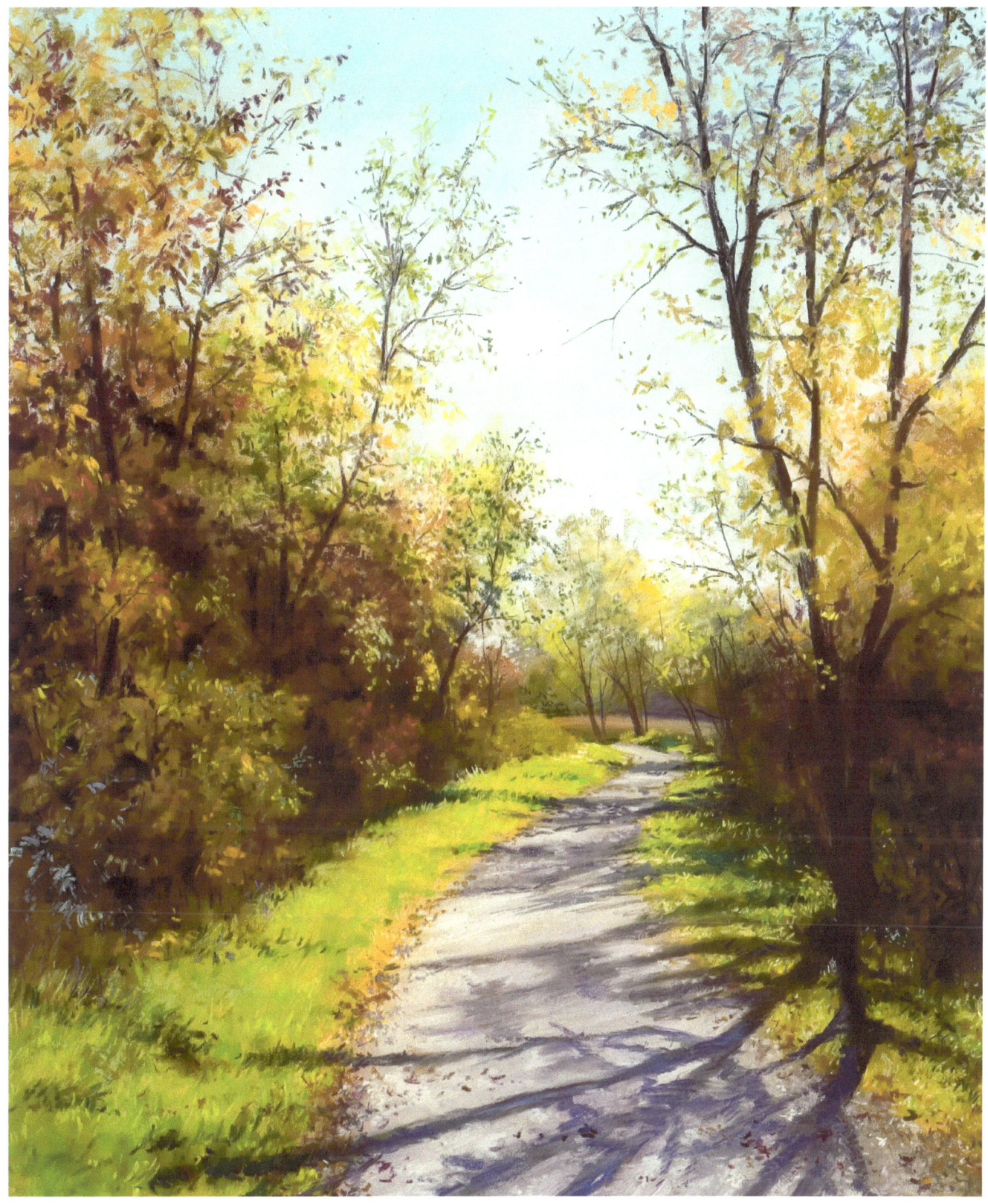

Woodland Trail 20 x 20 in.

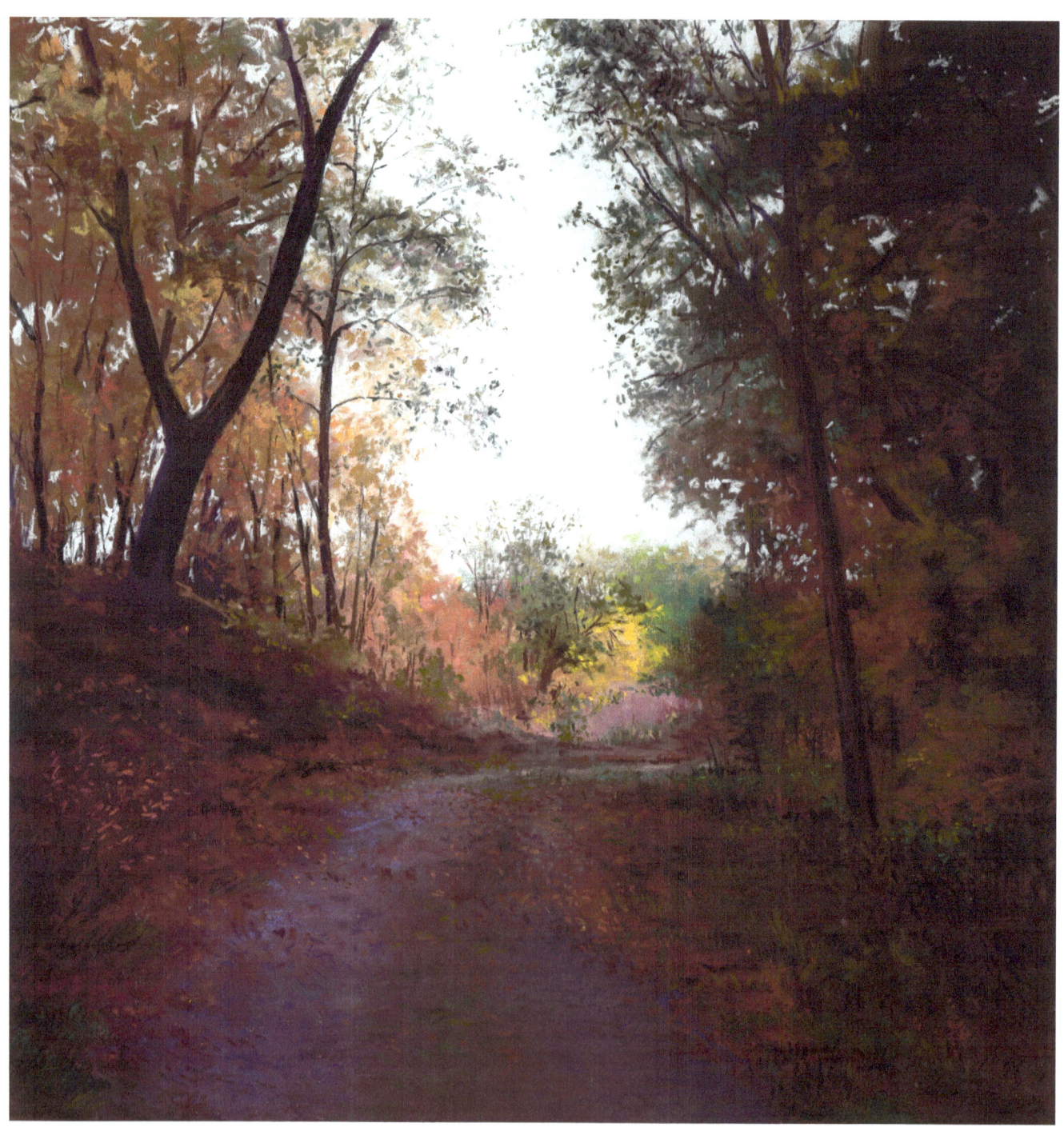

Autumn Trail, Loess Hills 20 x 20 in.

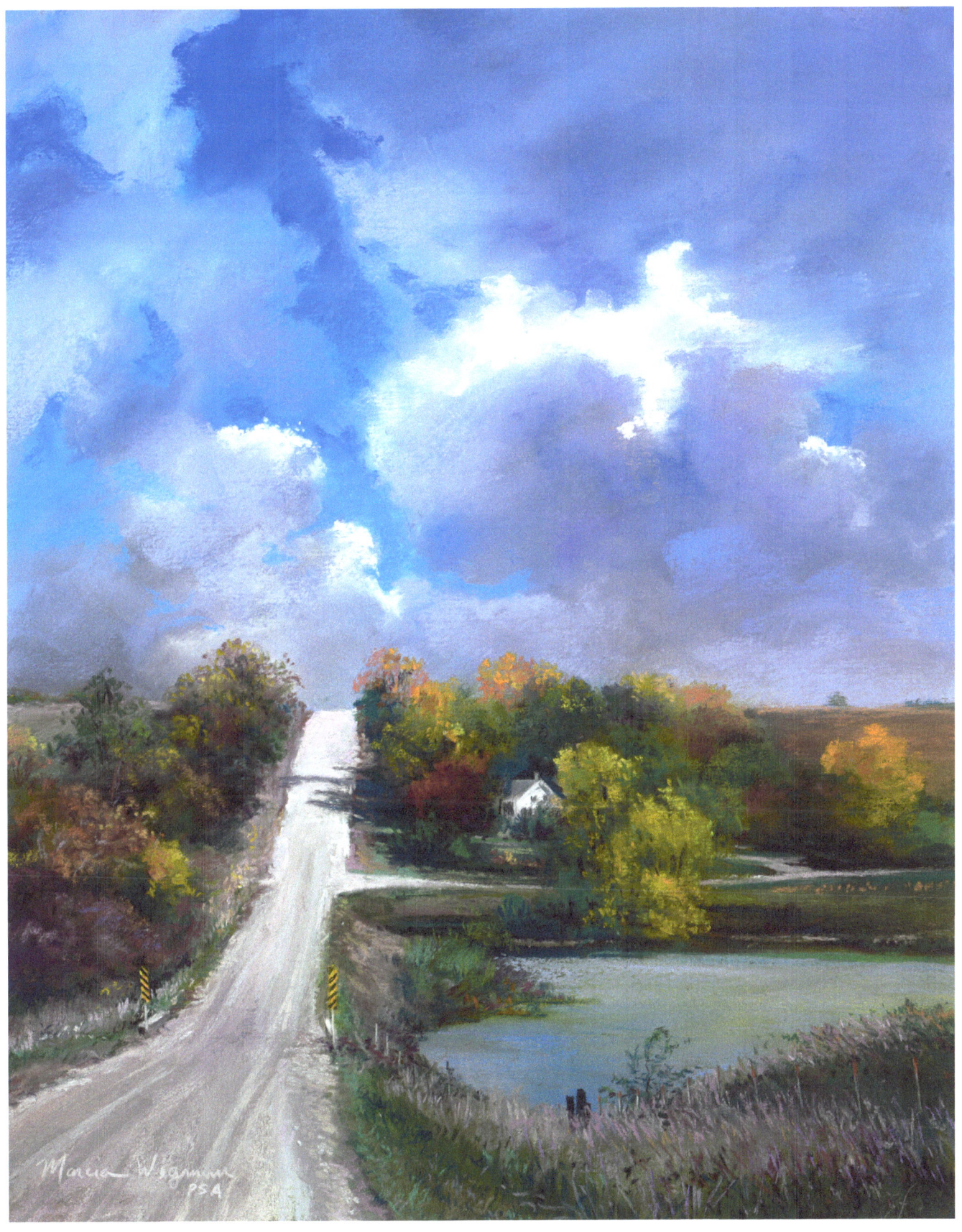

Pond, Road, and Sky 20 x 16 in.

Diptych, Triptych, and Quadriptych

My studio is relatively small. I do all the pastel paintings either flat on a table or upright on a tabletop easel. This limits the size of the sanded pastel paper on which I can work. Also limiting the size is the framing of a finished pastel painting. I like to have pastels framed with glass, as plexiglass tends to attract the pastel particles to the surface. Occasionally, I have been commissioned to do a larger work for both public and private spaces. Although matted and framed separately, and hung several inches apart, the paintings read as one scene. I always enjoy the challenge of doing these larger pieces.

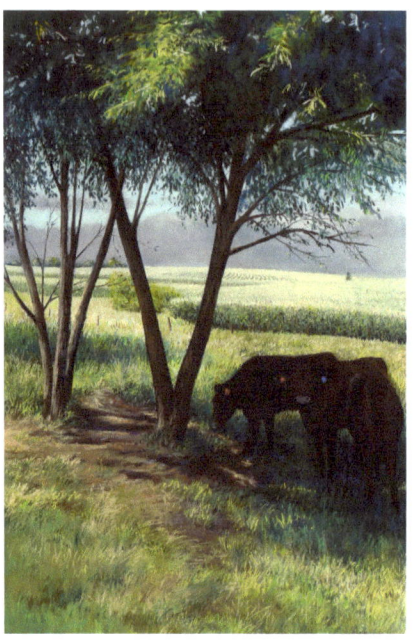
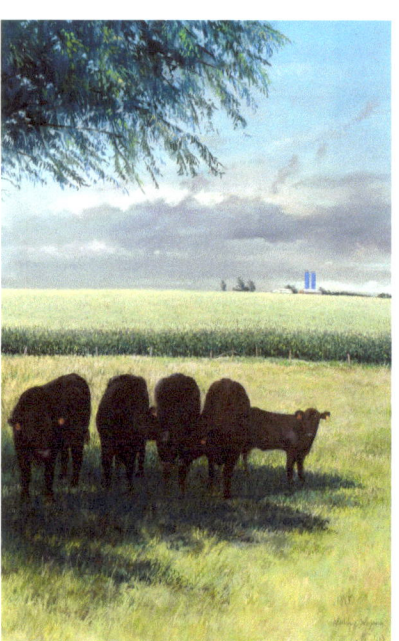

Shaded Cattle 36 x 48 in.

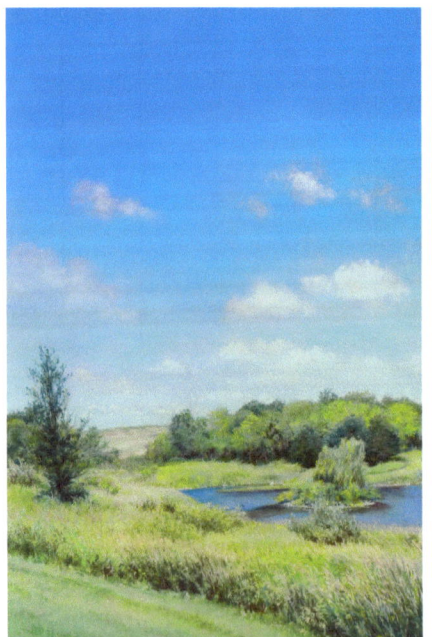
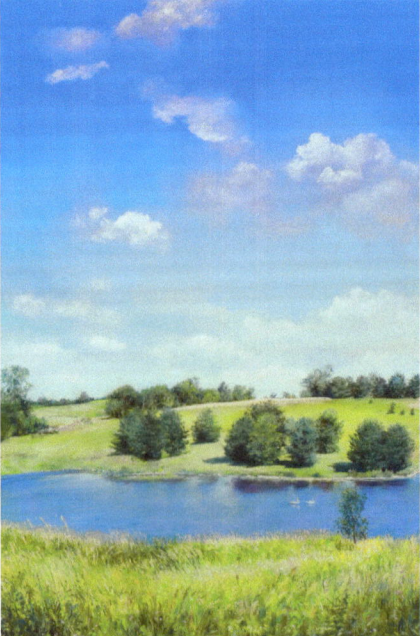
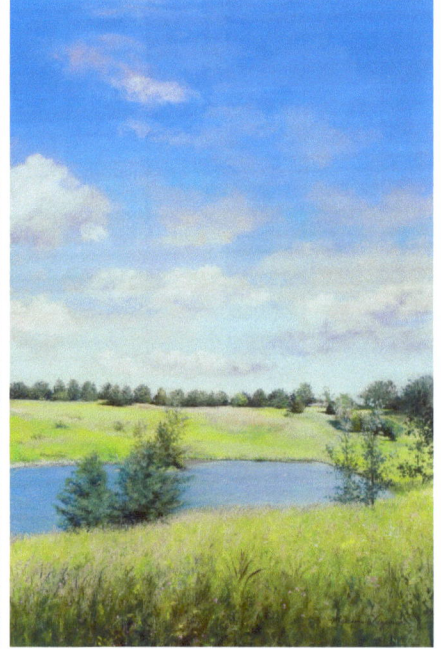

Davis Pond 36 x 72 in.

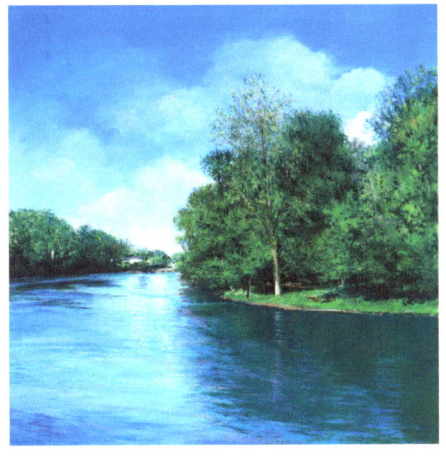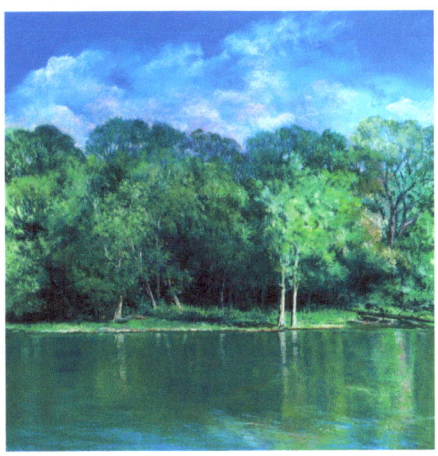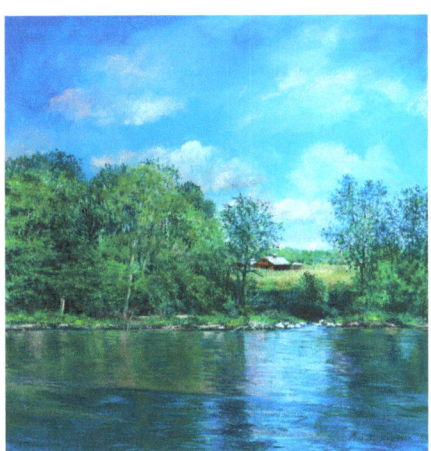

River Bend 24 x 72 in.

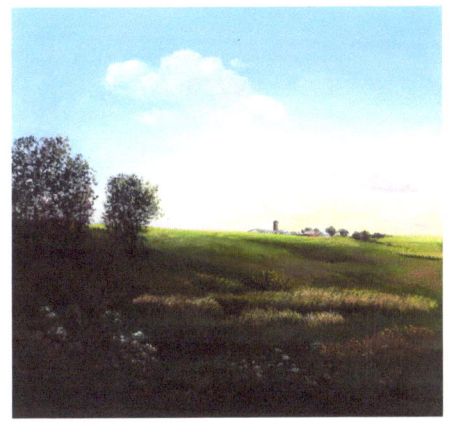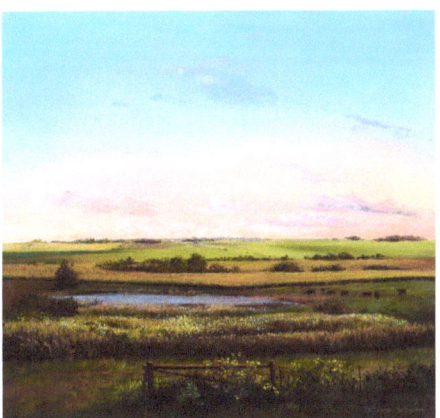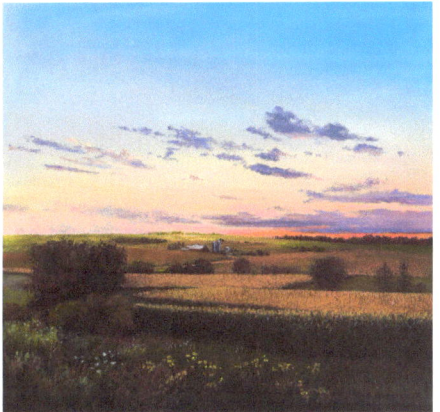

Evening Pastorale 24 x 72 in.

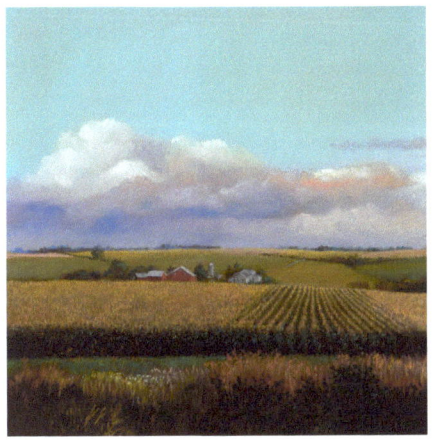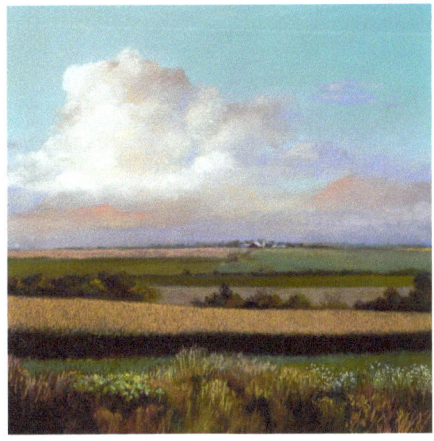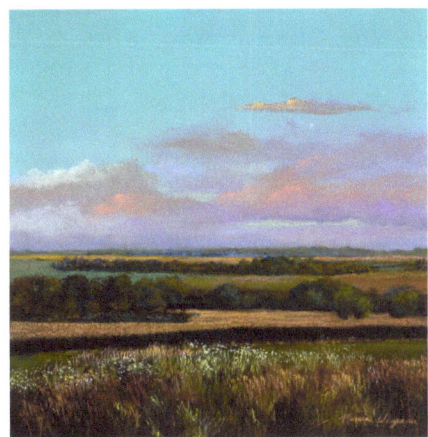

Oceans of Corn 18 x 54 in.

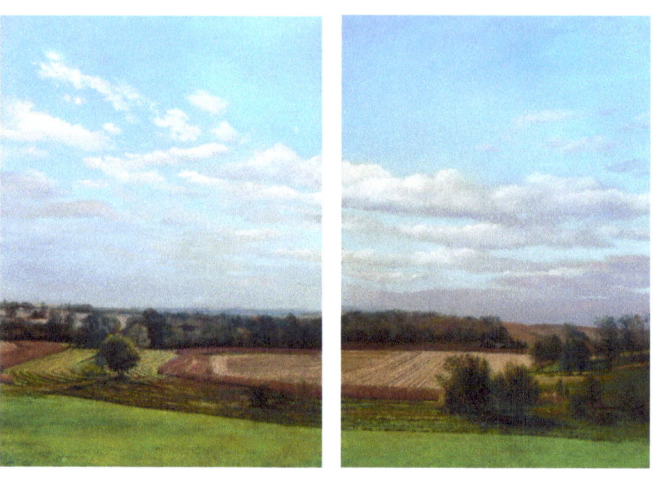

View Across the Land 31 x 46 in.

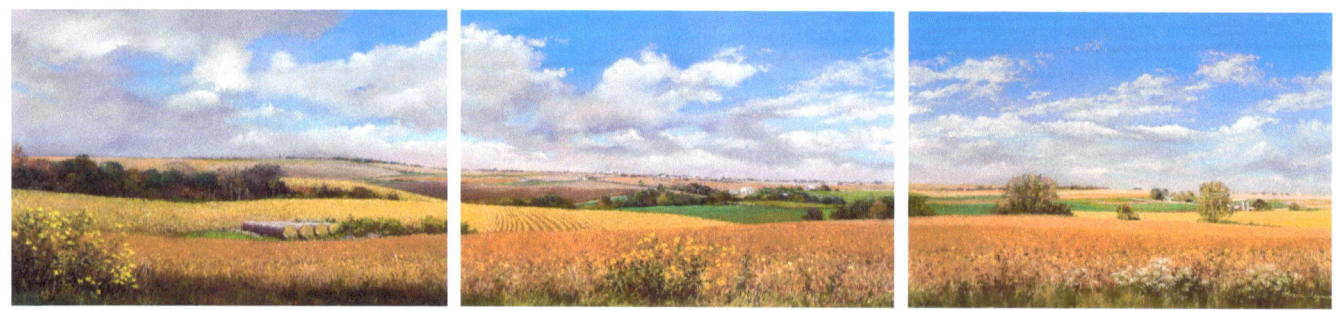

Soybean and Cornfields 16 x 72 in.

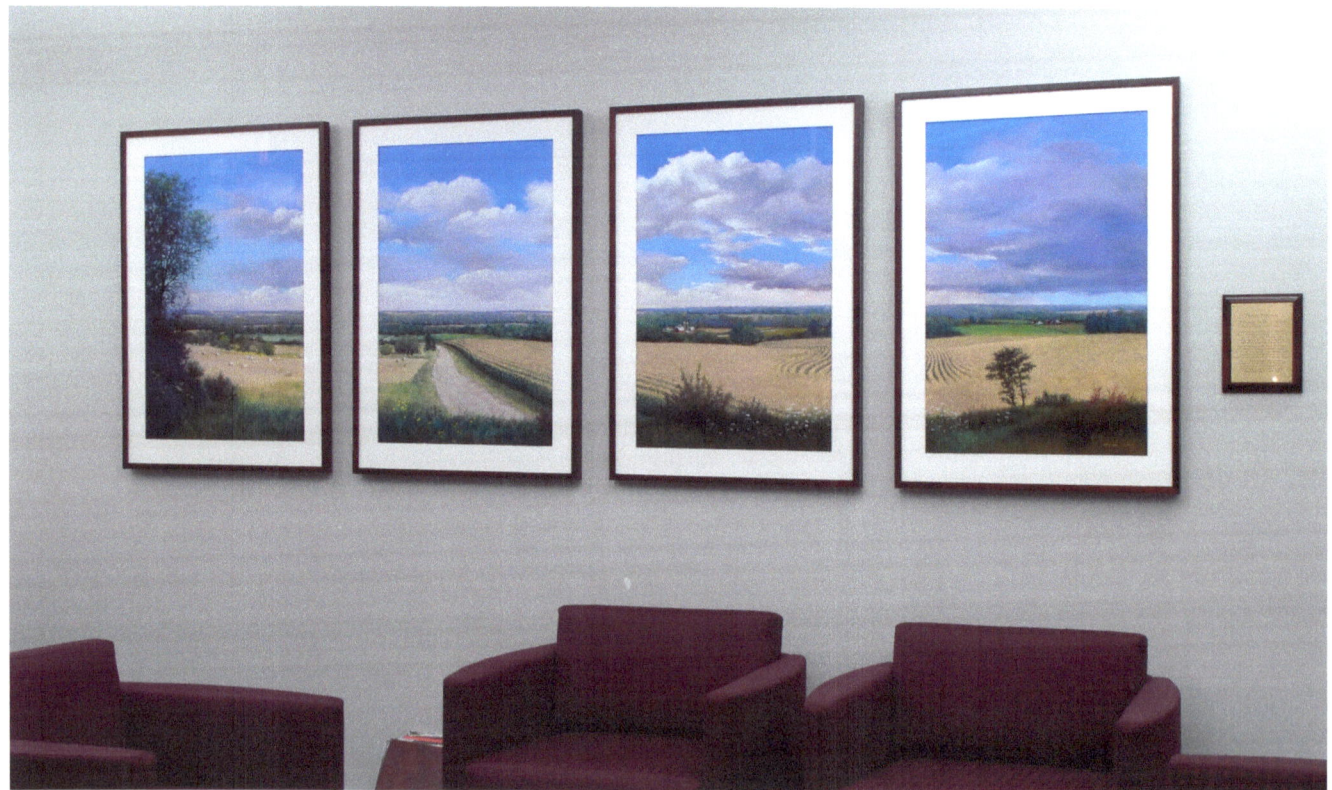

Summer Fields in Iowa 36 x 96 in.

Use of Photographs for Developing Paintings

Beginning of Summer in Iowa

From the 8-1/2 x 10-inch reference photograph, I changed the proportions of the painting to 17 x 36 inches to stretch out the image. I kept the cluster of farm buildings and trees close to the photograph other than eliminating the structure in front of the barn. I cropped the picture to the right of the farm and extended it to the left. Since the patterns of the rows of young soybeans undulating over the swells of land is what attracted and challenged me to do the painting, I brought them closer to the viewer by overlapping them with the foreground vegetation.

I wanted to emphasize the contrast between the liveliness of the foreground and the serenity of the soy patterns. Lightening the tone of the fields helps to create contrast between farm and foreground. This also helps to lead your eye back to the bright strip of yellow on the left and back to the very distant farm. The gray clouds bring your eye back around to the farm.

I chose the colors and direction of the clouds to frame the farm. The bits of bright blue sky give more depth and contrast to the dominating green.

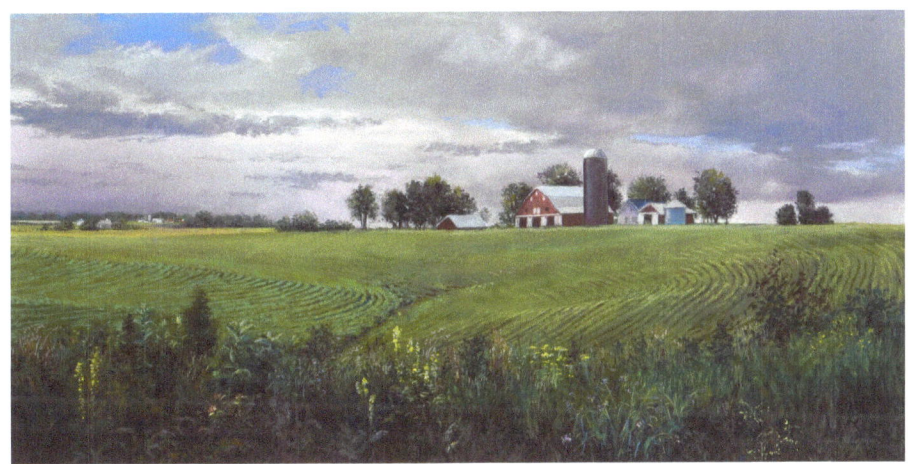

Beginning of Summer in Iowa 17 x 36 in.

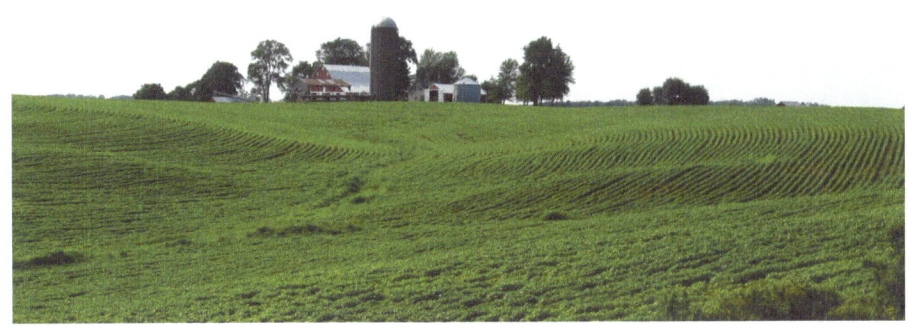

Reference photograph

Country Lane

The first version of the painting I composed horizontally, similar to the photograph. I eliminated the gate, the sign with red circles to the left, the sign to the right and the large tree trunk to the right. The rest of the painting is similar to the photograph.

For the vertical painting that was requested by the customer, I extended the trees upward. I always tell a customer who wishes to commission a painting similar to an existing one that I am willing to paint the same image a second time to see if I can improve upon the original.

Reference photograph below, pastel at bottom

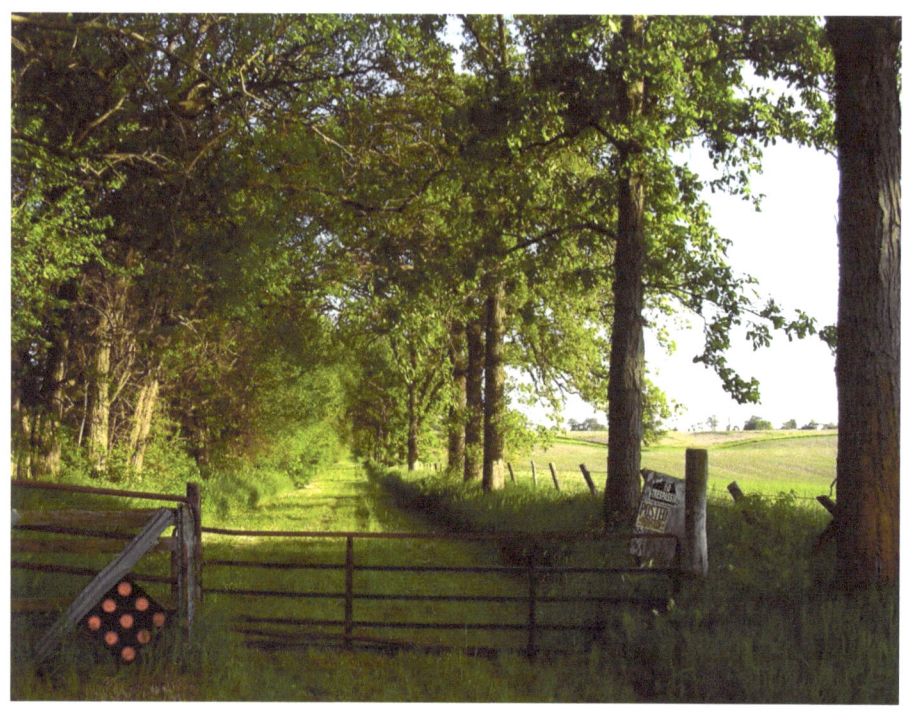

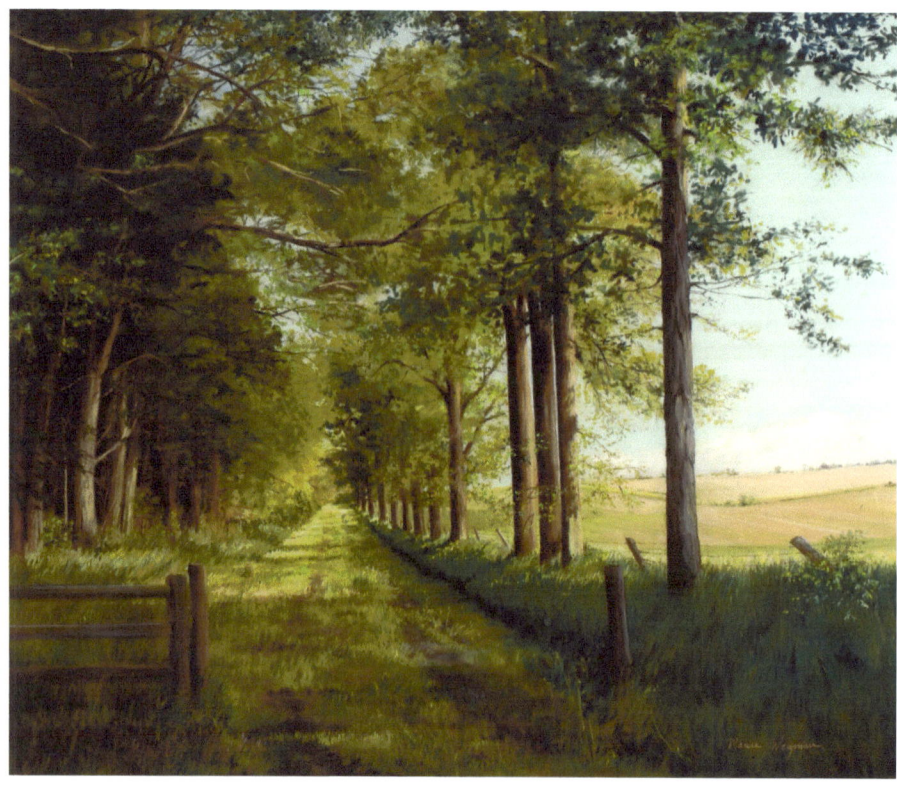

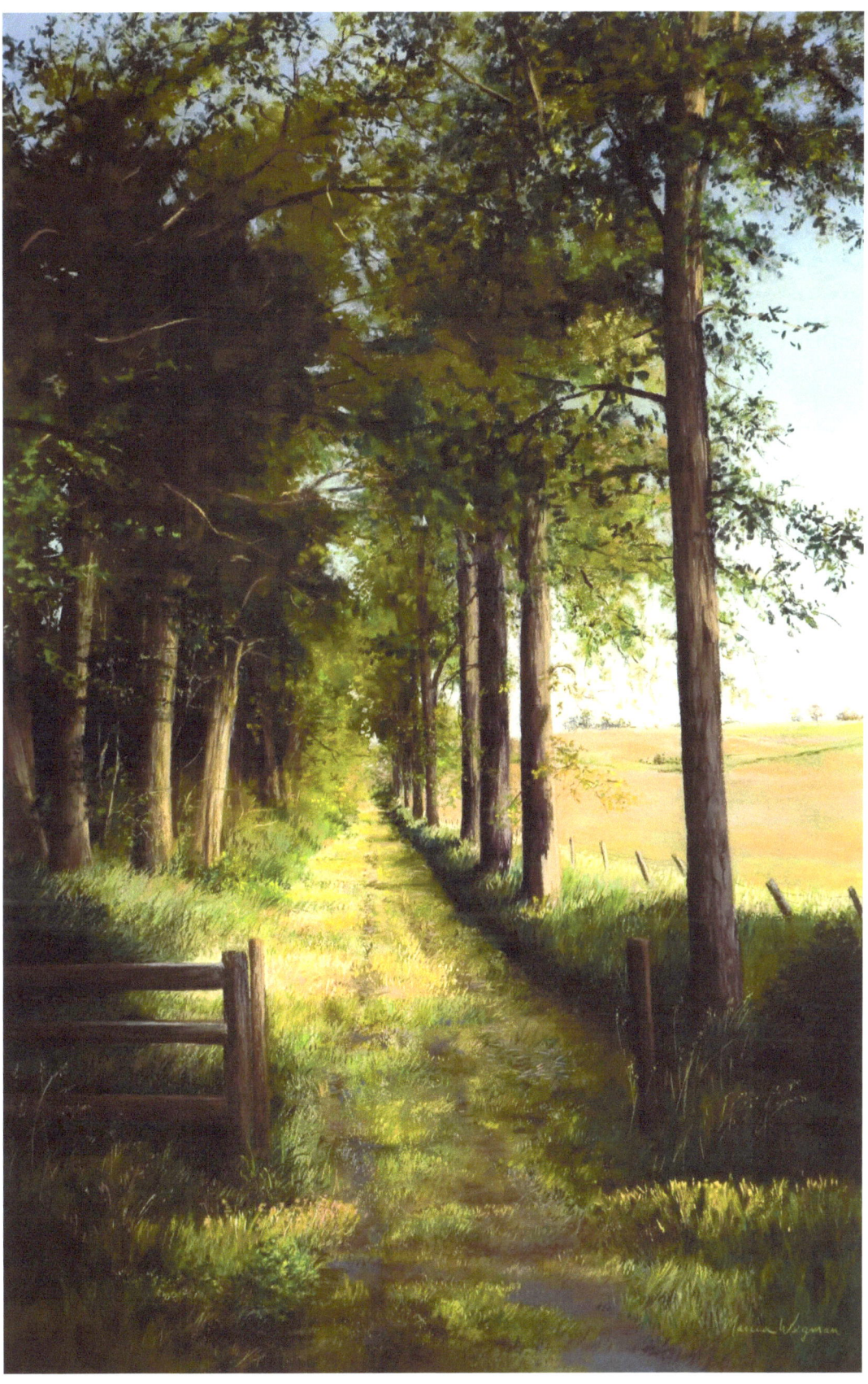

Above: *Vertical Country Lane II* 36 x 24 in.
Left below: *Horizontal Country Lane I* 32 x 36 in.

Blue Sky, Golden Fields

My inspiration for this painting was a photo of the sky I had recently taken in downtown Iowa City. Since it was the gorgeous cloud formation I wanted to emphasize, I chose photo references for the land that would fit a narrow proportion in the lower quarter of the composition and would work well with the colors in the sky. I returned to a scene I photographed on October 6, 2008, in northeastern Iowa enroute to McGregor. I have used this set of photographs for many different paintings as I love the colors and the long, deep view of stretched-out crop fields with the accents of dark clustered trees and white farm buildings.

Obviously, I eliminated the buildings in the sky photo. I lightened the lower edge meeting the horizon and warmed and defined the lowest bank of clouds. I combined elements from both land photographs, lessened the space of the foreground soybeans and made the cornfields more prominent by lightening the colors. Finally, I added the wildflowers to the foreground in a contrasting green. With this addition, I was taking artistic license as those wildflowers probably would be dried and brown in October. I have quantities of photos of roadside vegetation that I can slip into paintings as needed.

Reference photographs below.

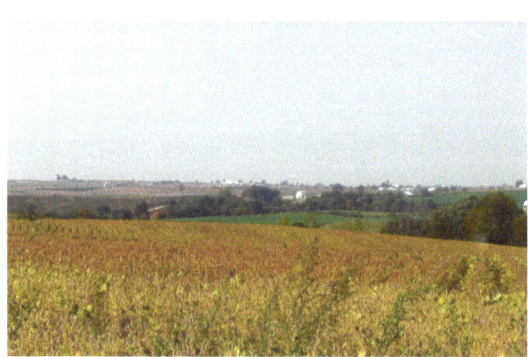
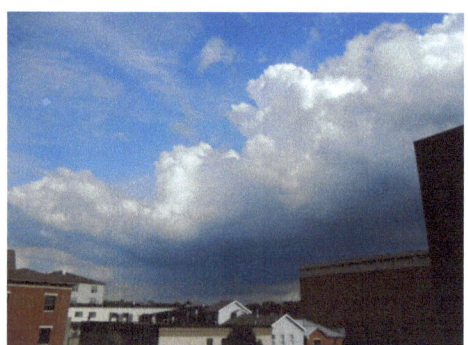

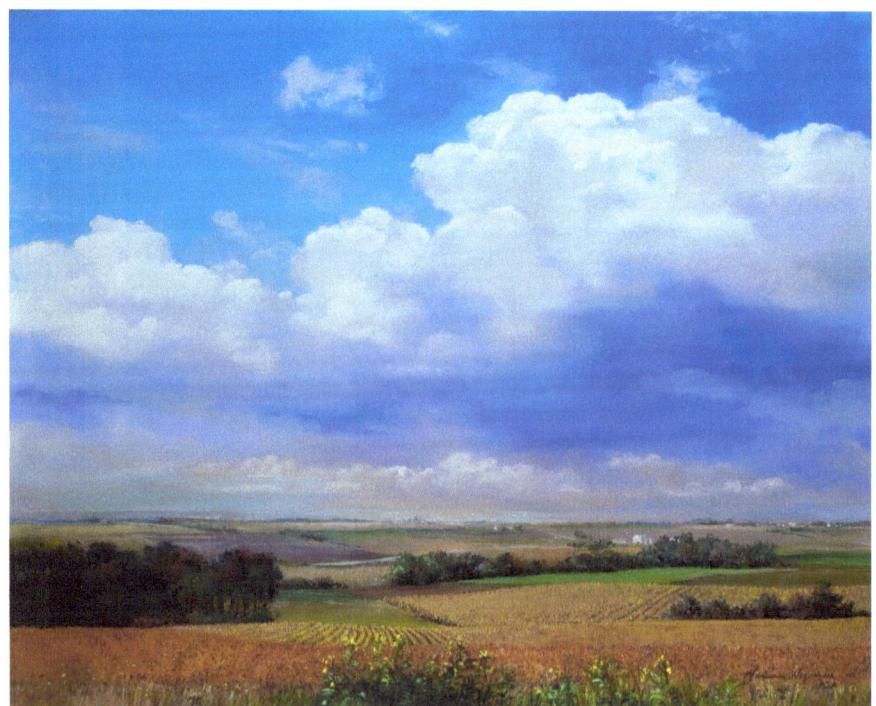

Blue Sky, Golden Fields 21 x 27 in.

Hay, Corn, and Beans

The reference landscape photos I used for this painting were taken along the twenty-mile stretch of road in northeastern Iowa called Little Switzerland. It is an exceptionally beautiful part of Iowa.

These photographs are shown below. I repositioned the wildflowers across the lower front of the painting and added a more dramatic and colorful sky to contrast with the hayfield.

Reference photographs below.

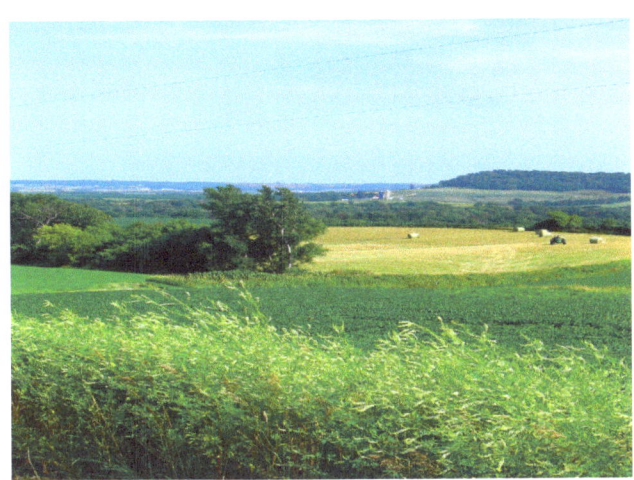
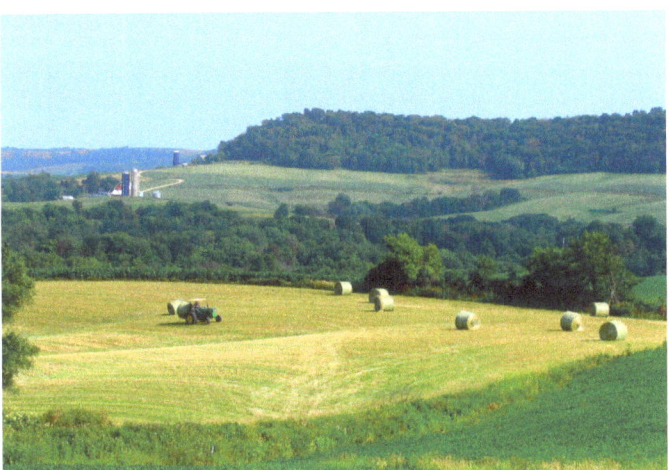

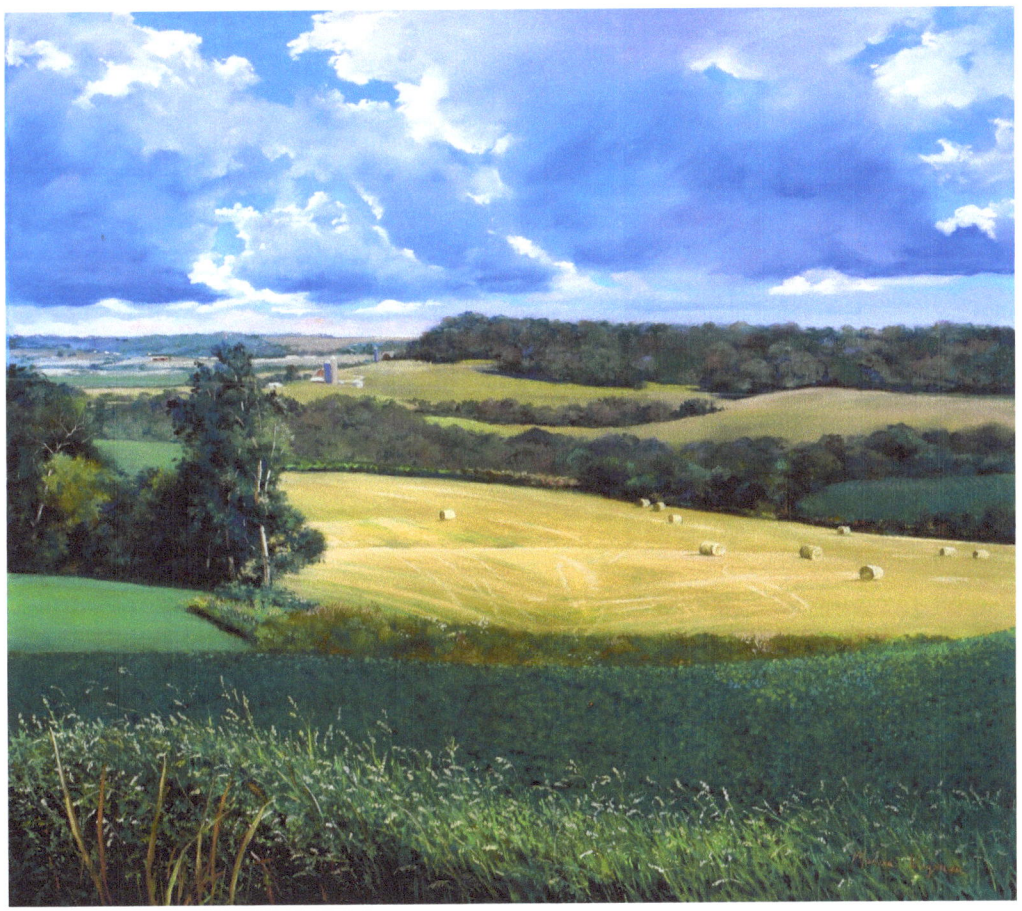

Hay, Corn, and Beans 28 x 32 in.

www.ingramcontent.com/pod-product-compliance
Lightning Source LLC
Chambersburg PA
CBHW041931240526
45473CB00034B/724